# Bloom's Modern Critical Views

# Bloom's Modern Critical Views

*Bloom's Modern Critical Views*

# Langston Hughes
## *New Edition*

*Edited and with an introduction by*
## Harold Bloom
Sterling Professor of the Humanities
Yale University

BLOOM'S
LITERARY CRITICISM
*An imprint of Infobase Publishing*

Editorial Consultant, Brian L. Johnson

**Bloom's Modern Critical Views: Langston Hughes—New Edition**

Copyright ©2008 by Infobase Publishing

Introduction ©2007 by Harold Bloom

Bloom's Literary Criticism
An imprint of Infobase Publishing
132 West 31st Street
New York NY 10001

**Library of Congress Cataloging-in-Publication Data**

Langston Hughes / edited with an introduction by Harold Bloom.
       p. cm. — (Bloom's modern criticial views)
 Includes bibliographical references and index.
 ISBN-13: 978-0-7910-96123 (hardcover : alk. paper)
 1. Hughes, Langston—Criticism and interpretation. I. Bloom, Harold.
PS3525.I5256Z5637 2007
812'.52—dc22                    2006102701

Cover design by Takeshi Takahashi/Joo Young An

Printed in the United States of America

Bang BCL 10 9 8 7 6 5 4 3 2 1

This book is printed on acid-free paper.

# Contents

# *Editor's Note*

My Introduction suggests that the major work of Langston Hughes was his honorable career as a writer, rather than the individual writings themselves. I intend that suggestion as homage, not irony, since it seems to me equally true of that heroic survivor, Norman Mailer.

Jonathan Scott sets the career of Hughes in the historical context of our Cold War with the now vanished Soviet Union, and William Hogan relates the poet's sense of place to a Harlem of his own imaginings.

Hughes's writings for children are surveyed by Steven Tracy, while Anita Patterson invokes jazz as a context for Hughes's lyrics.

Robert O'Brien Hokanson rather unconvincingly (for me) finds the Be-Bop aesthetic in Hughes, and H. Nigel Thomas worries an issue of patronage in regard to the poet.

Jazz, really a limited aspect of Hughes, who actually owed more to the poetry of Carl Sandburg than he did to the greatest African-American contribution to the arts, is seen by David Chinitz as Hughes's self-therapy.

The Gospel plays of Hughes are judged as surmounting social protest by Joseph McLaren, while Karen Jackson Ford reduces the poetry to an ethics of simplicity.

The sad issue of prejudice within African-Americans, based upon different degrees of pigmentation, is applied by Germain Bienvenu to Hughes's play, *Mulatto*.

This volume's first and best essay is by the distinguished literary biographer, Arnold Rampersand, who argues persuasively that *Fine Clothes to the Jew* was Hughes's masterpiece in poetry.

HAROLD BLOOM

## *Introduction*

LANGSTON HUGHES (1902–1967)

I

Twentieth-century black American literature is so varied that adequate critical generalization is scarcely possible, at least at this time. A literary culture that includes the fiction of Ellison and Hurston, the moral essays of Baldwin, and the extraordinary recent poetry of Jay Wright is clearly of international stature. Langston Hughes may be the most poignant and representative figure of that culture, more so even than Richard Wright. Clearly an authentic poet, Hughes nevertheless seems to lack any definitive volume to which we can turn for rereading. His best book of poems is certainly *Fine Clothes to the Jew* (1927), which retains some freshness and yet has palpable limitations. Folk traditions ranging from blues to spirituals to jazz songs to work chants to many other modes do get into Hughes's poetry, but his poems on the whole do not compare adequately to the best instances of those cultural models. Other critics find Hughes Whitmanian, but the subtle, evasive, and hermetic Whitman—still the most weakly misread even as he is the greatest of our poets—had little real effect upon Hughes's poetry. The authentic precursor was Carl Sandburg, and Hughes, alas, rarely surpassed Sandburg.

Social and political considerations, which doubtless will achieve some historical continuity, will provide something of an audience for Hughes's poetry. His first autobiography, *The Big Sea*, may be his most lasting single book, though its aesthetic values are very mixed. Rereading it, plus his second autobiography, *I Wonder as I Wander*, his *Selected Poems*, and *The Langston Hughes Reader*, I come to the sad conclusion that Hughes's principal work was his

1

life, which is to say his literary career. This conclusion is partly founded upon the contrast between Hughes's own writings and the admirable biography by Arnold Rampersad, *The Life of Langston Hughes, Volume 1, 1902–1941* (1986). Reading Rampersad's *Life* is simply a more vivid and valuable aesthetic and human experience than reading the rather faded verse and prose of Hughes himself. Hughes's courage and his persistence made the man more crucial as a representative figure than his intrinsic strength as a writer by itself might have allowed him to have become.

Rampersad, a biographer of uncommon distinction, memorably condenses the essence of Hughes's personal vision in the fifth paragraph of his *Life:*

> As successful as his life seemed to be by its end, with honors and awards inspired by more than forty books, and the adulation of thousands of readers, Hughes's favorite phonograph record over the years, spun in his bachelor suite late into the Harlem night, remained Billie Holiday's chilly moaning of "God Bless the Child That's Got His Own." Eventually he had gotten his own, but at a stiff price. He had paid in years of nomadic loneliness and a furtive sexuality; he would die without ever having married, and without a known lover or a child. If by the end he was also famous and even beloved, Hughes knew that he had been cheated early of a richer emotional life. Parents could be so cruel! "My theory is," he wrote not long before he died, "children should be born without parents—if born they must be."

Most of Hughes's writing, like his overt stances in life, is a reaction-formation away from that origin. Rampersad's skilled devotion uncovers the trace of sorrow that moves remorselessly from a grim family romance (or lack of it) through a refusal to abide or end in alienation. The refusal may be ascribed to Hughes's profound, almost selfless love for his own people, and makes him an authentic and heroic exemplar for many subsequent black American writers. Whatever the inadequacies of Hughes's various styles, his place in literary history is an assured one.

Rampersad shrewdly notes the mixture of will and passivity that combines in Hughes's art, and relates the passivity to Hughes's apparent asexuality. I wish only that the poetic will in Hughes had been stronger, as it was in Whitman and is now in John Ashbery and Jay Wright, among other contemporaries. What Hughes lacked, perhaps, was a sufficient sense of what Nietzsche called the will's revenge against time, and time's "It was." Absorbing his own plangencies, Hughes chose not to take revenge upon his familial past. His pride in his family and in his race was too great for that, but what made him a hero of a pioneering black literary life may also have weakened his actual achievement as a poet. Rampersad defends Hughes by comparing him to Whitman, who also had the sense that his life was a larger poem than any he could write. But the poet of "Crossing Brooklyn Ferry" and "As I Ebb'd with the Ocean of Life" could afford that sense better than could the poet of "The Weary Blues" and "Reverie on the Harlem River."

Yet there are moments in Hughes that are unique and testify to a mode of irony almost his own. In *The Big Sea*, Hughes recalls an exchange with his friend of Harlem Renaissance days, the black writer Wallace Thurman. The brief sketch of Thurman, followed by the wise passivity of Hughes's self-revelation, is like a fragment of an art, humorous and wise, that cultural and personal circumstances did not permit Hughes to perfect. Still, it remains a strong testament:

> Wallace Thurman laughed a long bitter laugh. He was a strange kind of fellow, who liked to drink gin, but didn't like to drink gin; who liked being a Negro, but felt it a great handicap; who adored bohemianism, but thought it wrong to be a bohemian. He liked to waste a lot of time, but he always felt guilty wasting time. He loathed crowds, yet he hated to be alone. He almost always felt bad, yet he didn't write poetry.
>
> Once I told him if I could feel as bad as he did all the time, I would surely produce wonderful books. But he said you had to know how to write, as well as how to feel bad. I said I didn't have to know how to feel bad, because, every so often, the blues just naturally overtook me, like a blind beggar with an old guitar:
>
> > You don't know,
> > You don't know my mind—
> > When you see me laughin',
> > I'm laughin' to keep from cryin'.

ARNOLD RAMPERSAD

# *Langston Hughes's* Fine Clothes to the Jew

As prolific as Langston Hughes strove to be in a variety of genres—
poetry, fiction, drama, and essays notably—he saw himself from first to
last primarily as a poet. Of his many collections of verse, nine must be
considered major in his career by almost any accounting: *The Weary Blues*
(1926); *Fine Clothes to the Jew* (1927); *Shakespeare in Harlem* (1942); *Fields of
Wonder* (1947); *One-Way Ticket* (1949); *Montage of a Dream Deferred* (1951);
*Ask Your Mama* (1961); and *The Panther and the Lash* (posthumously in 1967,
the year of his death). To these efforts might be added the volume published
by the leftist International Workers Order, *A New Song* (1938); although it
contained no new poems, the verse in that slender pamphlet was unusually
radical and had not been collected previously.

Of these volumes, the least successful both in terms of sales and of
critical reception, at least among black reviewers, was unquestionably *Fine
Clothes to the Jew*. I would like to argue that, paradoxically, this volume was
by far Hughes's greatest collection of verse, that the collection marked the
height of his creative originality as a poet, and that it remains one of the
most significant single volumes of poetry ever published in the United States.
In fact, despite its failure to gain recognition, *Fine Clothes to the Jew* may
stand in relationship to black American poetry in a way not unlike Walt

*Callaloo: A Journal of African American and African Arts and Letters*, 1986 Winter; 9 (1 (26)):
pp. 144–158. Copyright 1986 Johns Hopkins University Press.

Whitman's 1855 edition of *Leaves of Grass* stands in relationship to white American poetry, or to the poetry of the nation as a whole.

*Fine Clothes to the Jew* appeared almost ten years after Hughes first began to write poetry. While his work in Lincoln, Illinois (where by his own account he wrote his first poem, in 1916), is lost, almost all of his poems written in high school in Cleveland and thereafter are available to scholars. They may be found in the *Central High School Monthly, Crisis, Opportunity,* and other magazines published largely by blacks, as well as in white magazines that cover the broad ideological spectrum from *Vanity Fair,* on one hand, to the communist *New Masses,* on the other. The work of these first years culminated in the appearance from Knopf of Hughes's first book of any kind, *The Weary Blues. Fine Clothes to the Jew,* the next, built on elements found in the previous volume and in the magazines, but with such emphases and revisions that it marked, in effect, an unparalleled rethinking by Hughes about poetry in the context of black America.

Once Hughes shed his most youthful approaches to poetry and felt the stirring influence of Walt Whitman, whose lines he echoed unmistakably in his first published free verse poem, "A Song of the Soul of Central" (*Central High School Monthly,* January 1919) and Carl Sandburg ("my guiding star"), his poetry fell almost inevitably into three distinct areas.[1] The first area found Hughes dwelling on isolation, despair, suicide, and the like—conventional themes for a young, romantic poet, to be sure, but notions strongly felt by Hughes personally as he struggled to overcome the effects of his father's desertion and his mother's flighty compromise of her relationship with her son. A poem such as "Suicide's Note" ("The calm / Cool face of the river / Asked me for a kiss") exemplifies this mode.[2] The second area, also present virtually from the start of Hughes's career as a poet and fiction writer, reveals an aggressive socialist, non-racial intelligence, as for example in the very titles of two poems written later, in 1932: "Good Morning Revolution" and "Goodbye Christ." The third area, for which Hughes is almost certainly best known, finds him creating in direct response to the needs of black people—epitomized by "The Negro Speaks of Rivers," published in 1921.

Whatever distinction as a poet Hughes possesses almost certainly derives from his work in this last, racial vein. In his poetry of race, one again notes relatively clear subdivisions. Some poems protest the social conditions of blacks specifically; some are boldly declarative of the beauty and dignity of the race; still others—perhaps the most revered—transcend both angry protest and bold declaration to affirm quietly the dignity and historicity of blacks. Hughes's best known poems, such as "The Negro," "Dream Variations," and "When Sue Wears Red," almost all fall into one or another of these categories.

In its most representative work, however, *Fine Clothes to the Jew* falls outside of these categories. Although all of the poems in the various categories naturally involve a poetic concern with the manipulation of form, *Fine Clothes to the Jew* is based in essence on what one might acknowledge as a separate aesthetic, a different approach to poetic art. In the other work, Hughes writes—in spite of his concern with race—as a poet impelled by the literary tradition as defined by certain major poets of the language—in particular, Walt Whitman and his epigones, notably Carl Sandburg and Vachel Lindsay. But in *Fine Clothes* Hughes attempted to work in a way no black or white poet had ever attempted to work: deliberately defining poetic tradition according to the standards of a group often seen as sub-poetic—the black masses.

In the interest of accuracy, it must be noted that although the two approaches are presented here as contradictory, Hughes would probably never have attempted the latter if he had not found the encouragement and the signs to do so in the former, especially in Whitman's historic vision of democratic voices and his primary search for an authentic, American language of poetry. On the other hand, in his dignifying of certain Afro-American forms, Hughes explored areas which Whitman had not conceived, and of which Whitman, with his documented biases against blacks in spite of his attractive portraits of them in a few places in *Leaves of Grass*, probably would not have approved.

Hughes himself did not suddenly become enlightened by his finest insights into Afro-American form. Until 1923, perhaps the closest he had come to letting the black masses speak through his art was in "Mother to Son." This apparently simple poem amounted to nothing less than a personal reclamation of black dialect (Dunbar's "jingle in a broken tongue") for the black poet; surely "Mother to Son" takes us beyond the poles of low comedy and pathos identified by William Dean Howells (in praising Dunbar's use of dialect) as the range of the black race.[3] In Hughes's poem, black speech is invoked in the context of the race's courage, endurance, and sense of duty. But dialect would be only incidental to the major initiative of Hughes in the question of poetic form; at the center of his effort would be the recognition of a link between poetry and black music, and in particular the music not of the dignified and Europeanized spirituals, so often lauded, but of the earthy, almost "unspeakable" blues.

For his first few years as a poet, even as he grew technically proficient, Hughes had no idea what to do with a form he had heard first as a child in Lawrence, Kansas, and in Kansas City, Missouri. Even then he had responded emotionally, as he would assert, to the deep, piercing sadness of the music; later, no doubt, he began to marvel at its curious, accompanying impulse toward laughter. But how was he to effect a link between his learned standards of formal poetry and songs created by the artist among the masses? This question masquerades as one simply of technique; however, it concerns not only the realities of political power—the social powerlessness of blacks translated into the declassification of their art—but the ability of the individual to attain a sufficiently deep identification with his people and their modes of utterance so that, on an individual initiative, he is able to affect a dignified fusion of learned poetic values with those of the despised masses.

When Hughes opened his greatest essay, "The Negro Artist and the Racial Mountain" (1926) by equating the desire of a certain young black poet to be seen as nothing but a poet with the desire to be white, he was (perhaps reductively) stating his understanding of the most complex problem facing the young black writer. Hughes and, no doubt, some other young black writers had no literal desire to be white. Nevertheless, the domination of white poetic standards through the many unquestionably alluring volumes of white verse, backed ultimately by the domination of white culture, effectively made their dilemma forbiddingly close to that of a racial death-wish described by Hughes at the start of the essay. Because his will to solve this conundrum was so strong, however, Langston Hughes progressed where others stagnated. But he progressed only in stages.

Not long after "The Negro Speaks of Rivers," Hughes began to offer, as poetry, the barely mediated recording of the sounds and sights of black life, notably in religion. One poem, "Prayer Meeting" (1922–1923), may stand here as an example.

> Glory! Hallelujah!
> The dawn's a-comin'!
> Glory! Hallelujah!
> The dawn's a-comin'!
> A black old woman croons
> In the amen-corner of the
> Ebecaneezer Baptist Church—
> A black old woman croons—
> The dawn's a-comm'![4]

In his willingness to stand back and record, with minimal intervention, aspects of the drama of black religion (and, later, of music and dance), Hughes clearly showed that he had begun to see his own learned poetic art, even with his individual talent, as inferior to that of "ordinary" blacks—inferior, for example, to an old black woman in the amen corner who cries to Jesus, "Glory! Hallelujah!" At the heart of his sense of inferiority—which empowered rather than debilitated Hughes—was the knowledge that he (and other would-be poets) stood to a great extent *outside* the culture he worshipped. Perhaps Hughes stood at a greater distance from the masses than did most other black poets. Raised in relative isolation and with a haunting sense of parental abandonment, he stood outside because much of his life had been spent away from consistent involvement with the very people whose affection and regard he craved.

A more fateful step came one night in March, 1923, after a visit to a cabaret in Harlem, when he finally wrote himself and his awkward position *vis à vis* his race accurately into a poem, "The Weary Blues."

> Droning a drowsy syncopated tune,
> Rocking back and forth to a mellow croon,
>     I heard a Negro play.
> Down on Lenox Avenue the other night
> By the pale dull pallor of an old gas light
>     He did a lazy sway . . . .
>     He did a lazy sway . . . .
> To the tune o' those Weary Blues . . .

The distance between the persona or narrator of the poem (what is his race, for example, if he hears "a Negro" play and for whom is he writing?) and the black bluesman is the distance between the would-be black poet and his people. The poem has sprung equally from the poet's isolation and his will to admire. But Hughes, in an unprecedented step, also allowed the black bluesman a chance to sing his song, with minimal interference from conventional white poetic values.

> "Ain't got nobody in all this world,
> Ain't got nobody but ma self.
> I's gwine to quit ma frownin'
> And put ma troubles on the shelf."
> Thump, thump, thump, went his foot on the floor.
> He played a few chords then he sang some more. . .[5]

Within a poem based in conventional form, Hughes sets blues lyrics he had heard as a child in Kansas. The result is that, in one and the same work, the poet honors both the tradition of Europe (out of necessity, since he is writing in English) and the tradition of black America (achieved *in spite of* the English language). The latter tradition, in fact, invades the former; one must measure the opening lines of the poem against the cadences of urban black speech, derived from the South. This invasion was so unprecedented that the persona (and the poet, of course) does not know what to make of it. By his own admission, Hughes had a hard time ending the poem. For two years, he kept the poem, "whose ending I had never been able to get quite right," unpublished—at a time when he was trying to publish almost everything he wrote.[6] Rather than share this "beauty of a cabaret poem" with anyone, Hughes kept it from sight.[7] Meanwhile, he struggled to shape its ending—"I could not achieve an ending I liked, although I worked and worked on it."[8] Finally, the end confirms the persona's bewilderment and the bluesman's mystery:

> And far into the night he crooned that tune.
> The stars went out and so did the moon.
> The singer stopped playing and went to bed
> While the Weary Blues echoed through his head
> He slept like a rock or a man that's dead.

Hughes was for two years indecisive about how to end the poem. During that period, he spent a few months in a Paris nightclub in 1924, where the entertainers were black American jazz singers and musicians. He then became bolder in his incorporations of black music and dance into his poetry. One poem frames the cry of an exuberant black dancer: "Me an' ma baby's / Got two mo' ways, / Two mo' ways to do de buck!"[9] In "To A Negro Jazz Band in a Parisian Cabaret," he urges the black musicians to "Play that thing" for the white lords and ladies, "whores and gigolos," and "the school teachers out on a spree. Play it!"

> May I?
> *Mais oui.*
> *Mein Gott!*
> *Parece una rumba.*
> *!Que rumba!*
> Play it, jazz band!
> You've got seven languages to speak in
> And then some.
> Can I?
> Sure.[10]

A year in Washington, D.C., 1925, away from Parisian nightclub glitter but closer to the more elemental art forms of the black masses, only deepened his respect for the power of black music and its "lowly" source. "Like the waves of the sea coming one after another," he would write, "like the earth moving around the sun, night, day—night, day—forever, so is the undertow of black music with its rhythm that never betrays you, its strength like the beat of the human heart, its humor, and its rooted power." More and more he let the common people, and not the poets deemed great by the master culture, guide him. "I tried to write poems like the songs they sang on Seventh Street—gay songs, because you had to be gay or die; sad songs, because you couldn't help being sad sometimes. But gay or sad, you kept on living and you kept on going.[11]

The publication of *The Weary Blues* (January, 1926) did not entirely reflect this commitment; the manuscript was accepted in May of the previous year, and mainly comprised poems written much earlier. Apart from the quotation of blues in the title poem, and even briefer quotations in "Blues Fantasy" ("Hey! Hey! / That's what the / Blues singers say . . ."), the blues is not present in the book—in spite of its sonorous title.[12] For every "race poem," another exists that has nothing to do with black culture. The result is a mulatto-like text. This should not be surprising since the mulatto theme—and its transcendence—is one of the most prominent in Hughes's work. But to many readers *The Weary Blues* had gone much too far toward the black masses. Countee Cullen questioned in print whether the jazz poems were poems at all, and Hughes received a frightening reminder of black snobbishness when the veteran poet George M. McClellan wrote to tell him that while he liked the poems in *The Weary Blues,* he had scissored from the dustjacket (designed by Covarrubias) "that hideous black 'nigger' playing the piano."[13]

While *The Weary Blues* was in press and in the months following its appearance, Hughes went through certain experiences that revolutionized his aesthetic. First was his sojourn, already mentioned, among the black poor in Washington. Second was his entry into black Lincoln University a few days after *The Weary Blues* appeared, when for the first time since he was nine or ten, Hughes went to school with a majority of blacks (and all male)—an experience of incalculable effect on his sense of race. Third was the impact of the brilliant circle of young stars—the key members of the Harlem Renaissance—in Harlem at the same time: Aaron Douglass, Arna Bontemps, Wallace Thurman, Bruce Nugent, and Zora Neale Hurston, for whom Hughes's *Nation* essay of June 1926, "The Negro Artist and the Racial Mountain," was manifesto; to these should be added the names of musicians Hall Johnson, Paul Robeson, Clarence Cameron White, and W. C. Handy (often called the father of the blues), with whom Hughes either worked or consulted in the summer of 1926, especially in connection with a musical, to star Robeson, called "O Blues!" (from "The Weary Blues"). The fourth experience was the reaction of the black press to Carl Van Vechten's Harlem novel, *Nigger Heaven,* and to the appearance of *Fire!!* magazine.

The younger writers in general enthusiastically approved of *Nigger Heaven* ("Colored people can't help but like it," Hughes had predicted; the novel read as if it were written by "an N.A.A.C.P. official or Jessie Fauset.

But it's good").[14] To almost all the young black writers, Van Vechten's troubles were their own. The attack on him was an attack on what they themselves, or most of them, stood for—artistic and sexual freedom, a love of the black masses, a refusal to idealize black life, and a revolt against bourgeois hypocrisy. They decided to publish their own magazine, instead of relying on the staid *Crisis* and the like. For their pains, *Fire!!* received a withering reception in the black press. "I have just tossed the first issue of *Fire* into the fire," the reviewer in the *Baltimore Afro-American* fumed; Aaron Douglass had ruined "three perfectly good pages and a cover" with his drawings, while Langston Hughes displayed "his usual ability to say nothing in many words."[15]

These experiences prompted Hughes to go where no poet had gone before; in the summer of 1926 he wrote poems that differed sharply from the spirit of *The Weary Blues* and that contested the right of the middle class to criticize the mores and manners of the black masses. (The rebellious campaign continued into the fall, when Hughes wrote his first short stories since high school, the "West Illana" sequence of stories set on a ship much like the one on which he had sailed to Africa in 1923. Hughes's fiction navigated more sensual waters than ever before; whatever their limitations as art, the stories that resulted steam suggestively of miscegenation, adultery, promiscuity, and the turmoil of sexual repression—subjects all taboo to the critics who hated *Fire!!.)* During the summer he wrote almost feverishly; back in Lincoln for the fall term, he soon gathered his new poems into what he hoped would be his second book.

On Sunday, October 3, he visited New York and delivered the manuscript to Carl Van Vechten, to whom the collection was dedicated. As with Hughes's first book, they went over each of the poems; exactly what part Van Vechten played now is unclear. Three weeks later, Langston presented the revised collection to him to take to Knopf. By this time it had a name: "Fine Clothes to the Jew," after a line from Hughes's "Hard Luck":

> When hard luck overtakes you
> Nothin' for you to do
> Gather up yo' fine clothes
> An' sell 'em to de Jew . . .[16]

Knopf accepted "Fine Clothes to the Jew," but not without balking at the title (the firm had published *Nigger Heaven* apparently without difficulty). After Van Vechten personally defended the name, as he recorded in his journal, it was allowed to stand. Van Vechten perhaps had also chosen it, as he had chosen "The Weary Blues." Certainly, Hughes had been thinking of using "Brass Spitoons," from one of his poems. The choice was unfortunate. Apparently no one alerted Hughes to the effect his title would have on sales, which proved to be opposite to the result of Van Vechten's own crudeness. But he later regarded the title as one of the main reasons for the failure of the book: it was "a bad title, because it was confusing and many Jewish people did not like it."[17]

By mid-January, 1927, Hughes had copies of *Fine Clothes to the Jew.* The first reports were encouraging. Far from objecting to the title, his friend and supporter, Amy Spingarn, liked the book even more than *The Weary Blues,* because it seemed "more out of the core of life."[18] Her brother-in-law, Arthur Spingarn, who was also Jewish, noted the title but found the book a "splendid" work, in which "Jacob and the Negro come into their own."[19] The black conservative George Schuyler praised Hughes as "the poet of the modern Negro proletariat."[20] But after the attacks on *Nigger Heaven* and *Fire!!,* Hughes was nervous. "It's harder and more cynical," he explained defensively to Dewey Jones of the Chicago *Defender,* and "limited to an interpretation of the 'lower classes,' the ones to whom life is least kind. I try to catch the hurt of their lives, the monotony of their 'jobs,' and the veiled weariness of their songs. They are the people I know best."[21]

On February 5, just as he prepared to set out on a tour for Negro History Week, the black critics opened fire. Under a headline proclaiming Hughes a "SEWER DWELLER," William M. Kelley of the New York *Amsterdam News,* denounced *Fine Clothes to the Jew* as "about 100 pages of trash. . . . It reeks of the gutter and sewer." The regular reviewer of the *Philadelphia Tribune* adamantly refused to publicize it; Eustance Gay confessed that *Fine Clothes to the Jew* "disgusts me." In the *Pittsburgh Courier,* historian J. A. Rogers called it "piffling trash" that left him "positively sick." The Chicago *Whip* sneered at the dedication to Van Vechten, "a literary gutter-rat" who perhaps alone "will revel in the lecherous, lust-reeking characters that Hughes finds time to poeticize about. . . . These poems are unsanitary, insipid and repulsing." Hughes was the "poet 'low-rate' of Harlem." The following week, refining its position, the *Tribune* lamented Hughes's "obsession for the more degenerate elements" of black life; the book was "a study in the perversions of the Negro." It is questionable whether any book of American poetry, other than *Leaves of Grass,* had ever been greeted so contemptuously.[22]

To these and other black critics, Hughes had allowed the "secret" shame of their culture, especially its apparently unspeakable or unprintable sexual mores, to be bruited by thick-lipped black whores and roustabouts. How could he have dared to publish "Red Silk Stockings"?

> Put on yo' red silk stockings,
> Black gal.
> Go out an' let de white boys
> Look at yo' legs.

> Ain't nothin' to do for you, nohow,
> Round this town,—
> You's too pretty.
> Put on yo' red silk stockings, gal,
> An' tomorrow's chile'll
> Be a high yaller.
> Go out an' let de white boys
> Look at yo' legs.

Or "Beale Street Love"?

> Love
> Is a brown man's fist
> With hard knuckles
> Crushing the lips,
> Blackening the eyes,—
> Hit me again
> Says Clorinda.

By pandering to the taste of whites for the sensational (the critics ignored their own sensationalism, demonstrable in the scandal-ridden sheets of most black weeklies), Hughes had betrayed his race.[23]

In spite of this hostility, *Fine Clothes to the Jew* marked Hughes's maturity as a poet after a decade of writing, and his most radical achievement in language. While *The Weary Blues* had opened with references to the blues and poems written in dialect, before presenting the sweeter, more traditional lyrics, a prefatory note ("the mood of the *Blues* is almost always despondency, but when they are sung people laugh") now indicated the far greater extent to which *Fine Clothes to the Jew* falls deliberately within the range of authentic blues emotion and blues culture. Gone are the conventional lyrics about nature and loneliness, or poems in which the experience of the common black folk is framed by conventional poetic language and a superior, sometimes ironic poetic diction. Here few poems are beyond range of utterance of common black folk, except in so far as any formal poetry by definition belongs to a more privileged world. *Fine Clothes to the Jew* was the perfect companion piece to Hughes's manifesto, "The Negro Artist and the Racial Mountain."

As a measure of his deeper penetration of the culture and his increased confidence as a poet, three kinds of poems are barely present in *Fine Clothes to the Jew*—those that praise black people and culture directly, those that directly protest their condition, and those that reflect his own personal sense of desolation. For example: "Laughers," which celebrates blacks as "Loud laughers in the hands of Fate," is also probably the earliest piece in the book, having been published first as "My People" in June, 1922. "Mulatto" lodges perhaps the strongest protest, but is staged dramatically:

> . . . The Southern night is full of stars,
> Great big yellow stars.
>> O, sweet as earth,
>> Dusk dark bodies
>> Give sweet birth
> To little yellow bastard boys.

>> *Git on back there in the night.*
>> *You aint white.*

> The bright stars scatter everywhere.
> Pine wood scent in the evening air.
>> A nigger night,
>> A nigger joy.

> *I am your son, white man!*

>> A little yellow
>> Bastard boy.

Only one poem, "Sport," proposes life as an empty nothingness—as "the shivering of a great drum / Beaten with swift sticks."

Sorrow and despair dominate *Fine Clothes to the Jew*, but mainly through the expressive medium of the blues and its place in the lives of poor black men and women. In "Hey!" the blues is mysterious: "I feels de blues a comin', / Wonder what de blues'll bring?" It is also, as in "Misery," soothing, or even cathartic:

> Play de blues for me.
> Play de blues for me.
> No other music
> 'Ll ease ma misery . . .

Although the blues drifts in most often on the heels of lost love, the feeling can come for other reasons and still have poetic power. "Homesick Blues":

> De railroad bridge's
> A sad song in de air.
> De railroad bridge's

A sad song in de air.
Ever time de trains pass
I wants to go somewhere . . .

In *Fine Clothes to the Jew*, the singers and mourners are mainly women. By comparison, men are almost shallow; one man ("Bad Man") beats his wife and "ma side gal too": "Don't know why I do it but / It keeps me from feelin' blue." Men may be hurt in love, like the fellow in "Po' Boy Blues" who met "a gal I thought was kind. / She made me lose ma money / An' almost lose ma mind." But the blues are sung most often, and most brilliantly, by black women. Sometimes they sing to warn their sisters ("Listen Here Blues"):

Sweet girls, sweet girls,
Listen here to me.
All you sweet girls,
Gin an' whiskey
Kin make you lose yo' 'ginity . . .

Or, as in "Lament Over Love," their daughters:

I hope ma chile'll
Never love a man.
I say I hope ma chile'll
Never love a man.
Cause love can hurt you
Mo'n anything else can.

Women lament being cheated, for having been done wrong by "a yellow papa," who "took ma last thin dime" ("Gypsy Man"); or, as in "Hard Daddy," they grieve over male coldness:

I cried on his shoulder but
He turned his back on me.
Cried on his shoulder but
He turned his back on me.
He said a woman's cryin's
Never gonna bother me.

Sometimes the sorrow is greater when loss or the prospect of loss is mixed with profound self-abnegation and despair. "Gal's Cry For A Dying Lover":

. . . Hound dawg's barkin'
Means he's gonna leave this world.
Houng dawg's barkin'
Means he's gonna leave this world.
O, Lawd have mercy
On a po' black girl.

Black an' ugly
But he sho do treat me kind.
I'm black an' ugly
But he sho do treat me kind.
High-in-heaben Jesus,
Please don't take this man o' mine.

But the blues can reflect great joy as well as sorrow, as in "Ma Man," where a black woman's emotional and sexual ecstasy is so overpowering it drives her into song:

When ma man looks at me
He knocks me off ma feet.
When ma man looks at me
He knocks me off ma feet
He's got those 'lectric-shockin' eyes an'
De way he shocks me sho is sweet.

He kin play a banjo.
Lordy, he kin plunk, plunk, plunk.
He kin play a banjo.
I mean plunk, plunk . . . plunk, plunk.
He plays good when he's sober
An' better, better, better when he's drunk.

Eagle-rockin',
Daddy, eagle-rock with me.
Eagle-rockin',
Come and eagle-rock with me.
Honey baby,
Eagle-rockish as I kin be!

The last stanza of this poem, the second to last in the book (as if Hughes tried to hide it), was among the most sexually teasing in American poetry—to those who understood that "eagle-rocking" was possibly more than a popular dance step.

His critics had not howled without cause, but Hughes did not retreat. First at a Baptist church and then before an African Methodist Episcopal congregation in Philadelphia, he fulfilled engagements to read his poems. Then he coolly faced Floyd Calvin of the *Pittsburgh Courier* at the Knopf office on Fifth Avenue. In spite of the reviews, Hughes said, he declined to write about Vanderbilts and Goulds. At least two-thirds of all blacks were lower-class—"even I myself, belong to that class." In any event, "I have a right to portray any side of Negro life I wish to." He defended the blues singers Bessie Smith and Clara Smith as equal to the best of European folk singers, who were honored in America; and he declared that Carl Van Vechten had done more than anyone else for black artists.[24] To the white Cleveland *Plain Dealer,* curious about the hubbub in the black press over poetry, he explained that the black reviewers still thought that "we should display our 'higher selves'—whatever they are," missing the point "that every 'ugly' poem I write is a protest against the ugliness it pictures."[25]

When the *Pittsburgh Courier* invited Hughes to defend himself against his critics, he did not hesitate. In "These Bad New Negros: A Critique on Critics," he identified four reasons for the attacks: the low self-esteem of the "best" blacks; their obsession with white opinion; their *nouveau riche* snobbery; and their lack of artistic and cultural training "from which to view either their own or the white man's books or pictures." As for the "ill-mannered onslaught" on Van Vechten: the man's "sincere, friendly, and helpful interest in things Negro" should have brought "serious, rather than vulgar, reviews of his book." A nine-point defense of his own views and practices ended in praise of the young writers, including Toomer, Fisher, Thurman, Cullen, Hurston, and the Lincoln poet Edward Silvera. And Hughes himself: "My poems are indelicate. But so is life," he pointed out. He wrote about "harlots and gin-bibers. But they are human. Solomon, Homer, Shakespeare, and Walt Whitman were not afraid or ashamed to include them."[26] (Van Vechten thought the situation easy to explain; "you and I," he joked to Hughes while making an important distinction, "are the only colored people who really love *niggers*.")[27]

Hughes was not without friends in the black press. The *New York Age* found the book evocative of the joy and pathos, beauty and ugliness of black Americans, if of the more primitive type. The poet Alice Dunbar-Nelson, once married to Paul Laurence Dunbar, compared the book to Wordsworth and Coleridge's once maligned yet celebrated venture, *Lyrical Ballads,* which used the lives and speech of the common people; Hughes was "a rare poet."[28] Theophilus Lewis praised the book in the *Messenger,* and in the *Saturday Review of Literature* Alain Locke was deft about *Fine*

*Clothes to the Jew:* "Its open frankness will be a shock and a snare for the critic and moralist who cannot distinguish clay from mire."[29] And Claude McKay wrote privately to congratulate Hughes on having written a book superior to his first.

Among white reviewers, perhaps the most perceptive evaluation came from the young cultural historian Howard Mumford Jones. Using black dialect austerely, Hughes had scraped the blues form down to the bone, and raised the folk form to literary art. "In a sense," Jones concluded, "He has contributed a really new verse form to the English language." Although, like Wordsworth, he sometimes lapsed into "vapid simplicity." But if Hughes continued to grow, he was "dangerously near becoming a major American poet."[30] V. F. Calverton, Margaret Larkin, Arthur Davison Ficke, Hunter Stagg, Abbe Niles, Babette Deutsch, Julia Peterkin, and a wide range of reviewers praised the stark lyrical simplicity and beauty of most of the verse. More than once he was compared to Coleridge and Wordsworth's *Lyrical Ballads;* the critics understood that Hughes was trying to effect a historic change in poetry by compelling both blacks and whites to admit the power of black language. Other critics were not so sympathetic. The Boston *Transcript* flatly preferred Countee Cullen's work and called some of the Hughes verse "tawdry"; the *Nation* reviewer thought that Hughes was merely transcribing folklore, not writing poetry; the *New York Times* judged the volume "uneven and flawed."[31]

The ignorant blasts of the black press were nicely offset when Hughes accepted an invitation ("a great honor for me") from the Walt Whitman foundation to speak at the poet's home on Mickle Street in Camden, New Jersey. Stressing Whitman's humane depictions of blacks in his poetry, Hughes went on to claim that modern free verse, and his own work, descended from Whitman's great example. "I believe," Langston told the little gathering, "that poetry should be direct, comprehensible and the epitome of simplicity."[32] Suspicious of theory, Hughes had nevertheless identified one of the main ideas behind his theory of composition—the notion of an aesthetic of simplicity, sanctioned finally by democratic culture but having a discipline and standards just as the baroque or the rococo, for example, had their own. That simplicity had its dangers both extended its challenge and increased its rewards. The visit to Whitman's home left Hughes elated; to Van Vechten he mailed a postcard imprinted with an excerpt from Whitman's "Song of the Open Road": "All seems beautiful to me."[33]

Although Hughes would place the emphasis in his poetry in a different direction in the 1930s, when he wrote his most politically radical verse, he continued to write the blues even during this period. After the Depression, when Knopf published his *Shakespeare in Harlem*, the blues dominated the volume. When in the late 1940s and 1950s he allowed first be-bop (as in *Montage of a Dream Deferred*) and then increasingly "progressive" jazz (as in *Ask Your Mama*) also to shape his poetry, he was applying a basic principle he had first learned in the context of the blues. He never abandoned the form, because the blues continued as perhaps the most fertile form of black expressivity; *Ask Your Mama,* for example, is explicitly based on the "Hesitation Blues."

His initiative in the blues remains the only genuinely original achievement in form by any black American poet—notwithstanding the excellence of much of the work of writers such as Countee Cullen, Melvin Tolson, Gwendolyn Brooks, Robert Hayden, and even the rebel Amiri Baraka (surely the greatest names in modern black poetry). Their art is largely derivative by comparison. Afro-American poets did not rush to build on Hughes's foundation; most remained black poets who wished to be known simply as poets. But some poets followed the lead. Sterling Brown's *Southern Roads,* the most distinguished book of verse by an Afro-American in the 1930s, was certainly indebted to Hughes, although Alain Locke—anxious to be seen by Mrs. R. Osgood Mason ("Godmother") as opposed to Hughes after the "Mule Bone" controversy involving Hughes and Zora Hurston—used a review of *Southern Roads* to dismiss Hughes's blues and jazz writing as faddish, and to hail Brown as the authentic master of black folk poetry—a judgement without merit in spite of Brown's brilliance. Richard Wright, initially a poet, tried to write the blues, and even published one poem in collaboration with Hughes. Among whites, Elizabeth Bishop tried her hand at the form, with results certainly no worse than Wright's—the blues, they learned, is not as simple as it seems.

Black poetry, however, had to wait until the late 1960s and 1970s, with the emergence of writers such as Sherley Anne Williams, Michael S. Harper, and Raymond Patterson, to capitalize fully on Hughes's historic achievement. Ironically, because of the obscurity in which *Fine Clothes to the Jew* remains, and because the full extent of Hughes's artistic revolution has not been appreciated, many young black poets are unaware of the history of the form that they nevertheless understand as providing the only indisputably honorable link between their literary and cultural ambitions as blacks and the language compelled on them by history.

## Notes

1. Langston Hughes, *The Big Sea* (New York: Knopf, 1940).

2. "Suicide's Note," *The Weary Blues* (New York: Knopf, 1926): p. 87.

3. Paul Laurence Dunbar, "The Poet," *Complete Poems* (New York: Dodd, Mead, 1913): p. 191.

4. Hughes, "Prayer Meeting," *Fine Clothes to the Jew* (New York: Knopf, 1927): p. 46.

5. "The Weary Blues," *Weary Blues,* pp. 23–24.

6. *Big Sea,* p. 215.

7. LH to Countee Cullen, 7 April 1923; Countee Cullen Papers, Amistad Research Center, New Orleans.

8. *Big Sea,* p. 92.

9. "Negro Dancers," *Crisis,* 29 (1925): p. 221.

10. "To a Negro Jazz Band in a Parisian Cabaret," *Crisis,* 31 (1925): p. 67.

11. *Big Sea,* p. 209.

12. "Blues Fantasy," *Weary Blues,* p. 37.

13. George M. McClellan to LH, 14 July 1926; Langston Hughes Papers, Beinecke Rare Books and Manuscript Library, Yale University.

14. Langston Hughes to Alain Locke, 12 August [1926]; Alain Locke Papers, Moorland-Spingarn Research Center, Howard University.

15. *Big Sea,* p. 237.

16. "Hard Luck," *Fine Clothes to the Jew,* p. 18.

17. *Big Sea,* p. 264.

18. Amy Spingarn to Langston Hughes, ;[n.d.]; Langston Hughes Papers.

19. Arthur Spingarn to Langston Hughes, 3 February 1927; Langston Hughes Papers.

20. George Schuyler to Langston Hughes, 27 January 1927; Langston Hughes Papers.

21. James A. Emanuel, *Langston Hughes* (New York: Twayne, 1967): pp. 31–32.

22. *New York Amsterdam News* February 5, 1927; *Philadelphia Tribune,* February 5, 1927; *Pittsburgh Courier,* February 5, 1927; *Chicago Whip,* February 26, 1927; *Philadelphia Tribune,* February 12, 1927.

23. "Red Silk Stockings," *Fine Clothes to the Jew,* p. 73; "Beale Street Love," p. 57; "Laughers," pp. 77–78; "Mulatto," p. 71; "Sport," p. 40; "Hey!" p. 17; "Homesick Blues," p. 24; "Bad Man," p. 21; "Po' Boy Blues," p. 23; "Listen Here Blues," p. 85; "Lament Over Love," p. 81; "Gypsy Man," p. 22; "Hard Daddy," p. 86; "Gal's Cry For A Dying Lover," p. 82; "Ma Man," p. 88.

24. *Pittsburgh Courier,* February 26, 1927.

25. *Cleveland Plain Dealer,* March 27, 1927.

26. "Those Bad New Negroes," *Pittsburgh Courier,* April 16, 1927.

27. Carl Van Vechten to Langston Hughes, March 25 (1927); Papers.

28. *Washington Eagle,* March 11, 1927.

29. *Saturday Review of Literature,* 3 (April 9, 1927): 712.

30. *Chicago Daily News,* June 29, 1927.

31. *Boston Transcript,* March 2, 1927; *New York Times Book Review,* March 27, 1927.

32. *Camden Evening Courier,* March 3, 1927.

33. Langston Hughes to Carl Van Vechten, March 1, 1927.

GERMAIN J. BIENVENU

# *Intracaste Prejudice in Langston Hughes's* Mulatto

It is obvious that Langston Hughes's 1935 play *Mulatto: A Tragedy of the Deep South* concentrates on the unrelenting abuse that Southern blacks suffered at the hands of whites in the first part of the twentieth century. Continually, grotesque white characters come in and out of the play like ogres, ready to pounce upon nonwhite victims at the slightest provocation. But while such racist abuse is perhaps the most prominent feature of this story of racial mixing in the Deep South, it is certainly not the only concern to which Hughes calls attention. Like many writers of the Harlem Renaissance, Hughes is also concerned with prejudice *within* the black race. *Mulatto* displays, as effectively as any Renaissance work, the peculiar situation of blacks' harboring prejudices against fellow blacks. In this essay, I will examine how intracaste prejudice, as harbored and projected by Robert Lewis, the tragic mulatto of the play, contributes significantly to his tragic experience.

Before beginning my argument, I must stress that I am not supposing that, if Bert Lewis had been free of white racist views concerning blacks, he would not have experienced the problems with his father and with other whites that eventually lead to his death. No person of color possessing talents such as Bert's would have gone unmonitored by whites in the area and era depicted in *Mulatto*. Bert is an intelligent, capable, insightful black man

*African American Review,* Volume 26, Number 2; Summer 1992: pp. 341–353. © 1992 Germain J. Bienvenu.

with leadership skills, and even if Bert were an Uncle Tom, he would have
been a threat to all white racists who defend their notions of supremacy on
an insecure belief in non-white inferiority. I must also stress that I am not
exonerating the white racist characters— above all, Colonel Norwood—for
their complicity in Bert's tragedy. After all, if the racist regime established
and maintained by people similar to Colonel Norwood, Fred Higgins, and
the various members of the mob had not existed, a promising youth of Bert's
potential—not to mention his birthright—would likely have risen to the top
of his society instead of being smashed to the bottom. In addition, it is clear
that Colonel Norwood's brutal treatment of Bert as a racial inferior and his
rejection of Bert as a son bring about the main conflicts that propel Bert
toward destruction. What I wish to show in this essay is that Bert has shut
himself off from the reciprocal support, advice, affection, and acceptance
of the black community, and that such rejection of his black side in favor
of a white side that will not accept him figures directly in his downfall and
makes his "exorcism" at the hands of whites all the more tragic.

The first information that the reader gets about Robert Lewis occurs in
the opening description of the characters, in which Hughes notes that the
youngest mulatto son of Colonel Thomas Norwood and his black mistress
Cora Lewis *"resent[s] his blood and the circumstances of his birth"* (2). Hughes,
interestingly enough, does not specify white or black blood here. Robert's
*"blood"* would seem to include both black and white, and it is plausible that
the mixing of the two strains is *"the circumstance of his birth"* that Robert
most resents. While it might seem from this initial description that Robert
hates both bloodlines equally, the circumstances of the play reveal that he
has a predisposition toward one side over the other.

Early exposition reveals that, since Bert's return to the Norwood plantation, he has reminded both blacks and whites of his white parentage. Fred
Higgins, in a condemning manner, informs Colonel Norwood how Bert is
doing this among the townspeople, and William Lewis tells Cora how his
brother is doing it among the plantation blacks. After Cora inquires how
her grandchild Billy has come to speak boldly about his white grandfather,
William says, "Bert's the one been goin' all over de plantation since he
come back from Atlanta remindin' folks right out we's Colonel Norwood's
chilluns. . . . He comes down to my shack tellin' Billy and Marybell they
got a white man for grandpa" (13). Furthermore, when Bert first appears in
the play, he refers to himself as *"Mister* Norwood" (15)—defying the fact
that he is an illegitimate son of the Colonel—and starts recounting what he
believes to be the benefits of his white paternity. Thus, the earliest reports
of Bert's activity as well as the words that accompany his appearance show

Bert's insistence on publicizing his white lineage—not his black ancestry—in the expectation that people will treat him deferentially because of it.

In addition to his futile attempts to stress his whiteness over his blackness, Bert sets himself up for further frustration by harboring contempt for both blacks and whites in the area. Among whites, it is ironically his father—the person on whom Bert has built his white identity—against whom Bert holds the deepest grievances. But Bert's rebellious contempt for Norwood is not surprising, since it results from almost a lifetime of abuse heaped upon Bert by a father who will not acknowledge the paternity of his mulatto offspring. More specifically, Bert's bitter feelings toward his father stem principally from two instances in which the Colonel had not treated Bert as a white son.

The first cause for Bert's filial bitterness was a traumatic childhood episode that not only altered his relationship with his father but also affected his entire outlook on the racial politics of the South. Cora and William discuss this critical turning point in Bert's life, an occurrence that took place long before the play begins:

> **Cora:** [Bert] went runnin' up to Colonel Tom out in de horse stables when de Colonel was showin' off his horses—I 'members so well—to fine white company from town. Lawd, dat boy's always been foolish! He went runnin' up and grabbed a-holt de Colonel and yelled right in front o' de white folks' faces, "O, papa, Cora say de dinner's ready, papa!" Ain't never called him papa before, and I don't know where he got it from. And Colonel Tom knocked him right backwards under de horse's feet.
> **William:** And when de company were gone, he beat that boy unmerciful.
> **Cora:** I thought sho' he were gonna kill ma chile that day. And he were mad at me, too, for months. Said I was teaching you chilluns who they pappy were. Up till then Bert had been his favorite little colored child round here.
> **William:** Sho' had.
> **Cora:** But he never liked him no more. That's why he sent him off to school so soon to stay, winter and summer, all these years. (13–14)

Colonel Norwood fails to "blacken" his son by slapping any notion of whiteness out of the child just as he fails to break any remaining filial bonds by imposing academic exile on the youth.

Norwood remains powerless to change Bert's feelings of both kinship and whiteness because, prior to the episode in the stables, the Colonel himself had been the one who, through preferential treatment of his youngest son, had inadvertently encouraged such sentiments. (Cora, after all, had not dared to stress to her children "who they pappy were.") Similar notions of whiteness and kinship to the Colonel had not surfaced among Norwood's other mulatto children precisely because they had grown up "in their place," enjoying none of the partialities lavished upon the Colonel's "favorite little colored child." Bert, on the other hand, the spit and image of Thomas Norwood, grew to recognize both his resemblance to his father and the special treatment that it elicited from the Colonel. By the time of the important white guests' visit to the stables, Bert felt secure enough to proclaim publicly his relationship to the most prominent white man in the area, while at the same time denying any ties to blacks—referring, for example, to his mother as *Cora* instead of *Ma*. That Norwood publicly rejected the relationship and replaced the preferential treatment with brutality at the very moment when Bert was most sure about his identity accounts for both the trauma engendered by the episode and the intense hurt and indignation Bert felt from then on.

For Bert, the scene at the horse stables was very much like the crisis experience that many mixed bloods of American fiction encounter upon realizing that they are not part of the white class to which they have previously thought they belonged.[1] It is through Cora and William's retelling of the stables episode that the audience begins to sympathize with Bert's plight and to understand, in part, his obsession with being recognized as Norwood's true heir and, hence, as a white man. Ordered by the ruling class to remove all notions of whiteness from his mind, after his white father has indirectly encouraged such notions, Bert still refuses to replace his self-concept of white scion with that of "yard nigger." This stance propels him into and feeds the unending conflict of his life. William rightly tells his mother, "Bert thinks he's a real white man hisself now" (14). As will be seen in other passages, the more Bert is forced to remember his blackness, the more he insists upon his whiteness.

The second cause of Robert's filial belligerence is the type of work that his father has forced upon him since his return to the plantation after years of absence. Norwood himself recounts his degrading treatment of his intelligent, college-educated son, and offers his opinion of the youth in complaining to Cora about Bert's use of the Norwood car:

> He's no more than any other black buck on this plantation—due to work like the rest of 'em. I don't take such a performance from nobody under me—driving off in the middle of the day to town, after I've told him to bend his back in that cotton. How's Talbot going to keep the rest of those darkies working right if that boy's

allowed to set that kind of an example? Just because Bert's your son, and I've been damn fool enough to send him off to school for five or six years, he thinks he has a right to privileges, acting as if he owned this place since he's been back here this summer. (4)

The fact that Norwood wishes to have Bert treated in the same fashion as the lowliest field hand, and not even as a house or yard servant, is made more clear as Norwood continues:

There's no nigger-child of mine, yours, ours—no darkie—going to disobey me. I put him in that field to work, and he'll stay on this plantation till I get ready to let him go. I'll tell Talbot to use the whip on him, too, if he needs it. If it hadn't been that he's yours, he'd-a had a taste of it the other day. (4)

The indignation that Bert must be feeling under the harsh treatment that Norwood himself describes evokes a sympathetic response from the audience. For even if the Colonel does refuse to recognize Bert as a son, his blatant lack of good judgment in assigning an educated and highly capable "servant" to do the work of an unskilled laborer is foolish, if not unpardonable. Norwood's action probably would have been viewed even by his land-owning peers as a waste of potential, since Bert's abilities could have been channeled into more profitable service. It would not have been out of the question—and it might even have been deemed appropriate—to have a black of Bert's caliber (not to mention his relationship to the owner) in a supervisory position on the plantation.

Nonetheless, Cora and William implicitly condone Norwood's disciplining of Bert, however unjust and/or unwise, following the youth's return to the plantation. Cora, for example, observes that

De Colonel say he's gonna make Bert stay here now and work on this plantation like de rest of his niggers. He's gonna show him what color he is. Like that time when he beat him for callin' him "papa." He say he's gwine to teach him his place and make de boy know where he belongs. Seems like me or you can't show him. Colonel Tom has to take him in hand, or these white folks'll kill him around here and then—oh, My God! (14)

Because Cora views Norwood's intervention as necessary for Bert's protection, she can accept the Colonel's manner of discipline. Above all, she and William believe that Norwood's actions will be more effective than theirs in saving Bert's life, for Cora and William realize that they cannot bring Bert to the fundamental realization that surviving as a black person in their part of Georgia means living within the confinements imposed by white society. The two have repeatedly reminded Bert of this reality, but in vain. Rather than see Bert die at the hands of a white mob for refusing to follow the racial codes of the area, Cora and William would prefer to have him under the protective, if punitive, discipline of the most powerful white man in their locale. Furthermore, recognizing that Bert considers himself better than any other black in the area and, hence, that he will not listen to their advice, Cora and William view the tight reins that the Colonel attempts to impose on Bert as the only means of insuring the youth's continued existence. To their way of thinking, if Colonel Norwood can "break" Bert and put him "in his place," then perhaps Bert will be with them a little longer. They, like Norwood, fail to see that Bert cannot function in or tolerate a system that denies his rights and capabilities and that confines him to a position that he considers beneath his dignity.

While it could be argued that Bert's indignation arises over the injustice of his particular work assignment as well as the injustices of the entire Southern labor system, Bert's feelings seem more clearly to be governed by the racial preferences on which he has based his identity. As Bert tells his mother of the labor his father has imposed on him, "He thinks I ought to be out there in the sun working, with Talbot standing over me like I belonged in the chain gang. Well, he's got another thought coming! (*Stubbornly*) I'm a Norwood—not a field-hand nigger" (18). While Bert's reaction to the work is, in large part, justifiable, considering his intelligence and education, the intense indignation that he feels springs from something deeper than the injustices done to his capabilities. He is in no way sensitive to the indignation that other blacks must feel in being relegated to certain types of demeaning labor and barred from more rewarding forms of work. Bert is enraged over the summer assignment above all because it places him in the role of what he considers to be the lowest of all blacks—the field hand. This reduction in status is especially cloying since Bert not only considers himself not black but a Norwood heir. Bert goes on to assert that he is not going to do the work assigned to him, work which he views as being as much beneath his capabilities and his training as it is beneath his (white) race and his (assumed) name. Thus, Bert's protest is framed in terms of pride and self-interest, not universal human rights.

After Colonel Norwood recounts his treatment of Bert, the attention shifts to Bert's sister Sallie. Contrary to what Darwin T. Turner claims (299), the scene with Sallie is not a distracting digression from the action of the play; Sallie serves as a direct foil for Bert both in her character and in the better treatment she receives from Norwood. The Colonel allows Sallie to return to school after she has worked and resided in the "big house" during the summer, whereas Bert is prevented from returning to school and forced to live in a shack in the quarters. Sallie has even had servants such as Sam at her beck and call while on vacation, whereas Bert is ordered to "bend his back" in the field. When Norwood observes Sam carrying out Sallie's luggage, he remarks, "Huh! Darkies waiting on darkies! I can't get service in my own house. Very well" (5). Norwood's comments regarding his half-white daughter's privileges indicate resentment over the situation in his household, yet he allows the privileges to continue. Such preferential treatment of Sallie contrasts markedly with the abuse he heaps upon Robert, especially considering the fact that Bert was once Norwood's favorite.

The discrepancies between Norwood's treatment of Sallie and Bert are the direct result of each child's behavior; and that behavior, likewise, is a direct result of how the mulatto offspring views his or her whiteness and blackness. Sallie treats her peculiar situation diplomatically. Above all, she does nothing to rile her father, and that improves her chances of getting what she wants from him. Sallie's farewell words to Norwood indicate an astuteness that some might easily mistake for servile self-effacement:

> I just wanted to tell you goodbye, Colonel Norwood, and thank you for letting me go back to school another year, and for letting me work here in the house all summer where mama is. (Norwood *says nothing. The girl continues in a strained voice as if making a speech.*) . . . You been mighty nice to your—I mean to us colored children, letting my sister and me go off to school. The principal says I'm doing pretty well and next year I can go to Normal and learn to be a teacher. (*Raising her eyes*) You reckon I can, Colonel Tom? (6)

It is evident from this passage that Sallie knows that placating the man whom she cannot openly recognize as her father and assuming the role of a meek black servant around him and his ilk are the best means of getting what she wants from him and from the white world in general. And she gets it.

After Norwood utters a few lines that indicate that he has not been paying attention to Sallie, she continues, ". . . I want to live down here with mama. I want to teach school in that there empty school house by the Cross Roads what hasn't had a teacher for five years" (6–7). Apparent in this passage is the fact that Sallie, though perhaps the whitest of Norwood's offspring, does not deny her blackness. Rather, she openly acknowledges it—above all, by revealing her ambition to return to the area after graduation to teach black children who have been denied an education for years. Instead of scorning ignorant blacks, as Robert has done after receiving his education, Sallie wants to better herself in order to help the less fortunate members of her race. If the price to be paid for that opportunity is kowtowing at times to whites, the goal for Sallie is worth the seeming, yet actually disingenuous, self-effacement. As William tells his black mother about his sister, "Sallie takes after you, I reckon. She's a smart little crittur, ma" (12).

"A smart little crittur" like her mother, Sallie has fooled the white world in the same way that Cora has. By disingenuously remaining "in their place," Cora and Sallie have milked the white overlord for all that they can. Though the two might be referred to officially as the Norwood maids, neither undertakes many of the tasks of domestics. Rather, Cora and Sallie have domestics in their service and enjoy many of the luxuries that a white wife and a white daughter of a rich planter would. As long as they disguise their privileges under seeming servility to Norwood, as long as they forego the use of the front door and do not proclaim their true relationship to the Colonel (Cora calls him "Tom," but only in private), the benefits to be reaped from the white authority are innumerable. In the end, these advantages are invested in the future of the black community. Even though Sallie enjoys the white luxuries that other blacks do not have, she will return to the black community to teach black youth the skills necessary for getting ahead in American society.

On the other hand, Bert—like his white father, headstrong, stubborn, and as blind as he is proud—does not have the insight or the inclination to use covert means to secure benefits from the white world. This is not surprising, since everything Bert desires is overt: From whites he wants to be recognized as more white than black, and from his father he seeks public recognition as a legitimate heir. Obsessed with these futile goals, Bert cannot direct his energies toward efforts that would prove more beneficial to himself and to other blacks. Nor can he content himself with the advantages to be sapped by the cleverly clandestine manipulation that some blacks have learned to exert upon their white bosses. On the surface, Bert's cause might seem more honorable and sincere than Sallie's or Cora's, since what Bert openly demands is honesty from his father and equality with others of white parentage. But at its base, Bert's campaign is egocentric and inconsiderate (to state it mildly) of blacks. Bert argues for better treatment for himself—not better treatment for all blacks—on the grounds that he is part-white. Furthermore, as a Norwood, he considers himself better than most full-blooded whites. However honest he may be in expressing what he wants, Bert is not working for the good of others. The same cannot be said for Sallie and Cora, however sly they may seem to be in procuring what they desire.

Bert's obsessive sensitivity to being discriminated against in any fashion leads him into militant behavior that would not be accepted even from a white youth. When Fred Higgins comes to visit Norwood, Higgins complains that Bert nearly ran his car off the road and that Bert left a trail of dust in his wake, a lack of courtesy and respect that any older person might report to the parent of a child committing such an offense. Furthermore, Higgins discloses that Bert had been bickering with a postal worker over a policy of not providing refunds on money orders, a policy that probably would not have been breached even for a white customer. To make matters worse, Bert's reckless driving in town poses a threat to both black and white lives. Higgins adds that Bert

> comes in my store and if he ain't waited on as quick as the white
> folks are, he walks out and tells the clerk his money's as good as a
> white man's any day. Said last week standing out on my store front
> that he wasn't *all* nigger no how; said his name was Norwood—
> not Lewis, like the rest of his family—and part of your plantation
> here would be his when you passed out—and all that kind of stuff,
> boasting to the walleyed coons listening to him. (10)

Even when filtered through Higgins's racist language, it is apparent that Bert's belligerence stems from the fact that he wants to be treated the same as a white man not because he feels that all blacks should be treated equally with whites but because he is part-white himself. Also implied in Higgins's paraphrasing is Bert's sense that he is different from his non-white relatives and more affiliated with Norwood than they are. *They* may be Lewises, but he is a Norwood. That Bert haughtily considers himself apart not only from other blacks but even from members of his own family is further revealed when he and Cora discuss his upcoming meeting with the Colonel:

> **Robert:** Maybe he wants to see me in the library, then.
> **Cora:** You know he don't 'low no colored folks in there 'mongst
> his books and things 'cept Sam. Some o' his white friends goes in
> there, but none o' us.
> **Robert:** Maybe he wants to see *me* in there, though. (21)

It is a curious elitism derived from an awareness of his paternity, his resemblance to his father, and his individuality that causes Bert to expect as his lot more than might be due him even if he were a full-blooded white man.

Hence, when Cora reminds Bert that his sister Bertha is passing for white up North, he responds bitterly—not from any disapproval of what

Bertha is doing but from the fact that she has surpassed him on the color and social scales. His uncharacteristically terse response, "I know it" (18), indicates embarrassment: He, the true heir of Colonel Thomas Norwood, has not been able to achieve what a female Lewis has; he is too yellow to pass for white, too rusty at the elbows, as Norwood will remind him in their climactic confrontation (23).

Bert's hyper-elitist stance and his hypersensitivity to any racial prejudice directed toward him also blind him to the rather exceptional privileges that he has been granted—no matter how enmeshed with racial inequality and parental rejection or abuse these privileges may be. The Colonel tells Bert in a last-ditch (albeit stern and patronizing) attempt to end the conflict between them,

> . . . to Cora's young ones I give all the chances any colored folks ever had in these parts. More'n many a white child's had. . . . Sent you to college. Would have kept on, would have sent you back today, but I don't intend to pay for no darky, *or white boy either if I had one,* that acts the way you've been acting. (22; emphasis added)

Implied in the Colonel's last statement is an explanation of his previous disciplining of Bert through the summer work assignment—an explanation that might be lost on the audience if not highlighted for discussion. Norwood has treated Bert in a harsh manner over the summer as much for the latter's filial disrespect as for his disregard of other people. Norwood's discipline has also been intended as a chastisement aimed at calming Bert down, at making him realize what he has been offered, and at stopping him from striving after what he cannot attain. While Norwood is far from admirable in both his role of father and that of plantation owner, he has given Bert more advantages and more leeway than many other white men would give the mulattos or even the white children they have fathered.

It is also interesting to note that Norwood, despite his harsh treatment of Bert, has still cut the youth some slack. For example, early in the play Norwood warns that he will let Talbot use the whip on Bert if he needs it, but Bert has long been behaving in a way that Talbot would have returned with violence had it not been for the Colonel's intervention. Norwood's Freudian slip accounts for why he has been postponing Talbot's punishing Bert: Bert is a "nigger-child of mine, yours, ours," Norwood tells Cora (4). However much Norwood may refuse to acknowledge this fact outwardly, it is still an operating factor in his treatment of Bert. It may even account for Bert's "exile" having been academic rather than overtly punitive. Equally operant is the affection for Cora that Norwood cannot suppress.

In his final argument with Bert, the Colonel reveals perhaps the most remarkable privilege that someone of his racist bent could extend to Bert:

> I don't usually talk about what I'm going to do with anybody on this place. It's my habit to tell people *what to do,* not discuss it with 'em. But I want to know what's the matter with you—whether you're crazy or not. In that case, you'll have to be locked up. And if you aren't, you'll have to change your ways a damn sight or it won't be safe for you here, and you know it—venting your impudence on white women, parking the car in front of my door, driving like mad through the Junction, and going, everywhere, just as you please. Now, I'm going to let you talk to me, but I want you to talk right. (22)

Even though the Colonel belittles Bert in this invitation to dialogue, he is interested in learning why Bert is behaving in a way that the Colonel cannot understand. In addition, one cannot help noticing some parental concern on Norwood's part when he says that, if Bert does not change his ways, "it won't be safe for [him] here" (22). Perhaps Norwood's eventual banishment of Bert is intended as much as a protection of the mulatto son as a removal of an ugly problem. Unfortunately, Norwood's telling Bert to "talk like a nigger should to a white man" (23) does not facilitate communication; and the pride of both father and son breaks off dialogue, refuses compromise, and results only in continued conflicts for Bert with Norwood, with the whites of the area, and even with the local blacks.

Bert's prejudice against what he considers the lowest type of black is clearly seen in William's account of what Bert has been telling the Norwood plantation hands:

> . . . you can't talk to him. I tried to tell him something the other day, but he just laughed at me, and said we's all just scared niggers on this plantation. Says he ain't no nigger, no how. He's a Norwood. He's half-white, and he's gonna act like it. (14)

It is William above all who receives the brunt of Bert's prejudicial criticism. After William chides Robert for using the front door of the Norwood mansion (mainly because of the repercussions William fears such "impudence" might visit upon his family and the other Norwood blacks), Robert, whose natural speech approximates standard white, mimics his brother and inflicts a racial slur: "Yes, like de white folks. What's a front door for, you rabbit-hearted coon?" It is evident in this passage that Bert detests his brother's behavioral resemblance to "Uncle Tom" blacks.

That William, the darkest of Norwood's mulatto children, is not ashamed of the complacent lifestyle that he has adopted by choice is made clear when he retorts, "Rabbit-hearted coon's better'n a dead coon any day." Bert continues to defend himself, reminding William that they themselves are "only half-coons." Then the younger brother reveals what is at the center of his difficulties: ". . . I'm gonna act like my white half, not my black half" (16). Clearly, Bert believes that any step toward self-improvement and strength is characteristic of whites and that self-denigration and cowardice are the lot of blacks, who are by nature Uncle Tomish—although Bert makes a major exception in the case of his mother. For Bert, proof of such correlations is to be found in looking at the skin and behavior of himself and his darker brother.

There can be no doubt as to Bert's grievances against his blackness and his wishing to disaffiliate himself from blacks. Even when he says, a few lines later, "I might stay here awhile and teach some o' you darkies to think like men . . ." (16), he is speaking as would a white man who considers himself superior to his black listeners. That Bert is thus condescending toward his elder brother—and even to his mother, who is also listening—implies a rejection of them. Bert continues to blast his family's conformity:

> *You* can do it if you want to, but I'm ashamed of you. I've been away from here six years. (*Boasting*) I've learned something, seen people in Atlanta, and Richmond, and Washington where the football team went—real colored people who don't have to take off their hats to white folks or let 'em go to bed with their sisters. . . . Back here in these woods maybe Sam and Livonia and you[2] and mama and everybody's got their places fixed for 'em, but not me. (*Seriously*) Nobody's gonna fix a place for me. I'm old man Norwood's son. Nobody fixed a place for him. (*Playfully again*) Look at me. I'm a 'fay boy. (*Pretends to shake his hair back*) See these gray eyes? I got the right to everything everybody else has. (*Punching his brother in the belly*) Don't talk to me, old slavery-time Uncle Tom. (16)

Although Bert speaks about "real colored people" in this passage, he seems to bring them into the argument for the benefit of his mother and William, whom he considers far more "colored" than himself. What prompts Bert into demanding better treatment for himself is, again, not a belief in equality for all but indignation over the fact that he, the son of the most prominent white landowner in the area, an "[o]fay boy" with gray eyes, is treated like what he considers a common black. As in his other loud demands for better treatment for himself, Bert here voices, more than anything else, his feelings of superiority— a superiority that he bases on his independence, his education, his travels, and, above all, his paternal ancestry and resemblance to whites.

Bert's dislike of William arises from Bert's seeing in his brother too little of what he deems white and too much of what he detests in rural Southern blacks. In addition, Bert mocks the town blacks and reveals his scorn of them, just as he has mocked and scorned his brother. When he tells his mother about his encounter with the whites at the Junction that morning, he points out, pejoratively:

> 'Bout a dozen colored guys standing around, too, and not one of 'em would help me—the dumb jiggaboos! They been telling me ever since I been here, (*Imitating darky talk*) "You can't argue wid whut folks, man. You better stay out o' this Junction. You must ain't got no sense, nigger! You's a fool." (18)

Bert's scorn for the locals is further revealed as he tells his mother, "Besides you, there ain't nobody in this country but a lot of evil white folks and cowardly niggers" (18). Obviously, one of Bert's main grievances against the local blacks is that they are not "real colored people," like the blacks he has seen in Atlanta, Richmond, and Washington—or even like his mother. But, again, Bert seems to distinguish between blacks here chiefly for his mother's benefit. At the same time, he fails to realize that the local blacks refuse to band with him as much out of protest against his outrageous behavior as from fear of white retaliation. He asserts, in a typical refrain, that he is "half-white" and "no nigger," and implies again that since he is the son of the richest white man in the county he is superior not only to blacks but also to most whites in the area (18). Elitism remains at the core of Bert's scorn, his indignation, and his insistence on better treatment for himself.

Bert's most vehement denial of blackness and his loudest acknowledgment that he is obsessed with being recognized as Norwood's son occur during his penultimate conflict with his father. Bert and Norwood quickly become heated over Bert's twofold insistence on recognition when they encounter each other in the hallway of the big house:

> **Robert:** . . . I'm not a nigger, Colonel Tom. I'm your son.
> **Norwood:** (*Testily*) You're Cora's boy.
> **Robert:** Women don't have children by themselves.
> **Norwood:** Nigger women don't know the fathers. You're a bastard.
>         (Robert *clenches his fist*. . . .)
> **Robert:** I've heard that before. I've heard it from Negroes, and I've

heard it from white folks. Now I hear it from you. (*Slowly*) You're
talking about my mother.
**Norwood:** I'm talking about Cora, yes. Her children are bastards.
**Robert:** (*Quickly*) And you're their father. (23)

Perhaps what is most distressing to Bert in this exchange is that for the
first time he hears his father denying his children's paternity, something
Norwood had not done vocally even when he had beaten Bert at the stables.
But now the Colonel brutally echoes what blacks and whites have been telling Bert all along: that he is just a black bastard who cannot claim with any
certainty who his father is. These words coming from Norwood's mouth
are especially damaging to Bert, since he knows that he is unquestionably
the Colonel's son and since he even considers himself legitimate because of
Cora's fidelity to Norwood.

As his outrage continues to be fueled by Norwood's taunting denials,
Bert proceeds desperately:

> **Robert:** How come I look like you, if you're not my father?
> **Norwood:** Don't shout at me, boy. I can hear you. (*Half-smiling*)
> How come your skin is yellow and your elbows rusty? How come
> they threw you out of the post office today for talking to a white
> woman? How come you're the crazy young buck you are? (23)

Norwood now uses the stereotypes associated with mulattos to push Bert
back into the "nigger night" (an image for the black world Hughes uses in
his poem "Mulatto" [*Selected Poems* 160]) and to disaffiliate the youth from
the white world. Bert has what the white racist views as the unquestionable
physical markings of African ancestry—yellow skin and rusty elbows—that
linger long after miscegenation has occurred. Norwood also views the youth
as having the mental disorders some believe to result from the mixing of
black and white blood.

Bert, incensed by his father's stereotypic dismissal of mulattos and in-
dignant over being thrown in with blacks of the lowest status, asserts that
Norwood "had no right to raise that cane today when I was standing at the
door of this house where *you* live, while *I* have to sleep in a shack down the
road with the field hands. (*Slowly*) But my mother sleeps with you."

> **Norwood:** You don't like it?
> **Robert:** No, I don't like it.
> **Norwood:** What can you do about it?
> **Robert:** (*After a pause*) I'd like to kill all the white men
> in the world.

**Norwood:** (*Starting*) Niggers like you are hung to trees.
**Robert:** I'm not a nigger.
**Norwood:** You don't like your own race? (Robert *is silent.*) Yet you don't like white folks either? (23)

At the same time that he is asserting his whiteness most vehemently, Robert is forced to view as never before his denial of his blackness. Norwood's accusations of Bert's denial of blackness—no matter how full of ludicrous stereotypes these accusations may be—halt Bert as much as Bert's boast of killing all the white men in the world startles Norwood. (A boast, it should be noted, that occurs only after Bert is rejected summarily by the white father on whom he has built his white identity.) Instead of listening to Bert, on whom Norwood feels he has squandered many an indulgence that even white children could not expect from their fathers, Norwood links Bert to what whites consider the worst of blacks—the savage brutes, the would-be murderers, rapists, and insurrectionists that are hung from trees. As is evidenced by Bert's momentary silence, Norwood's remarks—as familially devastating as they are racist—drive an important message home: Bert cares for neither white nor black, nor anyone other than himself.

It is noteworthy that Robert ends up killing the person who gets him to recognize his prejudiced and self-supremacist stance. The last thing Bert tells his father before he starts choking the white man is that "I'm not your servant. You're not going to tell me what to do. You're not going to have Talbot run me off the place like a field hand you don't want to use any more" (24). Similarly, Bert will, later in the play, not let the white mob murder him as they would a detested or scapegoat black. Insisting on being his father's son, Bert follows his father in death. Having killed Norwood with his own hands, Bert will end his own life as well.

In a fleeting moment of truth immediately after killing his father, Bert finally owns up to his blackness—and to the repercussions of being black in Georgia. But it is too late for such realizations to save his life:

**Robert:** (*Wildly*) Why didn't he shoot, mama? He didn't want *me* to live. Why didn't he shoot? (*Laughing*) He was the boss. Telling me what to do. Why didn't he shoot, then? He was the white man.
**Cora:** (*Falling on the body*) Colonel Tom! Colonel Tom! Tom! Tom! (*Gazes across the corpse at her son*) He's yo' father, Bert.
**Robert:** He's dead. The white man's dead. My father's dead. (*Laughing*) I'm living.
**Cora:** Tom! Tom! Tom!
**Robert:** Niggers are living. He's dead. (*Picks up the pistol*) This is what he wanted to kill me with, but he's dead. I can use it now.

Use it on all the white men in the world, because they'll be coming
looking for me now. (24–25)

Bert, in killing his white father, obviously feels that he has killed his own
whiteness; for much of his identity as a white man has been tied up with
being Colonel Norwood's son. As Arthur P. Davis notes, "We sense that[,]
with the death of the Colonel, the bottom has really dropped out of Bert's
world" (200). For the first time, Bert refers to his father and to himself as
racial opposites. *The white man,* a phrase Bert uses repeatedly here to refer
to his dead father, implies a distancing of his father from himself that Bert
has heretofore not allowed. At the same time, in saying, "I'm living," followed by "niggers are living," Bert equates himself with blacks in a way he
has not done previously. The equation, at this point, can bring with it only
a recognition of doleful consequences. Bert knows that what awaits him,
as the non-white killer of a white man, is a gruesome death at the hands
of an angry white mob—an abuse that the white world reserves for those
it considers the most contemptible of blacks.[3] Unfortunately, Bert's awareness of all the ramifications associated with being black in Georgia, as well
as his identification with blackness, comes too late to do him any good.
Rather than suffer the inescapable disgraces—torture, mutilation, hanging,
burning—at the hands of whites, Bert kills what he has just recognized as
his black self.

If any doubt remains as to which parental line Hughes depicts his tragic
mulatto as preferring before the latter's admission of his blackness, one need
only go to Hughes's 1927 poem "Mulatto," in which the only words that the
audience knows for sure that the title character speaks are: *"I am your son,
white man!"* (*Selected Poems* 160). It is equally clear that the mulatto is trying
to convince his white half-siblings of his kinship to them, for they tell him,

> *Naw, you ain't my brother*
> Niggers ain't my brother.
> Not ever.
> Niggers ain't my brother. (160–161)

Full-blooded white half-siblings are absent from the play *Mulatto,* but
Colonel Norwood is all too similar to the white father of the poem, who
tells his mulatto son, *"You are my son! / Like hell!"* (160). The father, or the
half-siblings, or probably both then try to push the mulatto son back into
the dark world of the "nigger night": *"Git on back there in the night, / You ain't
white"* (161). But the mulatto son is like one of the "yellow stars" against the

"Southern night" (161), a similarity Hughes emphasizes by the way in which he places both son and stars in contrast to darkness in the poem:

> A nigger night,
> A nigger joy,
> A little yellow
> Bastard boy. (160)

and

> The Southern night is full of stars,
> Great big yellow stars. (161)

The yellow child does not fit into the black world, just as the yellow stars are separate entities from the Southern or "nigger" night. Undoubtedly, such imagery further illustrates that Hughes is stressing in both poem and play that his mulatto figure is one who seeks whiteness over blackness and that this futile, lifelong attempt is what makes Hughes's mulatto tragic, at least in these two works.

Arnold Rampersad notes that Hughes himself referred to *Mulatto* as an example of Afro-American defeatist literature (2: 14–15). Clearly, Bert does not come to the resolution that the mulatto narrator of Hughes's famous poem "Cross" (*Selected Poems* 158) does. Alive when the poem ends, the speaker of "Cross" forgives his white father in the first stanza and his black mother in the second; then, in the third and final stanza, he acknowledges with detached resignation that he himself is "neither white nor black" and does not know where his bloodline will lead him. On the other hand, Robert Lewis of the play *Mulatto* dies. Bitter to the end, *"resenting his blood and the circumstances of his birth"* (2), he hates his white father for not accepting him as a white son and rejects all that the race of his black mother has to offer. Bert has been forced to live in the shack but insists on dying in the big house. He must kill himself for the latter to happen.

## NOTES

1. For thorough discussions of the mixed blood's crisis experience as depicted in American literature, see Judith Berzon's *Neither White Nor Black*, especially chapter 5.

2. Bert here equates his mulatto brother William with full-blooded blacks, further indicating that Bert considers himself more white and, hence, better than William.

3. See Trudier Harris's *Exorcising Blackness* for a detailed examination of both historical lynchings and lynching as it figures in American literature.

## Works Cited

Berzon, Judith A., *Neither White Nor Black: The Mulatto Character in American Fiction.* New York: New York University Press, 1978.

Davis, Arthur P., "The Tragic Mulatto Theme in Six Works of Langston Hughes." *Phylon* 16 (1955): pp. 195–204.

Harris, Trudier. *Exorcising Blackness: Historical and Literary Lynching and Burning Rituals.* Bloomington: Indiana University Press, 1984.

Hughes, Langston. *Mulatto: A Tragedy of the Deep South.* 1935.

———. *Five Plays by Langston Hughes.* Ed. Webster Smalley. Bloomington: Indiana University Press, 1963: pp. 1–35.

———. *Selected Poems of Langston Hughes.* New York: Knopf, 1959.

Rampersad, Arnold. *The Life of Langston Hughes.* 2 vols. New York: Oxford University Press, 1986–1988.

Turner, Darwin T. "Langston Hughes as Playwright." *CLA Journal* 11 (1968): pp. 297–309.

KAREN JACKSON FORD

# *Do Right to Write Right: Langston Hughes's Aesthetics of Simplicity*

T he one thing most readers of twentieth-century American poetry can say about Langston Hughes is that he has known rivers. "The Negro Speaks of Rivers" has become memorable for its lofty, oratorical tone, mythic scope, and powerful rhythmic repetitions:

> I've known rivers:
> I've known rivers ancient as the world and older than
> the flow of human blood in human veins.

> (1656)

But however beautiful its cadences, the poem is remembered primarily because it is Hughes's most frequently anthologized work. The fact is, "The Negro Speaks of Rivers" is one of Hughes's most uncharacteristic poems, and yet it has defined his reputation, along with a small but constant selection of other poems included in anthologies. "A House in Taos," "The Weary Blues," "Montage of a Dream Deferred," "Theme for English B," "Refugee in America," and "I, Too"—these poems invariably comprise his anthology repertoire despite the fact that none of them typifies his writing. What makes these poems atypical is exactly what makes them appealing and intelligible to the scholars who edit anthologies—their complexity.

*Twentieth Century Literature: A Scholarly and Critical Journal,* 38 (4) Winter 1992: pp. 436–56. Copyright © 1992 *Twentieth Century Literature,* Hofstra University.

True, anthologies produced in the current market, which is hospitable to the African-American tradition and to canon reform, now include a brief selection of poems in black folk forms. But even though Hughes has fared better in anthologies than most African-American writers, only a small and predictable segment of his poetry has been preserved. A look back through the original volumes of poetry, and even through the severely redrawn *Selected Poems,* reveals a wealth of simpler poems we ought to be reading.[1]

Admittedly, an account of Hughes's poetic simplicity requires some qualification. Most obvious is the fact that he wrote poems that are not simple. "A Negro Speaks of Rivers" is oracular; "The Weary Blues" concludes enigmatically; "A House in Taos" is classically modernist in both its fragmented form and its decadent sensibility. Even more to the point, many of the poems that have been deemed simple are only ironically so. "The Black Christ," for example, is a little jingle that invokes monstrous cultural complexity. Likewise, two later books, *Ask Your Mama* (1961) and *The Panther and the Lash* (1967), contain an intricate vision of American history beneath their simple surfaces.[2] Nevertheless, the overwhelming proportion of poems in the Hughes canon consists of work in the simpler style; and even those poems that can yield complexities make use of simplicity in ways that ought not to be ignored.

The repression of the great bulk of Hughes's poems is the result of chronic critical scorn for their simplicity. Throughout his long career, but especially after his first two volumes of poetry (readers were at first willing to assume that a youthful poet might grow to be more complex), his books received their harshest reviews for a variety of "flaws" that all originate in an aesthetics of simplicity. From his first book, *The Weary Blues* (1926), to his last one, *The Panther and the Lash* (1967), the reviews invoke a litany of faults: the poems are superficial, infantile, silly, small, unpoetic, common, jejune, iterative, and, of course, simple.[3] Even his admirers reluctantly conclude that Hughes's poetics failed. Saunders Redding flatly opposes simplicity and artfulness: "While Hughes's rejection of his own growth shows an admirable loyalty to his self-commitment as the poet of the 'simple, Negro commonfolk' . . . it does a disservice to his art" (Mullen 74). James Baldwin, who recognizes the potential of simplicity as an artistic principle, faults the poems for "tak[ing] refuge . . . in a fake simplicity in order to avoid the very difficult simplicity of the experience" (Mullen 85).

Despite a lifetime of critical disappointments, then, Hughes remained loyal to the aesthetic program he had outlined in 1926 in his decisive poetic treatise, "The Negro Artist and the Racial Mountain." There he had predicted that the common people would "give to this world its truly great Negro artist, the one who is not afraid to be himself," a poet who would explore the "great field of unused [folk] material ready for his art" and recognize that this source would provide "sufficient matter to furnish a black artist with a lifetime of creative work" (692). This is clearly a portrait of the poet Hughes would become, and he maintained his fidelity to this ideal at great cost to his literary reputation.

In what follows I will look at some of that forgotten poetry and propose a way to read it that refutes the criticism that most of Hughes's poetry is too simple for serious consideration. I will first reconstruct Hughes's conception of the poet by looking at one of his prose characters who embodies his poetics; and, second, I will turn to a reading of *Shakespeare in Harlem* (1942), a volume of poetry that typifies Hughes's aesthetic program.

In his column in the *Chicago Defender* on February 13, 1943, Hughes first introduced the prototype of the humorous and beloved fictional character Jesse B. Semple, nicknamed by his Harlem friends "Simple." For the next twenty-three years Hughes would continue to publish Simple stories both in the *Defender* and in several volumes of collected and edited pieces.[4] Hughes called Simple his "ace-boy," and it is surely not coincidental that the Simple stories span the years, the 1940s to the 1960s, when Langston Hughes needed a literary ace in the hole.[5] The success of the Simple stories was an important consolation of the writer's later years, when his poetry was reviewed with disappointment, his autobiography dismissed as "chit-chat," his plays refused on Broadway, and his fiction diminished in importance next to Richard Wright's *Native Son* (1940) and Ralph Ellison's *Invisible Man* (1952).[6]

It seems obvious, however, that in the long association with his ace-boy Hughes found more than popularity and financial success. In fact, his prefatory sketches of Simple attest to the character's importance, in the sheer number of times Hughes sets out to explain him and in the specific details these explanations provide.[7] All of them depict Simple as an African American Everyman, the authentic—even unmediated—voice of the community that engendered him. For instance, in "Who Is Simple?" Hughes emphasizes the authenticity of his creation: "[Simple's] first words came directly out of the mouth of a young man who lived just down the block from me" (*Best* vii). Here and elsewhere Hughes asserts a vital connection between the fictional character and the people he represents: "If there were not a lot of genial souls in Harlem as talkative as Simple, I would never have these tales to write down that are just like him" (*Best* viii). The author's dedication to Simple is surely rooted in his conviction that Simple embodies and speaks for the very people to whom Hughes had committed himself back in the 1920s. But Hughes's affinity with Simple is more complete than this.

Commentators on the Simple stories have concentrated on two points: theme, "Hughes's handling of the race issue" (Mullen 20); and genre, "the generic nature of these prose sketches" (Mullen 20).[8] It is exclusively Hughes as prose artist we have acknowledged when considering these tales. However, I will argue that the Simple stories reveal a great deal about Hughes's poetic genius as well. Casting Simple as the figure of the poet illuminates Hughes's poetic program and explains his powerful affinity with his prose creation.

Crucial in tracing Simple's significance are the "Character Notes" to the 1957 musical comedy *Simply Heavenly*, which describe Simple in terms that stress his contradictions:

> Simple is a Chaplinesque character, slight of build, awkwardly graceful, given to flights of fancy, and positive statements of opinion—stemming from a not so positive soul. He is dark with a likable smile, ordinarily dressed, except for rather flamboyant summer sports shirts. Simple tries hard to succeed, but the chips seldom fall just right. Yet he bounces like a rubber ball. He may go down, but he always bounds back up.
>
> (*Plays* 115)

The parallel to Charlie Chaplin, an icon of contradiction, is telling. Like Chaplin, whose physical appearance announces internal tensions (his hat is too small, his shoes too large, his vest too tight, his pants too loose), Simple is awkward yet graceful, ordinary yet flamboyant. And, again as with Chaplin, these external tensions reveal deeper ones; he is obstinate yet fanciful, decent yet flawed, and—perhaps most poignant for Hughes—optimistic despite failure.

Simple is a compelling figure for Hughes precisely because of these tensions. For these contraries—even the apparently internal ones— hang about Simple like a fool's motley. The fool's motley, of course, traditionally implies chaos; yet while his multicolored costume reflects the intricacies and contradictions around him, the fool himself may often be a perfect simpleton. This is also true of Hughes's character: though his appearance and even to some extent his character express contradiction, his fundamental nature is unequivocally simple. Obstinate, positivistic, and optimistic, Simple is able to register contradictions without finally resolving them and therefore has special significance for Hughes's poetic project. Hughes, after all, claims that "where life is simple, truth and reality are one" (*Big Sea* 311). Yet, where in America is life simple for African Americans? The "where" Hughes invokes is not a place but a state of mind. The terms of his formulation—simplicity, truth, reality—are broad and vague because they are nearly synonymous to him. If one recognizes the simple facts of life, one will be able to see the truth; if one lives by the truth, one's reality will match one's ideals. Simplicity *is* truth in Hughes's vision.

Simple is the personification of such a poetics, a philosophy of composition that resorts to simplicity, not in response to singleness or triviality, but, ironically, in response to almost unspeakable contradiction. This is why he appears surrounded by complexities—his culture, his friends, even his clothing registering the confusion of the world around him. To shift the metaphor, simpleness, in both the character and the poetry, functions as a brick wall against which complexities collide. In its artless, uncomprehending refusal to incorporate contradictions, it exacerbates them. For a poet who equates simplicity with truth, cultivating a thematics and aesthetics of simplicity is essential— poetically and politically. Simplicity resists the pernicious subtleties and complexities of integrationist thought. Further, it reveals the inadequacies of such thought. But more important, it achieves these aims by reinstating the truth.

Let me turn to some examples. In "There Ought to Be a Law," Simple tells his friend Boyd that Congress ought to pass a law "setting up a few Game Preserves for Negroes" (*Reader* 181). Having seen a short movie about wildlife preserves, where "buffaloes roam and nobody can shoot a single one of them" (181), Simple concludes that "Congress ought to set aside some place where we can go and nobody can jump on us and beat us, neither lynch us nor Jim Crow us every day. Colored folks rate as much protection as a buffalo, or a deer" (181). Boyd, Simple's educated integrationist foil, first faults the plan for drawing a parallel between animals and humans: "Negroes are not wild," he asserts confidently. Yet, in observing Simple's logical flaw, he misses Simple's important point. Precisely because blacks are human beings, they should be treated better than animals. Boyd admits, "You have a point there" (181), but immediately discerns another shortcoming in Simple's argument. When Simple says that one of the things he would like about living on a preserve is that he could "fight in peace and not get fined them high fines" (182), Boyd recoils: "You disgust me. I thought you were talking about a place where you could be quiet and compose your mind" (182). Again Boyd reacts against the racist stereotype that black men are physically aggressive.

In fact, however, the freedom to fight was suggested to Simple by a scene in the movie showing two elks locking horns. While Boyd would replace one behavioral cliché (black men fighting) with another (men meditating in nature), he fails to see that both prescriptions curtail freedom. Once again, Simple makes the more substantial point: "I would like a place where I could do both" (182). While Simple's ideas always sound regressive at first, he ultimately articulates a far more radical position than Boyd's; and he does so by rejecting the falsifying complexities Boyd raises. Boyd's willingness to view all racial issues as hopelessly intricate finally renders him ineffective and conservative. Simple's obstinacy, on the other hand, enables him to view all issues in black and white, so to speak. Indeed, "There Ought to Be a Law" introduces, in a back-handed way, a black separatist position that Simple holds throughout the stories. Far from capitulating to white racist stereotypes about African-Americans, Simple advocates a complete break with the white world and, thus, a thorough rejection of white racist assumptions.[9]

When Simple tries his hand at poetry in two stories, we can begin to see how he embodies Hughes's conception of the poet. Ironically, in "Wooing the Muse" Simple is first inspired to compose poetry when he leaves the city to spend his vacation on the beach. Though the natural setting is a conventional pretext for poetry, Simple's verses ignore the romantic idealization of nature in favor of his characteristic realism regarding a subject that interests him more, human nature:

> Sitting under the trees
> With the birds and the bees
> Watching the girls go by. (*Best* 28)

In fact, he gently mocks Romantic clichés like "the birds and the bees" by incorporating such phrases into his irreverent lines. But it is precisely their status as clichés that Simple exploits, tossing off such lines as empty gestures toward figuration to contrast the way his poems barrel unmetaphorically toward their artless points (though his prose is highly figurative). And, of course, that second line is not just any cliché but a euphemism for sexual relations, and thus it receives a double reproof when Simple follows it with his blunt restatement, "Watching the girls go by."

Predictably, Boyd misses the poem's own logic and faults the verse for its failure to realize conventional Anglo-American form: "You ought to have another rhyme. *By* ought to rhyme with *sky* or something" (28). Boyd cannot read the poem on its own terms but views it only as an unfinished quatrain composed (ideally) of two rhymed (aa/bb) couplets. Simple, on the other hand, sees no reason why form should exceed meaning: "I was not looking at no sky, as I told you in the poem. I was looking at the girls" (30).

Simple's second poem is a free-verse composition about racism; "This next one is a killer," he tells Boyd. "It's serious" (30). In it he compares the treatment of non-black immigrants in the United States with the mistreatment of African-Americans:

> I wonder how it can be
> That Greeks, Germans, Jews,
> Italians, Mexicans,
> And everybody but me
> Down South can ride in the trains,
> Streetcars and busses
> Without any fusses.
> But when I come along—
> Pure American—

They got a sign up
For me to ride behind:
   COLORED
My folks and my folks' folkses
And their folkses before
Have been here 300 years or more—
Yet any foreigner from Polish to Dutch
Rides anywhere he want to
And is not subject to such
Treatments as my fellow-men give me
In this Land of the Free. (30)

Again, the poem is evaluated in terms of conventional literary standards when Joyce, Simple's fiancée, wants him "to change *folkses* to say *peoples*" in order to elevate its diction (31). But since Simple doesn't have an eraser, his original phrasing is preserved. This suggests another constituent feature of Simple's poetry: it is improvisational. Even when he writes poems, they are subject to the pressures of the immediate moment and cannot be polished or refined.

While the lack of an eraser might suggest the opposite, that the poem is fixed and unchangeable, it actually indicates that the process of composition—rather than the product (which is another matter and might receive revision at another time)—is spontaneous and improvisational. In fact, Simple thinks this poem should be longer, but he has to conclude it where he does because Joyce interrupts him during composition. And his sense that the poem should have been longer derives not from some external formal measure but from the integral relationship of structure and meaning. Boyd, on the other hand, thinks "It's long enough" because he doubts the poem's worth; but Simple asserts, "It's not as long as Jim Crow" (31).

After a lengthy discussion with Boyd about why he does not write more nature poems, Simple recites a third piece—a ten-stanza toast in the "counting rhymes" genre, structured in tercets (until the final stanza which is five lines) rhyming aab, like a blues stanza. The "b" line in each stanza is also a refrain line throughout, as in a ballad:

When I get to be ninety-one
And my running days is done,
Then I will do better. (33)

Simple has concocted this toast as a retort to people who tell him, as Boyd has just done, "You should be old enough to know better." Simple distinguishes between "knowing" and "doing":

"I might be old enough to know better, but I am not old enough
to *do* better," said Simple. "Come on in the bar and I will say you
a toast I made up the last time somebody told me just what you
are saying now about doing better. . . . That's right bartender, two
beers for two steers. . . . Thank you! . . . Pay for them, chum! . . .
Now, here goes. Listen fluently." (33)

Several points in this passage bear upon Simple's poetic practice. Most
important is the assertion that recognizing (knowing) social or literary
conventions need not result in enacting them (doing). When Simple orders
"two beers for two steers," he playfully supports this by infusing the poetical
(by virtue of the rhymes) into the mundane as easily as he has infused the
mundane into the poetical. Finally, when Simple cautions Boyd to "Listen
fluently," he coins a phrase that will appear again and again in the stories,
whenever Simple suspects that habitual ways of "reading" will obstruct the
proper reception of his compositions. The odd phrase pulls artist and audience together, insisting that writer and reader accompany each other in a
new literacy. "Listen fluently" also introduces orality, and appropriately so,
since it precedes the toast, an oral composition, and thus widens the scope
of poetry. As we have seen, many of Simple's poetic models are African-
American folk forms—ballads, blues, toasts—genres that can claim written
*and* oral status. Certainly Hughes, like Simple, "knows" about literary convention but chooses to "do" things his own way.

The opposition of correctness as knowledge and correctness as action
(in the context of poetry, "action" means writing truthfully) is central to
"Grammar and Goodness," another story that treats Simple's poetic production. Simple's formulation of this borders on the nonsensical, like many
of his wise sayings: "It is better to *do* right than to write right" (*Stakes* 182).
Simple reads two poems to the narrator (who in this story is apparently
not Boyd). The first is one that Joyce and Boyd have edited. Its conclusion
uneasily renders Boyd's accommodationist perspective in Simple's belliger-
ent style:

Now, listen, white folks:
In line with Rev. King
Down in Montgomery—
Also because the Bible
Says I must—
In spite of bombs and buses,
*I'm gonna love you.*
I say, I'm gonna LOVE you—
White folks, OR BUST! (181)

The "authorities"—Reverend King and the Bible (and behind them, certainly, Joyce and Boyd)—want Simple's poem to advocate loving the enemy.

However, this conciliatory theme is gainsaid by the imperative construction, the screaming capital letters, the allusions to white violence, and the threatening last line (which comes off as a warning to whites to *be* lovable rather than as a promise on Simple's part to love them "in spite" of themselves). Despite these obvious contradictions, the narrator extricates a coherent "message" from the piece by ignoring its style, and doubts whether Simple could have written such a poem: "You never wrote a poem that logical all by yourself in life" (181). Simple admits this freely and offers another, unedited, poem in its place; it is no surprise when it completely contradicts the first one. It begins,

> In the North
> The Jim Crow line
> Ain't clear—
> But it's here!

and ends,

> Up North Jim Crow
> Wears an angel's grin—
> But still he sin.
> I swear he do!
> Don't you? (181)

Though the narrator agrees with the sentiment of this poem, he chides Simple "for the grammar" (182). Simple once again rejects the notion that poems must meet formal standards, claiming, "If I get the sense right . . . the grammar can take care of itself" (182). Both "Wooing the Muse" and "Grammar and Goodness" repudiate the aesthetics of traditional poetry, especially adherence to conventional forms, elevation of diction, preference for written rather than oral forms, the necessity of polish and finish, and the subordination of content to form.

Simple is thus a folk poet in the African and African-American traditions. His poems are communal, colloquial, and often improvisational. When he uses existing verse forms, he chooses ballads, blues, toasts, and spirituals. Moreover, his speech is rendered lyrical through a high content of figuration and internal rhyme.[10] In addition to his status as folk poet, however, Simple is the embodiment of—and, considering his life span, perhaps the defender of—Langston Hughes's aesthetic program. His name, an epigrammatic poem in its own right, captures this aspect of the character.

In "Family History" Simple explains his highly suggestive name:

> "Grandpa's name was Jess, too. So I am Jesse B. Semple."
> "What does the *B* stand for?"
> "Nothing. I just put it there myself since they didn't give me no initial when I was born. I am really Jess Semple."
>
> (*Speaks* 179)

Simple's name invokes his family history, a heritage that the story reveals is multiracial. His name, then, links him to a diverse cultural past and thereby at least superficially legitimates him as a representative figure. A second interesting feature of his name is the self-defining middle initial "B." He says the "B" stands for nothing, but knowing him, we wonder if it doesn't signify "black." Or, it may derive from another story, "Bop," in which he explains to Boyd that the difference between the prefixes "*Re* and *Be*" (in "Re-Bop" and "Be-Bop") is that the "Be" signifies "the real thing like the colored boys play" (*Wife* 56). In such a reading, the middle initial "B" might indicate the integrity of self-authorship, a prerequisite for being an authentic representative of his larger culture. Even more suggestive are the puns involved in Simple's names. By giving himself the middle initial he transforms his given name from a negative description of himself—Jess Semple ("just simple")—into an imperative statement—Jess B. Semple ("just be simple"). The revised name, then, issues a commanding motto for Hughes's poetic program. And finally, "Semple" may also be an ironic appropriation of the middle name of Aimee Semple McPherson, the evangelist, who became a vicious and outspoken opponent of Hughes during the early forties.[11] It would be sweet revenge to name his irreverent, black-nationalist bard after a white evangelist who tried to censor and, failing that, publicly excoriated Hughes's poetry.

Simple's provocative name, his rich and original use of language, his obstinate literalism, his radical politics, and his eccentric appearance distinguish him as a poet figure and associate him with a long line of poetic simpletons—most important, with Shakespeare's fools. This is especially obvious in a story like "Cocktail Sip," where Boyd says Simple sounds like an Elizabethan poet, or "Midsummer Madness," in which Simple composes pithy proverbs. Like a Shakespearean fool, the Hughesian bard often encodes wisdom in nonsense.[12] Indeed, the cardinal point of the Simple stories is the wisdom of simplicity—a precept that, when applied to poetry, demands a daring aesthetic program.

*Shakespeare in Harlem* (1942), roughly contemporary with the Simple period, self-consciously engages in wooing Simple's muse. The volume is exemplary for two reasons: first, because it declares itself to be "A book of light verse," and second, because it has been largely overlooked by critics (the latter point undoubtedly due to the former). That is, its outspoken aesthetic recalcitrance has almost certainly doomed it to critical neglect. To read *Shakespeare in Harlem* we need an interpretive practice that accommodates these poems on their own terms, one that strives, as Simple would say, to "listen fluently."

From the prefatory note at the front of the book,

> A book of light verse. Afro-Americana in the blues mood. Poems syncopated and variegated in the colors of Harlem, Beale Street, West Dallas, and Chicago's South Side.

> Blues, ballads, and reels to be read aloud, crooned, shouted, recited, and sung. Some with gestures, some not—as you like. None with a far-away voice (viii)

to "A Note on the Type" on the last page of the book,

> The headings are set in Vogue Extra-Bold, a typeface designed in our time with the aim to express the utmost simplicity (125)

*Shakespeare in Harlem* equates the poetic with the simple. It declares itself to contain merely "light verse," "Afro-*Americana*"—a collection of folk materials—rather than high art. Like much of Hughes's canon, this book will employ folk forms—"blues, ballads, and reels"—that common readers are already familiar with from the oral culture. Indeed, the poet encourages readers to make the poems their own: they should be "read aloud, crooned, shouted, recited, and sung." Further, they can be acted out, "Some with gestures, some not." The preface, then, casts readers in the role of performers who will interpret the poems "as [they] like." The allusion to *As You Like It* is the first oblique reference to the namesake of the book. Yet, this Shakespeare, *in Harlem*, is near at hand, colloquial, folksy; he does not speak with the "far-away voice" of Elizabethan England or literary convention or classical poetry. Even his typeface expresses the "utmost simplicity."

But the appropriation of Shakespeare into simplicity in Harlem is not merely an adjustment undertaken for the audience, nor is it entirely a political maneuver. When Shakespeare goes to Harlem, he faces a crisis of language that is figured forth in extreme simplicity. The material and psychological conditions of Harlem as depicted here (elsewhere Hughes emphasizes its many positive aspects)—poverty, hunger, violence, lack of opportunity, unfathomable despair—render him almost speechless; it is only through the fool, conventionally a voice of simplicity amid overwhelming complexity, that the poet maintains expression. Like Virginia Woolf's imaginative "reconstruction" of the life of Julia Shakespeare in *A Room of One's Own,* in which she tries to imagine what would have been the fate of Shakespeare's sister (that is, of a talented female poet in the sixteenth century), Hughes is to some extent exploring what Shakespeare's fate would be were he an unemployed African-American in twentieth-century Harlem.

Little wonder, then, that the title poem—in which we first hear how Shakespeare sounds in Harlem—is half nonsense:

> Hey ninny neigh!
> And a hey nonny noe!
> Where, oh, where
> Did my sweet mama go?
>
> Hey ninny neigh
> With a tra-la-la-la!
> They say your sweet mama
> Went home to her ma. (111)

The poem's nonsense syllables, as might be expected, echo a song from *As You Like It* which two pages sing in honor of the fool's engagement:

> It was a lover and his lass,
>     With a hey, and a ho, and a hey nonino,
> That o'er the green cornfield did pass
>     In springtime, the only pretty ringtime,
> When birds do sing, hey ding a ding, ding.
> Sweet lovers love the spring. (V.iii.15–20)

*Shakespeare in Harlem* reverses this song: love cannot be idealized through images of springtime and green fields. *As You Like It* itself ridicules romantic equations about love, nature, and the simple life, and the nonsense syllables in the pages' song suggest the fatuousness of those idealized formulations. In the Hughes poem, by contrast, the allusion to Shakespeare seems to marshal the linguistic resources of the fool. Here the nonsense, rather than echoing the mindless babble of the clichéd lyrics, disrupts the portentousness of the lines that communicate the loss of love. Indeed, the first two lines of nonsense in each quatrain seem almost to make possible the utterance of the final two lines that admit loss.

The structure of the stanzas, then, which move from nonsense to sense, suggests that the incantatory energy of the nonsense—deriving from rhymes, alliteration, exclamation marks, and most of all from the liberating effects of nonreferential language—is necessary in order to accommodate the painful reality of the sense lines. The word "ninny" in Hughes's stanzas can thus be read simultaneously as a nonsense utterance and a direct address to the fool, "Hey, Ninny." In both cases the special capacities of foolishness are invoked. Similarly, the literal "no" that is released in the nonsensical "nonny noe" provides an aural negation of the otherwise ineluctable misfortune of the sense lines.

And though the poem sounds somewhat whimsical, lost love is not a comic subject in *Shakespeare in Harlem*. The "un-sonnet sequence" that opens the book (another revision of Shakespeare), "Seven Moments of Love," demonstrates what the rest of the book will reiterate: that to be abandoned by a lover is to be cast deeper into poverty. "Supper Time" moves from poverty as an image of loneliness to poverty as the literal result of being alone:

I look in the kettle, the kettle is dry.
Look in the bread box, nothing but a fly.
Turn on the light and look real good!
I would make a fire but there ain't no wood.
Look at that water dripping in the sink.
Listen at my heartbeats trying to think.
Listen at my footprints walking on the floor.
That place where your trunk was, ain't no trunk no more.
Place where your clothes hung's empty and bare.
Stay away if you want to, and see if I care!
If I had a fire I'd make me some tea
And set down and drink it, myself and me.
Lawd! I got to find me a woman for the WPA—
Cause if I don't they'll cut down my pay. (4)

The unsonnet sequence, indeed the entire book, treats love as a social rather than merely a private problem. Abandoned lovers are exposed to hunger and cold, to diminished wages and status. Details like the dry kettle, the empty breadbox, and the lack of firewood function simultaneously as metaphors for the speaker's isolation and as factual examples of the hardships he will face living on only one income.

The title poem begins a process of recontextualization of private life that the rest of the book develops. In "Shakespeare in Harlem" a speaker registers his loss of love in the first quatrain and another person answers him with the reports of still other people ("they say") in the second quatrain. The poem, in a section of the book called "Lenox Avenue," obviously invokes the voices of the people living along the street. A man arrives home, discovers his partner is gone, asks where she went, and is answered by a crowd of neighbors that she went home to her mother. The communal nature of the event is further registered in the appellation "sweet mama" and in the lover's retreat to her own "ma." This is clearly a family affair, not the isolated nuclear family of suburbia but the extended family of a population that is shifting from the rural south to the urban north. (The Harlem resident's responsibility to aid even remote family members who move north is a repeated theme of the Simple stories.) Romance in this context is not the usual stuff of sonnets but a relationship modeled on the family, as the similarity between the terms "sweet mama" and "ma" indicates. The speaker's "sweet mama" has not left for independence or romance but has retreated to another community, where she will receive care: to her family. There can be little doubt that she is shrinking from the kind of hardships that the "Supper Time" speaker faces.

The poem's simplicity, then, has a great deal of work to do. The nonsense lines allude to a tradition of empty love sentiments even as they also tap the special verbal resources of the fool. The plurality of voices situates love as a public issue. The appellations "sweet mama" and "ma" suggest a paradigm of need and dependence that love can support but not conquer. Though the speaker may to some extent employ nonsense in an effort at "laughing to keep from crying," this cannot wholly account for the poem. After all, this is Shakespeare, a master of the oxymoron and paradox; that he resorts to nonsense and repetition indicates that his relocation to Harlem has taken a heavy linguistic toll.

"Shakespeare in Harlem" probably has echoes of another fool's song. King Lear's Fool advises that nonsense is an appropriate response (it is the sign, in fact, of some vestige of sense) to the extreme emotional and physical hardships that Lear and the Fool experience on the stormy heath:

> He that has and a little tiny wit,
>     With a heigh-ho, the wind and the rain,
> Must make content with his fortunes fit,
>     For the rain it raineth every day. (III.ii.74–77)

The logic of the Fool's song turns on the double use of "little tiny wit": it argues that he who has a shred of sense left will employ a bit of humor to accept his situation, no matter how horrible it seems. The association of the fool's perspective with wisdom is here and elsewhere abbreviated in the word "wit" that refers at once to humor, to knowledge, and, most important, to a quality that humor and knowledge combined may inspire: ingenuity. In *As You Like It* Rosalind tells Touchstone what is true for nearly all of Shakespeare's fools at one time or another, "Thou speak'st wiser than thou art ware of" (II. iv.55). Hughes's simpletons are blood brothers to Shakespeare's fools.

The wisdom and ingenuity of the Ninny become apparent when we contrast two of the poems in *Shakespeare in Harlem*. In "Kid Sleepy" the title character, like Melville's Bartleby the Scrivener, prefers not to participate in life. To all of the speaker's efforts at imaginatively resuscitating him, Kid Sleepy responds, "I don't care":

> Listen, Kid Sleepy,
> Don't you want to get up
> And go to work down-
> Town somewhere
> At six dollars a week
> For lunches and car fare?
>
> Kid Sleepy said,
> *I don't care.* (24)

The prospect of working for a pittance, of earning just enough money to continue going to work, does not inspire Kid Sleepy. The speaker of "If-ing," on the other hand, is brimming with optimism and energy, though he has no more material resources than Kid Sleepy does. He has, instead, verbal ones:

> If I had some small change
> I'd buy me a mule,
> Get on that mule and
> Ride like a fool.
>
> If I had some greenbacks
> I'd buy me a Packard,
> Fill it up with gas and
> Drive that baby backward.
>
> If I had a million
> I'd get me a plane
> And everybody in America'd
> Think I was insane.
>
> But I ain't got a million,
> Fact is, ain't got a dime—
> So just by *if*-ing
> I have a good time! (32)

The difference between Kid Sleepy and this speaker is that the second speaker, as he proudly admits in stanza one, is a fool. He can acknowledge that he "ain't got a dime," but that "fact" is countered by another, more important, fact: he has had a good time.

Kid Sleepy, as his name indicates, has utterly succumbed to hardship, while the "*If*-ing" speaker has turned nonsense into a survival strategy. And notably that strategy is a linguistic game that finds new uses for even the most apparently unavailing words. The very contingency of the word "if" renders it susceptible to transformation. The fool Touchstone in *As You Like It* recognizes a similar indeterminacy in the word. Touchstone explains that quarrels can be resolved not by determining the truth or falsity of conflicting claims but by rejecting these inflexible categories:

> All these [quarrels] you may avoid but the Lie Direct, and you may avoid that too, with an If. I knew when seven justices could not take up a quarrel, but when the parties were met themselves, one of them thought but of an If: as, "If you said so, then I said so"; and they shook hands and swore brothers. Your If is the only peacemaker. Much virtue in If. (V.iv.96–103)

Hughes's speaker also has discovered the virtue in "if," and he exploits its contingency in order to imagine a better life.[13] Further, the speaker's word game employs rhyme, alliteration, metaphor, and rhetorical extravagance in order to conjure linguistic wealth. Kid Sleepy's response to poverty and unproductive work is more sensible than the second speaker's, but it is killing him. His name tells us he is on the brink of unconsciousness, he drowses in the harmful sun throughout the poem, and, most troubling, he has almost no language. His final utterance, the one that ends the poem and probably finishes off Kid Sleepy himself, lacks a subject and verb—lacks, that is, subjectivity and thus the capacity to act: "*Rather just / stay here*" (25). The "*If*-ing" speaker, by contrast, uses "I" nine times in his short poem and not only employs a range of action verbs but creates the most crucial one himself. Indeed, "coining" the word "*if*-ing" is another way he amasses his imaginary fortune.

These two poems suggest that the simpleton's penchant for verbal play saves him because it makes linguistic production possible. When Shakespeare gets to Harlem, he is dumbstruck. Having recourse to the voice of the fool is how he continues to write poetry. What I have been calling his crisis of language is an important theme in these and other poems. It is also, however, a structural principle in the volume. The book consists of eight sections of poetry, four of which have generic designations that are anticipated in the preface: "Blues for Men," "Mammy Songs," "Ballads," and "Blues for Ladies." Two other titles emphasize locale rather than genre: "Death in Harlem" and "Lenox Avenue" (the street where Simple's hangout is located).

All these sections answer to the interests of simplicity in their folk forms, common speakers, colloquial diction, everyday concerns, and uncomplicated ideas. Even more interesting are the first two sections: "Seven Moments of Love: An Un-Sonnet Sequence in Blues" and "Declarations" identify forms that are far simpler than ballads and blues: "moments," "declarations," a "statement," and one "little lyric." These new designations all emphasize brevity, bluntness, and simplicity, and they all take the thematics of simplicity to the structural level. As we will see, the poems themselves function like little elemental chunks of poetry that resist complication and elaboration. If we can find ways to read these atomic lyrics, we will have begun to achieve fluency in Hughes's poetry of simplicity.

I will conclude, then, by looking at several such poems in the "Declarations" section. The section title warns that these poems are not meditative or subtle in content, not figurative or lyrical in form. Instead, they are blurtings that make poetry out of the obvious or even the obtuse. "Hope," for example, reveals that the speaker's sense of possibility depends in an ironic way on her or his impoverished mental and linguistic resources:

> Sometimes when I'm lonely,
> Don't know why,
> Keep thinkin' I won't be lonely
> By and by. (16)

It is precisely the speaker's not knowing that makes hope possible. To know more, to think this out more thoroughly, would surely mean the eradication of all hope. The speaker's language supports the sense that inarticulateness is bliss; the last line, "By and by," is a phrase from spirituals and hymns, songs that turn from misery toward hope by positing another time when suffering will be alleviated and even rewarded.

The speaker seems not to know where this formulation originates, but it is nevertheless part of her or his severely limited verbal repertoire. The exhaustion and vagueness of "by and by," ironically, make it efficacious. Two insubstantial words create hope by putting the concreteness of a harsh reality (now) into relation with the abstractness of a better future time (then); and in the process the phrase conjures up an in-between realm of relation even though it cannot visualize hope in more decisive terms. Further, "by" is a homonym for the "bye" in "goodbye" and lends a sense of finality that shuts down further thought and thus staves off despair. "Hope" is achieved, then, by dwelling in an intellectual and linguistic limbo, by waiting in some state that is neither "here" nor "there"—a provisional state characterized by verbal simplicity. "By and by" defers all the mental and linguistic processes that would inevitably lead to the negation of hope.

"Statement" announces its simplicity in its title. And, true to its name, it offers only this bare fact:

Down on '33rd Street
They cut you
Every way they is. (28)

The speaker making this statement has no time for pondering the by-and-by, subject as he is to the perils of the present moment. The knife-wielding, anonymous "they" are not just the perpetrators of street violence but also other evils—hunger, poverty, unemployment, disappointment—that produce physical violence (as the dialect "they" for "there" suggests). The ubiquitousness of "they" and "every way" demands the full attention of this speaker, who can only state or declare the bald truth about life on 133rd Street. The conditions of his existence prevent him from analyzing, lyricizing, or elaborating his plight. The reader, of course, can do these things; in fact, to listen fluently *is* to analyze these brief utterances and elaborate recognitions and insights that move beyond them. But "Statement" itself remains a hard fact and thus an obstinate form that articulates the exigencies of Harlem.

Finally, "Little Lyric" self-consciously demonstrates the way that poetry will be altered when Shakespeare gets to Harlem: The poem's epigraph insists parenthetically that this little lyric is *"Of Great Importance"*:

I wish the rent
Was heaven sent. (21)

What is lost in reproducing the poem here is the way the tiny couplet is engulfed by the rest of the page. The white space that ominously surrounds it is as crucial to a reading of the poem as its two lines are. "Little Lyric" says visually that the sigh of desire expressed in the poem has been nearly extinguished by the vast emptiness around it. The visual hopelessness and fragility of the poem on the page are translated into language in the poem proper. Like "by and by," the idiomatic phrase "heaven sent" does not express a real confidence in divinity to pay the rent miraculously but rather employs the unavailing concept of heaven to figure forth dumb luck. Since there is obviously no heaven (as the hardships and injustices of Harlem seem to indicate), or at least no heaven that is willing to intervene, wishing "the rent / Was heaven sent" is merely an ironic way to acknowledge that the rent will not be paid. Again, the brevity of the poem, the sufficiency of its perfect rhymes, and the elemental simplicity of its point are features that defy further elaboration within the poem.

The "Little Lyric" enacts the near loss of language. It reveals in an extreme form what all the other poems in the volume suggest—that utter simplicity is the only adequate response to a dislocated life in an urban ghetto in a racist country. Simplicity, as we have seen, sometimes takes the form of nonsense and foolishness and sometimes takes the form of brevity and obviousness. Both manifestations of Hughes's aesthetics of simplicity forgo the complexities of "great poetry" in order to express something that is "of great importance." Such poems would rather do right than write right.

## Notes

1. Easily ninety percent of the poems in Hughes's canon are of the sort that I am describing as simple.

2. Jemie, Hudson, and Miller, among others, have persuasively demonstrated the intricacies of Hughes's jazz structures in these two late books.

3. Reviews in which these epithets appear are collected in Mullen.

4. The stories are collected in five volumes, *The Best of Simple, Simple Speaks His Mind, Simple Stakes a Claim, Simple Takes a Wife,* and *Simple's Uncle Sam.* Additionally, Hughes takes Simple to the stage with *Simply Heavenly,* a comedy about Simple's marriage.

5. In "Who Is Simple?"—the foreword to *The Best of Simple*—Hughes concludes, "He is my ace-boy, Simple. I hope you like him, too" (viii).

6. For a chronicle of Hughes's disappointments during these years, see Rampersad, especially chapter 8 of the second volume "In Warm Manure: 1951 to 1953." Ellison characterized *The Big Sea* as a "chit-chat" book during an interview with Rampersad in 1983 (202).

7. Hughes wrote at least four explanations of Simple: "The Happy Journey of 'Simply Heavenly,'" "Simple and Me," "Who Is Simple?" and the "Character Notes" to *Simply Heavenly.*

8. In his Introduction Mullen surveys the scholarship on the Simple stories; all the works he cites discuss either their racial politics or their prose structures.

9. One might wonder how a character described as an "Everyman" or a "black separatist"—that is, as a stereotype—can break stereotypes. That is, how can black separatism resist stereotypes when it, *by definition,* carries racist stereotypes with it? This is a subtlety that would not interest Simple, who accepts the necessity of his own racism and rejects the idea that African-Americans should "overcome" black nationalist stereotypes. As long as white racism prevails, he will resist it in kind. See "Color on the Brain" (*Stakes* 106–110) for one of many exchanges between Simple and Boyd about this issue.

10. In "Cocktail Sip," for example, Boyd's quotations of Elizabethan poetry are juxtaposed with Simple's rhyming prose: "Zarita is strictly a after-hours gal—great when the hour is late, the wine is fine, and mellow whiskey has made you frisky" (*Wife* 47).

11. Rampersad explains McPherson's antagonism to Hughes in chapter 14 of his second volume: "McPherson had a specific reason to harass Hughes. She was one of the allegedly fraudulent ministers of religion mentioned by name in his 'Goodbye Christ'" (390).

12. For discussions of the fool that emphasize the wisdom of his simplicity, see Welsford, Willeford, Weimann, and Goldsmith.

13. In his chapter on *Henry IV, Part I*, Holland makes a similar point, describing Falstaff's way of using "if" as a habit of speech that liberates him from the world of responsibilities and permits him to enter a "world of imaginings" (119).

## WORKS CITED

Baldwin, James. "Sermon and Blues." Mullen, pp. 85–87.

Goldsmith, R. H., *Wise Fools in Shakespeare*. East Lansing: Michigan State University Press, 1955.

Hollands, Norman N., *The Shakespearean Imagination: A Critical Introduction*. Bloomington: Indiana University Press, 1964.

Hudson, Theodore R., "Technical Aspects of the Poetry of Langston Hughes." *Black World* (1973): pp. 24–45.

Hughes, Langston. *The Best of Simple*. New York: Hill, 1961.

———. *The Big Sea: An Autobiography*. New York: Knopf, 1940.

———. *Five Plays by Langston Hughes*. Bloomington: Indiana University Press, 1968.

———. "The Happy Journey of 'Simply Heavenly.'" *New York Herald-Tribune* 18 Aug. 1957, sec. 4: pp. 1 +.

———. *The Langston Hughes Reader*. New York: Braziller, 1958.

———. "The Negro Artist and the Racial Mountain." *The Nation* CXXII (1926): pp. 692–694.

———. "The Negro Speaks of Rivers." *The Norton Anthology of American Literature*. Ed. Nina Baym et al. 2nd ed. New York: Norton, 1985.

———. *Selected Poems of Langston Hughes*. New York: Vintage, 1974.

———. *Shakespeare in Harlem*. New York: Knopf, 1942.

———. "Simple and Me." *Phylon* 6 (1945): pp. 349–352.

———. *Simple Speaks His Mind*. New York: Simon, 1950.

———. *Simple Stakes a Claim*. New York: Rinehart, 1953.

———. *Simple's Uncle Sam*. New York: Hill, 1965.

———. *Simple Takes a Wife*. New York: Simon, 1953.

———. *Simply Heavenly*. *Five Plays by Langston Hughes*. Bloomington: Indiana University Press, 1968.

———. "Who Is Simple?" *The Best of Simple*. New York: Hill, 1961: pp. vii–viii.

Jemie, Onwuchekwa. *Langston Hughes: An Introduction to the Poetry*. New York: Columbia University Press, 1976.

Miller, R. Baxter. *The Art and Imagination of Langston Hughes*. Lexington: University Press of Kentucky, 1989.

Mullen, Edward J., *Critical Essays on Langston Hughes*. Boston: Hall, 1986.

Rampersad, Arnold. *The Life of Langston Hughes, Volume II: 1941–1967*. New York: Oxford University Press, 1988.

Redding, Saunders. "Old Form, Old Rhythms, New Words." Mullen, pp. 73–74.

Welsford, Enid. *The Fool: His Social and Literary History*. London: Faber, 1935.

Wiemann, Robert. *Shakespeare and the Popular Tradition in the Theater: Studies in the Social Dimension of Dramatic Form and Function*. Baltimore: Johns Hopkins University Press, 1978.

Willeford, William. *The Fool and His Scepter: A Study in Clowns, Jesters, and Their Audiences*. Evanston: Northwestern University Press, 1969.

DAVID CHINITZ

# Rejuvenation through Joy: Langston Hughes, Primitivism, and Jazz

*It is not easy to identify in any simple way either "good guys" or "bad guys" in the history of Western primitivism.*

Marianna Torgovnick,
*Gone Primitive: Savage Intellects, Modern Lives*

The nature of Langston Hughes's engagement with the primitivism of the 1920s has been obscured from the beginning by a succession of myths. The oldest, propagated by hostile reviewers, has it that Hughes, led astray by his friend and editor Carl Van Vechten, was positively carried away with primitivist ardor to the great detriment of his art.[1] The second myth, circulated by Hughes himself in order to counteract the first, tells us that Hughes was never seriously involved with primitivism, which he recognized all along for the fad that it was.[2] The third myth, a later critical compromise, contends that after indulging for a few poems and a story or two, Hughes saw through the primitivist hoopla and simply repudiated all its tenets.[3]

The truth is more tangled than any of these stories acknowledges. Like T. S. Eliot, D. H. Lawrence, and other white modernists, Hughes reacted as both artist and social critic to the primitivist ferment of the early twentieth century. Hughes's position was of course complicated by his racial identity, which made him an object and not merely an observer of primitivist representations. The complex and often conflicted results are manifest in much

*American Literary History*, 9 (1); Spring 1997: pp. 60–78. © Oxford University Press.

of his early work. In this essay I explore Hughes's relation to the primitive as it evolved, gradually and arduously, over a period of approximately twelve years from the early 1920s to the mid-1930s. In extricating himself from the primitivist movement, Hughes struggled to disengage ideas long fused in primitivist discourse, attempting to rescue elements of primitivism that he continued to find meaningful—especially those pertaining to African-American jazz.

## I

The primitivism that confronted Hughes was somewhat removed from the anthropological and ethnological developments that inspired his white modernist counterparts; it postdated the primitivist artistic innovations of cubism, *Le Sacre de printemps* (1913), and *The Waste Land* (1922). What Hughes faced was rather the popularization of these intellectual currents. By the early 1920s, when the primitive had been avant-garde for a decade, it had also caught the attention of a much larger public. Those who, like Alain Locke, seriously valued African sculpture and other aspects of "primitive culture" found their ideas ever more commonly reduced to a core of enthusiastic platitudes and stereotypes.

In the US of the 1920s, the "vogue of the Negro" reached possibly even more voguish heights than in a Europe captivated by Josephine Baker and *négrophilie*. In Europe black culture was an exotic import; in America it was domestic and increasingly mass-produced. If postwar disillusionment judged the majority culture mannered, neurotic, and repressive, Americans had an easily accessible alternative. The need for such an Other produced a discourse in which black Americans figured as barely civilized exiles from the jungle, with—so the clichés ran—tomtoms beating in their blood and dark laughter in their souls. The African-American became a model of "natural" human behavior to contrast with the falsified, constrained and impotent modes of the "civilized."

Far from being immune to the lure of this discourse, for the better part of the 1920s Hughes asserted an open pride in the supposed primitive qualities of his race, the atavistic legacy of the African motherland. Unlike most of those who romanticized Africa, Hughes had at least some firsthand experience of the continent; yet he processed what he saw there in images conditioned by European primitivism, rendering "[the land] wild and lovely, the people dark and beautiful, the palm trees tall, the sun bright, and the rivers deep" (*Big Sea* 11). His short story "Luani of the Jungle," in attempting to glorify aboriginal African vigor as against European anemia, shows how predictable and unextraordinary even Hughes's primitivism could be. To discover in the descendants of idealized Africans the same qualities of innate health, spontaneity, and naturalness requires no great leap; one has only to identify the African-American as a displaced primitive, as Hughes does repeatedly in his first book, *The Weary Blues*:

> They drove me out of the forest.
> They took me away from the jungles.
> I lost my trees.
> I lost my silver moons.
> Now they've caged me
> In the circus of civilization. (100)

Hughes depicts black atavism vividly and often gracefully, yet in a way that is entirely consistent with the popular iconography of the time. His African-Americans retain "among the skyscrapers" the primal fears and instincts of their ancestors "among the palms in Africa" (101). The scion of Africa is still more than half primitive: "All the tom-toms of the jungles beat in my blood, / And all the wild hot moons of the jungles shine in my soul" (102).

For white Americans, access to these tom-toms often came in the form of jazz, an African-American cultural product widely misread as a simple transplantation of savage ritual music. According to the prevailing discourse, jazz in its original setting both expressed and incited the savagery of its creators. As one outspoken opponent explained to her readers, "Jazz originally was the accompaniment of the voodoo dancer, stimulating the half-crazed barbarian to the vilest deeds" of "brutality and sensuality" (Faulkner 16). There was no reason to assume that white Americans were immune to the effects of jazz; in fact a number of scientists, social scientists, and psychologists held the contrary. An article called "Why 'Jazz' Sends Us Back to the Jungle," for example, cited ethnologist Walter Kingsley as endorsing the view that "one touch of 'Jazz' makes savages of us all" by reawakening even "in the most sophisticated audience instincts that are deep-seated in most of us." This argument was a favorite with those who believed that the spread of jazz threatened to destroy Western civilization entirely. For those who espoused it, this prediction was borne out in the character of jazz dances, with their relatively free movement and indecorous contact between partners.

Of course the transformative potential of jazz could be singled out for approbation as well as for condemnation. If jazz liberated repressed instincts, then perhaps it could reenergize an exhausted and jaded civilization. This view, championed by Van Vechten and other devotees, helped to market jazz and all things "Negro" to the white American public. The accessibility of the primitive in the form of jazz encouraged the practice of slumming, in which whites would patronize black jazz cabarets to soak up the primitive atmosphere—and often to engage in some mildly primitive antics of their own. Uninhibited abandon was easier to achieve amidst crowds of dancing savages energized by primitive rhythms, and such a construction of African-Americans and their music made it possible for disaffected whites to join in (Ogren 164). Others who were less bold or merely curious came just to observe the primitives at play. Located in jazz, the primitive became "a tonic and a release" for whites who found their own culture comparatively bloodless (Huggins 89). Jazz fever and the primitivist euphoria supported each other throughout the 1920s in their mutual rise to celebrity.

·      The association of jazz with the primitive was reinforced by the many jazz musicians who understood that one vogue promoted another—witness song titles like "Futuristic Jungleism" (Mills Blue Rhythm Band) and "Jungle Jamboree" (Fats Waller and Andy Razaf). Duke Ellington had probably the greatest success of all in using primitivism to sell music, through spectacular jazz-accompanied jungle floor shows at the Cotton Club. That African-American writers should also have been pulled—some more, some less eagerly—into the jazz-primitivist discourse was inevitable. Claude McKay's controversial *Home to Harlem* (1928) was most famously immersed in the primitivity of the jazz scene. Zora Neale Hurston, too, invoked atavistic imagery in asserting that the music of a black jazz band brought out the savage in her: "I dance wildly inside myself; I yell within, I whoop; I shake my assegai above my head. . . . I am in the jungle and living in the jungle way" (154). The primitive element in jazz is a central feature of Hughes's poems as well between 1922 and 1926.

The jazz cabaret in Hughes is carnivalesque, its atmosphere thick with constitutionally prohibited alcohol, frankly sexual dancing (with sex itself not too far in the background), interracial fraternization, and of course the insinuations of jazz itself. Jazz conveys the liberating potential of the primitive to the world at large:

> White girls' eyes
> Call gay black boys.
> Black boys' lips
> Grin jungle joys. (*Weary* 32)

In Hughes's "Nude Young Dancer," a performer strips herself of all the accoutrements of civilization, behavioral as well as sartorial:

> What jungle tree have you slept under,
> Night-dark girl of the swaying hips?
> What star-white moon has been your mother?
> To what clean boy have you offered your lips? (*Weary* 33)

Under the influence of jazz, listeners too shed artificial skins to uncover their primitive selves.

If jazz was perceived by its opponents not merely as a music but as a subversive force, Hughes and other supporters defended jazz not by disputing but by reaffirming that view. Hughes read jazz, like the primitive itself, as an attractive and necessary corrective to prevailing American values: "[J]azz to me is one of the inherent expressions of Negro life in America: the eternal tom-tom beating in the Negro soul—the tom-tom of revolt against weariness in a white world, the world of subway trains, and work, work, work; the tom-tom of joy and laughter, and pain swallowed in a smile" ("Negro Artist" 4). Hughes readily accepted that jazz was a savage music, and this assumption strengthened his attachment to primitivist concepts. As Steven Tracy points out, Hughes was never particularly well informed about the relationship between African and African-American music (67); he was satisfied to assume that blues and jazz were essentially primitive so long as traditional hierarchies could be inverted and the primitivity of African-American music be seen as a positive distinction.

Supporting this inversion of values was a tempting but dangerous move. On the one hand, primitivism was empowering: it made the African-American suddenly an object of admiration. The characteristics of "exuberance, spontaneity, irresponsibility . . . and sexual freedom" long attributed to the race by demeaning stereotypes were now the very qualities sought after by whites in rebellion against conventional values (Huggins 156–157). On the other hand, the price of this newfound respect was the perpetuation of the old stereotypes. Atavistic conceptions assume and imply an inherent disparity between whites and blacks, dooming the latter to an irrevocable, if supposedly enviable, Otherness. For precisely this reason, most of the older generation of black writers, critics, and race leaders relentlessly opposed the primitivist representation of the African-American. And thus the association of jazz with the primitive made a socially unsavory music still more objectionable. Conceding the barbarity and unrespectability of the music, the black leadership generally chose to argue that jazz belonged only to the marginal "ugly side" of the African-American people (Ikonne 12).

Many of the talented younger black artists, by contrast, gravitated unapologetically towards primitivism as an affirmative racial discourse. For the "New Negroes," the primitivist ardor for what seemed distinctive and valuable in the African-American character constituted an auspicious new trend in white thinking. Primitivism also reinforced the importance of the black American's African roots, an appealing emphasis for a generation deeply influenced by Marcus Garvey. Moreover, the primitive was still avant-garde as well as popular, and its artistic avatars (cubism, jazz, etc.) remained abhorrent to the pillars of society—a definite attraction for a group of young creators determined to modernize the black artistic scene.

Finally, primitivism generated a market environment in which, for virtually the first time, African-American art could thrive. Primitivism helped make the Harlem Renaissance possible by developing a receptive audience and by encouraging patronage (Moses 40). At the same time, of course, it provided a potentially disastrous formula for earning white approval and the rewards of fame and fortune that went with it (Singh 36). It is not surprising that the younger writers, including Hughes, were regularly charged with pandering to the white primitivist appetite. For the most part these accusations were groundless, for the New Negroes' engagement with primitivism was if anything somewhat idealistic rather than mercenary. But as Langston Hughes came to see, it is not always easy to tell the difference.

## II

The first two myths concerning Hughes and primitivism are now easily disposed of. To begin with, Hughes did not merely dabble in primitivism; for several years it represented an important influence on his art and his thought. And since Hughes's jazz atavism preceded even Van Vechten's, the suggestion of some early critics that his white friend dragged Hughes into the primitivist vortex is unfounded.[4] At the same time, primitivism was not necessarily detrimental to Hughes's art. Some of his most effective and interesting poems of the early to mid twenties—poems like "Jazzonia" (25), "Negro Dancers" (26), "The Cat and the Saxophone" (27), "Lenox Avenue: Midnight" (39), and "Afraid" (101), collected in *The Weary Blues*—develop out of the jazz-primitivist mode.

In any event, most of the contemporary critical fire directed at Hughes's primitivism came in reaction not to *The Weary Blues,* which might arguably have merited the charge, but to his next collection, *Fine Clothes to the Jew.* In *Fine Clothes to the Jew,* a book shot through with the spirit, language, and form of the blues, Hughes fulfills the agenda defined in his seminal essay of the same period, "The Negro Artist and the Racial Mountain," with a naturalistic account of lower-class African-American life. The realism of *Fine Clothes to the Jew* makes the atavism of *The Weary Blues* seem almost quaint by comparison. Like the blues, the poetry of *Fine Clothes to the Jew* deals mostly with what Hughes calls "low-down folks" ("Negro Artist" 2)—abandoned lovers, the unemployed, "bad men" (21), battered women, and alcoholics. The romanticized primitives of *The Weary Blues* are entirely absent. What is striking about the contemporary response to *Fine Clothes to the Jew,* though, is that critics seem to have been unable to perceive the distinction. The association of the African-American with the primitive was so ingrained by 1927 that the working-class personae of *Fine*

*Clothes to the Jew* were apparently indistinguishable from the primitives of its predecessor.

In one supportive review, for example, Lewis Alexander claimed that *"Fine Clothes* reveals . . . that Mr. Hughes understands completely the lives of the more primitive types of Negro"; similarly, Julia Peterkin credited Hughes with rendering sensitively "the emotions of primitive types of American Negroes" (Mullen 7–8, 55). This extremely loose conception of the primitive worked less in Hughes's favor with the many African-American critics who considered *Fine Clothes to the Jew* thoroughly vulgar, a sensational portrayal of the sordid side of African-American life designed to appeal to voyeuristic white readers. Anything unwholesome, however much a reality in the lives of millions of black Americans, was to be considered exotic, and any attempt to write about it was, ipso facto, exploitative.

The proletarian realism of *Fine Clothes to the Jew* emerges from Hughes's increasingly conscious relationship to the black urban masses. His impressionistic earlier approach had exoticized the city "folk" as passionate latter-day savages; his new strategy focuses instead on their response to the adversity they face in daily life. But this is not to say that the people Hughes sketches in *Fine Clothes to the Jew* have not been romanticized in another way: "They live on Seventh Street in Washington or State Street in Chicago and they do not particularly care whether they are like white folks or anybody else. Their joy runs, bang! into ecstasy. Their religion soars to a shout. Work maybe a little today, rest a little tomorrow. . . . They furnish a wealth of colorful, distinctive material for any artist because they still hold their own individuality in the face of American standardizations" ("Negro Artist" 2). Even without atavism, Hughes's black working class are "natural" types, uncorrupted by the dehumanizing and falsifying forces of industrial capitalism. They may not be primitives per se, but they are still a race apart; their differences from the "civilized" Westerner remain essential. The progression from Hughes's cabaret poems to the blues poems of *Fine Clothes to the Jew* did not, then, mark a sudden about-face in the poet's sensibility. The naturalistic depiction of "ordinary" black lifestyles constituted a new emphasis, but otherwise continued the project intended by the primitivistic depiction of Harlem night life—the project of portraying African-American life in all its difference from white American life.

Although Hughes, like his critics, found the change in his representation of the African-American populace natural and continuous, it does mark the beginning of a significant ideological shift. Yet he had not thus far renounced primitivism on principle; on the contrary, even as he composed the poems that would make up *Fine Clothes to the Jew,* he was publishing his jazz cabaret poems in various journals and defending the quintessential work of pop primitivism, Van Vechten's *Nigger Heaven* (1926). Primitivism had not lost its value for Hughes, though he himself was shifting away from it.

Having more or less exorcised black atavism by the end of the decade, Hughes now worked to identify and to isolate the grains of truth that had attracted him to the primitivist movement in the first place. The legacy of 1920s primitivist discourse, which left Africa, the African-American, and jazz all but *defined* in terms of the primitive, made this process of refinement and redefinition an arduous one.

Hughes's struggle with these concepts may be usefully framed as part of a broader contest over the representation of the African-American in art—a manifestation of the "classic dialectic of difference" defined by Anthony Appiah: "[O]n the one hand, a simple claim to equality, a denial of substantial difference; on the other, a claim to a special message"—a celebration of difference (25). From the inception of his career, Hughes had to negotiate between these alternatives, gradually to formulate a synthesis between the poles of sameness and radical difference.

Hughes's 1931 novel, *Not Without Laughter*, endeavors, perhaps prematurely, to reach such a synthesis. In place of the atavism of *The Weary Blues* and the urban turmoil of *Fine Clothes to the Jew*, the novel offers a kind of pastoral, implicitly celebrating the freedom, vitality, and cultural richness of rural African-American folk life. The conservatism and piety of the folk are exemplified in characters like Annjee and Hager, while the irresponsible Jimboy and the lively Harriett embody the culture's musicality and free spiritedness. Predominantly, as Donald C. Dickinson points out, *Not Without Laughter* is a "quietly assimilationist" work, illustrating "that Negro life is neither sordid, spectacular or in most ways different from the life of any other people" (55). Yet Jimboy and Harriett, while hardly primitives, are also meant to exemplify talents and qualities specific to their race. Hughes is striving to reconcile Appiah's poles: the denial and the assertion of difference.

This attempt at reconciliation shapes most of all the ending of the novel. Harriett, who ran away earlier in the book, finally resurfaces as a successful performer, making a career of her unique racial spirit by imparting it, through song and dance, to her audiences. Drawing on the rich folk culture she has inherited from Jimboy, Harriett (now billed as "The Princess of the Blues") has achieved prosperity—a prosperity that will allow her nephew Sandy, Jimboy's son, to continue his education and "amount to something" (321). Harriett and Sandy embody Hughes's hope for the African-American future: equality and integration without loss of racial identity. In fact, their ability to infiltrate the American mainstream actually depends on the "special message"—in this case, the power of African-American art forms like blues and jazz—that Appiah identifies with the celebration of difference.

Many critics have found this happy ending too easy. Yet *Not Without Laughter* is also far from Hughes's last word on this subject; indeed, he is wrestling with the same issues twenty and more years later, with music still the pivotal element—the powerful yet dangerous key to a prospective racial success story.[5] Black music opens avenues to acceptance, empowerment, and enrichment; but these, in turn, threaten a dilution, and eventually the effacement, of blackness. Hughes's separatist aesthetic runs counter to his basically integrationist politics, an opposition which constantly challenges him to envision a satisfactory long-term resolution.

Primitivism, at any rate, fetched African-Americans credit at far too high a price. While it proffered a kind of respect, this respect made real acceptance and integration finally less rather than more achievable. Hughes found himself in a middle position, trying to affirm in effect that African-Americans were different, but not *that* different. His work is informed, as Arnold Rampersad has written, "by the notion that stereotypes are most often based on some underlying if distorted truth" (326). Hughes always sought to preserve those underlying truths, undoing their distortion as best he could.

In the case of primitivist stereotypes, Hughes's stance continued to evolve long after he wrote his last atavistic poems. Only gradually could he untangle sameness and difference, atavism and cultural heritage, jungles and jazz, to arrive at a more refined position than 1920s categories permitted. By 1930 and *Not Without Laughter,* Hughes knew that an unpretentious lifestyle rooted in folk origins did not depend on some primitive black essence; still, he could not resist describing Harriett's stage act in atavistic terms: "Suddenly the footlights were lowered and the spotlight flared, steadied itself at the right of the stage, and waited. Then, stepping out from among the blue curtains, Harriett entered in a dress of glowing orange, flame-like against the ebony of her skin, barbaric, yet beautiful as a jungle princess. She swayed towards the footlights, while Billy teased the keys of the piano into a hesitating delicate jazz" (317). Hughes still had not dissociated the power of African-American music from that of the primitive. In fact his rejection of primitivism was never a complete repudiation, for even as he left the primitivist movement behind Hughes strove to conserve what had attracted him to it and to distinguish that from what he was rejecting. This effort is intriguingly foregrounded in one of the best—and least discussed—stories from his 1934 collection, *The Ways of White Folks.*

### III

By the mid-1930s, far from having ushered in the end of racism, the cult of primitivism and the "vogue of the Negro" were for all intents finished. Hughes had outlasted his own period of primitivist ardor and had by now distanced himself still further through his increasingly radical politics. In

"Rejuvenation through Joy"—one of his longest stories and the only one to be considered for a Hollywood film (Rampersad 285, 308)—Hughes lampooned the primitivist cult in all its self-indulgence and absurdity. But beyond its cutting and often funny satire, the story also confronts two more complex problems. First, it seeks to identify the truths that inhered in the primitivist celebration of African-American culture. In particular, Hughes continues to believe, at times almost mystically, that jazz expresses and addresses a realm of the human psyche that Western civilization has suppressed; that the African-American retains easier and more immediate access to this spirit; and that implicit within jazz is an alternative mode of being. The ending of the story touches on a second and more painful issue: black complicity, including Hughes's own, in 1920s primitivist excesses.

"Rejuvenation through Joy" describes the rise and fall of the colony founded by the handsome and charismatic Eugene Lesche, who prescribes primitivism as a cure for the civilized ennui of his wealthy patrons. "Joy," Lesche's byword, is to be attained through music and motion, which survive in their primal forms today only in "the Negro." The Colony of Joy, presided over by Lesche and managed by his sidekick, Sol, enlists a Harlem band to supply the "primitive jazz" that together with some simple swaying exercises based loosely on jazz dance is to restore clients to psychical health. After scoring a great initial success, the colony begins to disintegrate over competition for Lesche's attention among its mainly female residents; finally it collapses when a melee touched off by the band incites the jealous patrons to violence and mayhem.

There is never a question but that Lesche's motives are pecuniary, his ideas reductive, and his language overblown; it is also clear that he does not fully understand the doctrine he preaches. The ludicrous side of Lesche's methods is obvious in, for example, the colony's re-Christening of all its inhabitants: "Lesche was called the New Leader. The Negro bandmaster was known as Happy Man. The dancers were called the Primitives. The drummer was ritualized as Earth-Drummer. And the devotees were called New Men, New Women" (89). The band leader's name had been Happy Lane to begin with; apparently even that was not cloying enough for Lesche's purposes.[6] And the biblical echo in "New Men, New Women" among so much else that is purportedly pagan serves to underscore the catch-as-catch-can quality of Lesche's secondhand rhetoric. Hughes's narrative acquires an increasingly acerbic tone by ironically adopting these terms rather than overtly deriding them.

Lesche is thoroughly indifferent to the merit of his ideas, which are for him only a means to entrepreneurial ends. Yet when we see (in flashback) Lesche first hit upon the idea that will make him rich, Hughes uses Sol's response to acknowledge his own mixed reaction to the scheme: "'Looks like to me,' said Lesche, 'a sure way to make money would be, combine a jazz band and a soul colony, and let it roll from there—black rhythm and happy souls.' 'I see,' said Sol. 'That's not as silly as it sounds'" (77). Similarly, when Sol remarks, "It's unbelievable how many people with money are unhappy," Lesche answers, with equal accuracy, "It's unbelievable how they need what we got" (73). Even while he decries its misuse, Hughes hints that Lesche's creed, and especially his theory of the life-giving powers of jazz, is indeed "not as silly as it sounds." When Sol asserts that he and Lesche "want to show 'em how much light there is in darkness" (83), he means only that they will portray the primitivity of "Negro" life as the key to happiness. But unknowingly, Sol is also defining Hughes's project in "Rejuvenation through Joy": to reveal the virtues obscured by the confusions and falsehoods of popular primitivism. Hughes, too, wants to show us the light in this darkness.

Lesche's conception of African-American life and culture is a jumble of primitivist stock ideas: "[H]e said, in substance, that Negroes were the happiest people on earth. He said that they alone really knew the secret of rhythms and of movements. . . . Move to music, he said. . . . [T]o music as modern as today, yet old as life, music that the primitive Negroes brought with their drums from Africa to America—that music, my friends, known to the vulgar as jazz, but which is so much *more* than jazz that we know not how to appreciate it" (70). Typically, Lesche does not distinguish between African-Americans and Africans, nor between the reality of Africa and its idealized projections. "See how the Negroes live," he tells his followers, "dark as the earth, the primitive earth, swaying like trees, rooted in the deepest source of life" (84). Primitives, he claims, "never sit in chairs:" where the hips and "life-center" are immobilized: "Look at the Negroes! They know how to move from the feet up, from the head down. Their centers live. They walk, they stand, they dance to their drum beats, their earth rhythms. They squat, they kneel, they lie—but they never, in their natural states, *never* sit in chairs. They do not mood and brood. No! They live through motion, through movement, through music, through joy!" (69). Adhering to this dubious sociology, Lesche furnishes his colony not with chairs but with backless African stools, and Sol remarks that he has hired a top-notch decorator "to do it over primitive—modernistic" (72). As usual, a mote of insight emanates from Sol's confusion.

To complete their plan of "combin[ing] a jazz band and a soul colony" (77), Lesche and Sol hire a talented group of black musicians from Harlem's Moon Club: "Happy Lane's African band, two tap dancers, and a real blues singer were contracted to spread joy, and act as the primordial pulse beat of the house. In other words, they were to furnish the primitive" (73). The irony of hiring a blues singer to "spread joy" is lost on the two schemers, who are determined only to provide, as Sol puts it, "music, the best music, jazz, real primitive jazz out of Africa (you know, Harlem)" (81). Ever concerned that the primitive be kept in control, however, Sol instructs the musicians "to be ladies and gentlemen (I know you are), to play with abandon, to give 'em all you got, but don't treat this like a rough house, nor like the Moon Club either" (81). Although the narrative remains focused on the white characters, Hughes gives the musicians just enough room to make clear that they are aware of being patronized and are not happy about it. The members of the band are not taken in for an instant by what impresses the rich and the educated.

Lesche's devotees have run the gamut of late nineteenth- and early-twentieth-century alternatives to Western rationalism, from hermeticism to psychoanalysis to Eastern religion and finally to pop primitivism. "Almost all of them," the narrative informs us, "had belonged to cults before—cults that had never satisfied" (86). Lesche's therapeutic blend of jazz and the primitive is so much in step with its time that its novelty seems inexplicable to them: "How did it happen that nobody before had ever offered them Rejuvenation through Joy? Why, that was what they had been looking for all these years! And who would have thought it might come through the amusing and delightful rhythms of Negroes?" (87). The concept of the "noble savage" had been absorbed long ago by popular philosophy; cynicism toward civilization was voiced incessantly in the postwar period; stereotypes of African-Americans as uncorrupted human "naturals" were ubiquitous; and the frenetic carpe diem ethos of the jazz age, to whatever extent a reality, was widely heralded and denounced. At the convergence of these ideas stood popular primitivism and the "vogue of the Negro." Add to them the various theories about jazz and "jazz emotions" then in circulation, and the wonder is really that Hughes (never mind Lesche) had to *invent* the Colony of Joy.[7]

A more significant surprise is that despite its quackery, Lesche's method does get results. Most of the "New Men" and "New Women" are quite satisfied with his treatment. Says one, "the rhythms have worked wonders" (86); for the rest "the house [is] full of life and soul" (88). In time they do experience gains in confidence and a loss of inhibitions (89–90). These successes are only partly attributable to Lesche's personal magnetism or to the credulity of the "New Ones." For at bottom, Langston Hughes *did* believe jazz to possess transformative powers, *was* convinced that rhythm carried transcendental energies, and *did* feel that African-American culture had special qualities of spontaneity, vitality and naturalness—not, by 1934, to be equated with primitivity—from which other races could benefit; *The Ways of White Folks* makes this last point over and over. Like other primitivists, including the early Hughes, Lesche has diluted these truths with quantities of nonsense. but enough good remains in his program to make it actually work.

In his 1954 *First Book of Rhythms,* we find Hughes, writing in propria persona, repeating parts of Lesche's lessons almost verbatim to children. More than once he stresses, for example, that "the most beautiful rhythms seem always to be moving upward . . . because the sun is above, and the growing things that start in the earth grow upward toward it" (18–19). This echoes Lesche's first lecture: "Splendid . . . beautiful and splendid! That's what life is, a movement up! . . . We need to *live* up, point ourselves at the sun, sway in the wind of our rhythms, walk to an inner and outer music" (68). The association of rhythm with the sun, which hovers around Lesche through the entire story, seems to be one that Hughes himself accepted readily enough to pass it on to his young readers. This mystical view of rhythm is elaborated by Lesche, who exhorts his followers to recover their natural selves by moving "to the gaily primitive rhythms of the first man." This recovery is to be accomplished "not by turning back time, but merely by living to the true rhythm of our own age," which may be discovered in jazz (70). Hughes, who had once asserted that "The rhythm of life / Is a jazz rhythm" (*Weary* 39), explains to the impressionable that "*All* the rhythms of life in some way are related" and that "Nature is rhythm" (*First Book* 18, 42). And however Lesche travesties it, his thesis—that the recovery of rhythm is crucial to spiritual health—is supported by Hughes's own assertions that success in any endeavor, whether athletic, culinary, or even political, depends on rhythm.[8] Here too, Hughes did not think Lesche's ideas as silly as they sounded.

"Joy," Lesche's keyword, is also a favorite with Hughes, who likewise associates it with African-American life. This association carries over from the primitivist context of "To Midnight Nan at Leroy's" (*"Jungle lover. . . . / And the moon was joy"* [*Weary* 30]) to the proletarianism of "The Negro Artist and the Racial Mountain" ("Their joy runs, bang! into ecstasy")—for as we have seen, it took Hughes some time to separate these concepts. The word reappears in Hughes's later poetry ("Juice Joint: Northern City" [1949], "Death in Harlem" [1935]), where it continues to represent the exhilaration and unrepressed freedom he admires in African-American culture. In identifying "joy" as the missing element in the lives of his clients, and in tapping African-American music as a source of this treasure, Lesche is again on target.

In another, more literary sense, Lesche is no ordinary charlatan. As Hughes's recurrent allusions make clear, Lesche is a false sun god, a modern Phaeton who preaches sun worship and then hubristically takes the god's place: "Every morning, *ensemble,* they lifted up their hands to the sun when the earth-drums rang out—and the sun was Lesche, standing right there"

(89). The first thing we learn of Lesche's origins is that he had worked his way across the country driving a chariot in a circus. He outdid Helios by riding "twice daily" (73). His progress carried him—naturally—from east to west until, finally abandoning his chariot in Los Angeles, he acquired an inseparable companion named Sol.[9] The end of his story comically recapitulates the destruction of Phaeton by Zeus's thunderbolt when he loses control of the chariot of the sun and scorches the earth. In the final catastrophe, Lesche disappears when a shot intended for him fires "upward toward the ceiling and crash[es] through the glass of the sun court, showering slivers on everybody" (94). Lesche's pretensions may be false, but they are high; his theories are a mockery, but a mockery of something important. The sun, as *The First Book of Rhythms* explains, is the source of ascending rhythms, and "the rhythms of the joyful spirit are rising ones" (26). If joy, rhythm, and the sun are all conceptually linked for Hughes, then one can at least say of Lesche that he usurps the right throne.

Two minor episodes in Hughes's autobiography *The Big Sea*—one in which a pupil of Hughes's falls in love with him (67–69), another in which a jealous German brewery master tries to shoot Hughes for his alleged dalliance with a young girl (74–77)—may have inspired some of Lesche's adventures. Still more remarkable, however, is Lesche's resemblance to another Harlem Renaissance writer: Jean Toomer. Physically, Lesche and Toomer are virtual twins—both tall and lean, with bodies conditioned by long hours devoted to physical training. Like Lesche, Toomer was considered "handsome beyond words"; like Toomer, Lesche is endowed with "a deep smooth voice" (66–67).[10] Hughes attributes Toomer's success as a Gurdjieffian guru, like Lesche's as the apostle of joy and jazz, to his personal beauty: "They liked him downtown because he was better-looking than Krishnamurti" (*Big Sea* 242). In his philandering Lesche is also modeled on Toomer, whose many lovers included Edna St. Vincent Millay, Margaret Naumburg (the wife of novelist Waldo Frank, his best friend), and the wealthy Mabel Dodge (Lewis 71–73). As a follower of Gurdjieff, Toomer preached "a regimen of 'inner exercises' and 'sacred gymnastics'" (Lewis 72), very likely the source of Lesche's "slow, slightly grotesque, center-swaying exercises" (88). And as Rampersad points out, even Lesche's first name, Eugene, seems to have been derived from Toomer's (285).

The kinship between Lesche and Toomer reveals something of Hughes's mixed feelings towards the latter; it also sheds light on the final twist that wrenches "Rejuvenation through Joy" to its ironic close. This comes in a brief denouement following the fracas that wipes out Lesche's colony: "The newspapers laughed about it for weeks, published pictures and names of the wealthy inmates; the columnists wisecracked. It was all very terrible! As a final touch, one of the tabloids claimed to have discovered that the great Lesche was a Negro—passing for white!" (95). One's first impulse is perhaps to dismiss this as a fabrication, the caustic last dig from a tabloid sneering at high society and its foibles. But looking back through the story, one finds that Hughes has actually left the question uneasily open. We know nothing of Lesche's past beyond the circus. His color is never specified, though his black hair is mentioned twice. Beyond that, there's not much to go on except for the resemblance to Toomer—and Toomer, significantly, was a light-skinned "racial chameleon" who was never quite sure where he belonged (Lewis 66). After Toomer wrote *Cane*, his dedication to Gurdjieff took him progressively farther from the African-American community; eventually he married a white woman and insisted on being considered, as Hughes puts it, "no more colored than white" (*Big Sea* 242). Hughes discusses Toomer's racial conversion in a tone of scrupulously inscrutable detachment. He obviously regrets that "the poet who, a few years before, was 'caroling softly souls of slavery' now refused to permit his poems to appear in an anthology of Negro verse," and he seems to resent Toomer's efforts to proselytize Harlemites who could ill afford the luxury of mysticism (241–242). But adding that Toomer had simply decided, "after Paris and Gurdjieff, to be merely American," Hughes avers, with an uncertain level of irony, that "one can't blame him for that" and concludes by asking enigmatically, "Why should Mr. Toomer live in Harlem if he doesn't care to? Democracy is democracy, isn't it?" (242–243). Complicating the picture still further is Hughes's awareness of his own racial indeterminacy as the product of European, African-American, and Native American ancestors. Though American mores defined him as black, he discovered to his surprise and disappointment that Africans considered him white (*Big Sea* 11, 102–103, 118). In this respect, too, the relations among Toomer, Hughes, and Lesche are fraught with tension and ambiguity.

With the concluding exclamation point of "Rejuvenation through Joy"—"passing for white!"—Hughes directs his sarcasm not, like the tabloid's, at the possibility but at the supposition of impossibility. There is no reason to believe that Lesche might *not* be passing. Certainly his exploitation of primitivist stereotypes indicates nothing to the contrary. In fact, the final doubt about Lesche's color packs a disturbing message from Hughes to his own race: that under the spell of primitivism it has been all too difficult to tell the victim of harmful stereotypes from the purveyor. Too many African-American cultural leaders—even the jazz genius Duke Ellington, even the genteel poet Countee Cullen, even Hughes himself—had contributed to the primitivist fraud, guilty in some cases of passively accepting primitivist discourse, in others of actively promoting it, at whatever cost in long-term social consequences. Lesche is neither a McKay nor a Van Vechten, neither a black primitivist nor a white. He is an archetype, equivocal of race.

"Rejuvenation through Joy" is not merely a satire on the perpetrators of popular primitivism and their dupes. By 1934 it hardly mattered who was to blame; the damage was done, and the African-American, represented in Hughes's story by a gifted band exploitatively billed as "The Primitives," continued to suffer for it. Hughes's anger, barely submerged beneath the story's good humor, flares over the reductive mischaracterizations of black culture, the commercialism, the sham sociology and the downright silliness of the primitivist fad and its concomitants, the "vogue of the Negro" and the debate over jazz. His anger is fueled by a frustrated sense that important particles of truth had been obscured by all the smoke and incense. For these were truths in which Hughes placed a great deal of personal faith and on which hung much of his hope for the future of his people.

## NOTES

1. J. A. Rogers, for instance, accused Hughes of "attempt[ing] to exploit the jazzy, degenerate, infantile and silly vogue" of primitivism (Mullen 47–48). Benjamin Brawley and Allison Davis each echoed this charge while specifically decrying the corrupting influence of Van Vechten, as did a still harsher anonymous reviewer in the *Chicago Whip* (Rampersad 140–141, 165; Davis 268–269). Hughes himself responds to these reactions in *The Big Sea* 271–272. See also Mullen 7–9 and Barksdale 24–27.

2. See *The Big Sea* 325, which should be read in conjunction with similar common sense denials (e.g., 228). Some recent critics have followed Hughes's lead in claiming that he "never used 'primitive' or African characteristics to explain American Negroes" (Huggins 164) or that he "did not try to develop a 'primitive' vision of modern life" (Ogren 128).

3. Donald C. Dickinson, for example, states baldly that "In 1930 [Hughes] renounced the whole body of primitivism" (30). Jean Wagner and David Levering Lewis similarly downplay the ultimate importance of African romanticism in Hughes's work while admitting its influence on his earliest poems (Wagner 454; Lewis 83–84).

4. *The Weary Blues* was in fact substantially complete by the time the two men met (Rampersad 108–110, 165).

5. This theme is developed extensively, for example, in *Montage of a Dream Deferred* (1951) and *Ask Your Mama* (1961).

6. Hughes appears to have adapted the name of Arthur "Happy" Rhone, at whose club he first met Van Vechten (Kellner 198).

7. Hughes did draw on the real-life career of the "Great Om" and his Westchester religious colony (Rampersad 284–285); however, the idea of basing a therapy on jazz and popularized primitivism was his own.

8. See *First Book* 39–40 and *Rhythms of the World*.

9. Hughes also has Lesche and Sol play repeatedly on "body" and "soul" (77, 78, 80).

10. On Toomer's appearance, voice, and physique see Lewis 62–66.

WORKS CITED

Appiah, Anthony. "The Uncompleted Argument: Du Bois and the Illusion of Race." *Critical Inquiry* 12 (1985–1986): pp. 21–37.

Barksdale, Richard K. *Langston Hughes: The Poet and His Critics.* Chicago American Library Association, 1977.

Davis, Allison. "Our Negro Intellectuals." *Crisis* Aug. 1928: pp. 268–269.

Dickinson, Donald C. *A Bio-Bibliography of Langston Hughes, 1902–1967.* Hamden: Archon, 1972.

Faulkner, Anne Shaw. "Does Jazz Put the Sin in Syncopation?" *Ladies' Home Journal* Aug. 1921: 16+.

Huggins, Nathan Irvin. *Harlem Renaissance.* London: Oxford University Press, 1971.

Hughes, Langston. *The Big Sea.* 1940. New York: Thunder's Mouth, 1986.

———. *Fine Clothes to the Jew.* New York: Knopf, 1927.

———. *The First Book of Rhythms.* New York: Watts, 1954.

———. "Luani of the Jungle." *Harlem* 1.1 (1928): pp. 7–11.

———. "The Negro Artist and the Racial Mountain." *Nation* 23 (June 1926): pp. 692–694. Rpt. in *Langston Hughes Review* 4.1 (1985): pp. 1–4.

———. *Not Without Laughter.* 1930. New York: Knopf, 1963.

———. *The Rhythms of the World.* Folkways, FC7340, 1955.

———. "Rejuvenation through Joy." *The Ways of White Folks.* 1934. New York: Vintage, 1971: pp. 66–95.

———. *The Weary Blues.* New York: Knopf, 1926.

Hurston, Zora Neale. "How It Feels To Be Colored Me." *I Love Myself When I Am Laughing, and Then Again When I Am Looking Mean and Impressive: A Zora Neale Hurston Reader.* Ed. Alice Walker. New York: Feminist, 1979: pp. 152–155.

Ikonne, Chidi. *From DuBois to Van Vechten: The Early New Negro Literature, 1903–1926.* Contributions in Afro-American and African Studies 60. Westport, Conn.: Greenwood Press, 1981.

Kellner, Bruce. *Carl Van Vechten and the Irreverent Decades.* Norman: University of Oklahoma Press, 1968.

Lewis, David Levering. *When Harlem Was in Vogue.* New York: Knopf, 1981.

Moses, Wilson Jeremiah. "More Stately Mansions: New Negro Movements and Langston Hughes' Literary Theory." *Langston Hughes Review* 4.1 (1985): pp. 40–46.

Mullen, Edward J., ed. *Critical Essays on Langston Hughes.* Boston: Hall, 1986.

Ogren, Kathy J. *The Jazz Revolution: Twenties America and the Meaning of Jazz.* New York: Oxford University Press, 1989.

Rampersad, Arnold. *The Life of Langston Hughes, Volume I: 1902–1941: I, Too, Sing America.* New York: Oxford University Press, 1986.

Singh, Amritjit. "Black-White Symbiosis: Another Look at the Literary History of the 1920s." *The Harlem Renaissance Re-Examined.* Ed. Victor A. Kramer. New York: AMS, 1987: pp. 31–42.

Torgovnick, Marianna. *Gone Primitive: Savage Intellects, Modern Lives.* Chicago: University of Chicago Press, 1990.

Tracy, Steven C. *Langston Hughes and the Blues.* Urbana: University of Illinois Press, 1988.

Wagner, Jean. *Black Poets of the United States.* Trans. Kenneth Douglas. Urbana: University of Illinois Press, 1973.

"Why 'Jazz' Sends Us Back to the Jungle." *Current Opinion* Sept. 1918: p. 165.

JOSEPH McLAREN

# From Protest to Soul Fest:
# Langston Hughes' Gospel Plays

In the 1960s, Langston Hughes, as dramatist and songwriter, was instrumental in defining the musical genre of the "gospel song-play," evident in a number of his productions: *Black Nativity* (1961), *The Gospel Glory* (1962), *Tambourines to Glory* (1963), *Jericho-Jim Crow* (1964) and *The Prodigal Son* (1965). The "song-play" concept can be distinguished from the musical play whose action more closely resembles that of a conventional drama.

Although other works using gospel music had preceded Hughes's 1960s presentations, among them Marc Connelly's *The Green Pastures* (1930) and Hall Johnson's *Run, Little Chillun!* (1933), Hughe's plays demonstrate how gospel music was "first used in a full-fledged sense to score a book musical" (Burdine 74). Alex Bradford called Hughes "the first gospel playwright," the one who created a "format" other than the concert for presenting gospel singing (Masterson, Lect. #3). Another possible progenitor of the gospel play would be James Baldwin, whose *The Amen Corner* (1954) also uses gospel songs but more as background for certain scenes rather than as the primary, substantive element of the play's structure.

Hughes recognized that gospel music, which has maintained a close link to folk traditions, could have an appeal to both black and white audiences (Sanders 114–115). He was inspired by its "soulful" power as well as its commercial potential as festival celebration derived from "theatrical

*Langston Hughes Review*, 15 (1); Spring 1997: pp. 49–61. © Langston Hughes Society.

ritual of the church service." Certain black church manifestations, such as call-and- response, offering, preaching, praying, testifying, and, of course, singing, are inherently theatrical though their use within an actual service is essentially spiritual (Weaver 58).[1]

Hughes has been connected most often to secular forms of African American music, especially jazz and blues, whose elements can be found in gospel music. Like jazz, gospel music also allows for spontaneous improvisation because it is a "free-wheeling art form not restricted by pre-formulated patterns which might tend to stifle the needed fervor of its composers and participants" (Masterson, Lect. #2).

Originating in the early twentieth century, gospel music was popularized in the twenties and thirties by the legendary Thomas A. Dorsey of Chicago.[2] Associated with the "sanctified" church rather than orthodox black churches, the musical form was furthered by the success of artists such as Mahalia Jackson, whose recording of "Move On Up a Little Higher" contributed to the international recognition of gospel singing in the 1950s (Brooks 156–159; Masterson, Lect. #2). Marian Anderson and William Warfield were also in the vanguard of those popularizing the form. By the 1960s, some five hundred amateur gospel groups were in existence as well as over fifty professional aggregations. Mahalia Jackson's "He's Got the Whole World in His Hands" had become a hit recording, and her 1962 European tour furthered recognition of gospel music as did the Staple Singers, who won the 1962 *Down Beat* magazine award for "best new vocal group," the first such honor to be accorded a gospel group (Masterson, Lect. #2).

As stage drama, the gospel play was extremely popular in New York productions such as Vy Higgensen's trilogy, *Mama, I Want to Sing*. Parts 1 and 2 stand as the longest running African American off-Broadway musical, appearing from 1983 to 1991; they were succeeded by *Let the Music Play Gospel* and *Mama, I Want to Sing III: Born to Sing*, staged in 1996 at the Union Square Theatre in New York.[3] Such films as *The Preacher's Wife* (1996), with Whitney Houston and Denzel Washington, also rely on the vitality of gospel singing.

It is ironic that Hughes, who did not have a reputation for Christian advocacy—especially as a result of his 1930s radical poems "Christ in Alabama" and "Goodbye Christ"—used traditional Biblical texts for dramatic ends in the 1960s. His ridicule of white evangelist Aimee Semple McPherson and black clergyman Reverend Dr. Becton, both of whom he considered charlatans, characterizes an earlier position from which Hughes distanced himself, especially concerning "Goodbye Christ," resulting in criticism from the left. To a degree, Hughes revised his anti-Christian reputation by the 1950s with such pieces as "The Glory Around His Head," an Easter cantata "solicited" by Albert Christ-Janer, editor of *American Hymns Old and New*. Unfortunately, during the civil rights era, Hughes would come into conflict with black church figures because of the implicit critique of clerical charlatanism in *Tambourines to Glory* (Hughes, *Big Sea* 275–278; Rampersad 1: 392–395; 2:261, 369–371).[4]

In general, however, Hughes's turning to the gospel play marked a positive portrayal of the black church and a retreat to a less politically charged arena. In a sense, Hughes revisited the black church experience he rejected at age twelve, as portrayed in "Salvation." Just as he had mined jazz and blues in cabarets and nightclubs, Hughes found that the storefront church was a site for imbibing gospel music (Berry 323–324). The gospel play appealed to audiences in ways that Hughe's more traditional plays did not, evoking various forms of audience participation. Alice Childress suggested certain artistic issues concerning audience response and the adaptation of gospel elements to the stage:

> He [Hughes] saw the beauty in the gospel material. I know at times I quarreled about some of the things, some of the gospel plays and shows. I felt that they were almost raucous. Sometimes I felt that he was losing something—sensitivity—and catering too much to crass audiences, stomping and jumping and clapping which would catch people up who knew nothing about the whole gospel background. But he said, "Alice, that's colorful. That's life." (Childress)

Although audience appeal and popularity were obvious reasons for choosing the gospel song format, Hughes was also extending his treatment of black icons developed in his thirties plays. He chose the central narrative of Christianity, the Nativity, as a subject for the song "The Ballad of the Brown King"—the Christmas carol, dedicated to Martin Luther King, Jr., drafted in May 1954 at the request of Margaret Bonds, who is credited with the score. The "widely acclaimed" composition, which premiered on 11 December 1960, was aired on New York television on Christmas Day ("Margaret Bonds" 17). One apparent intention of the ballad was to reinforce the image of African participation in the Nativity story by foregrounding color through the origins of the African "wise man" Balthazar. The song mentions Ethiopia, Egypt and Arabia as possible locations of Balthazar's origin, and color is used to connect the black persona of the song and the "Brown King" who is "dark" (Hughes, "Ballad").

Hughes went beyond the suggestion of African origins in framing the central characterizations of his most celebrated gospel play, *Black Nativity,* which explicitly uses black personas to re-figure the Christ story. Announced in early December in the New York African American newspaper the *Amsterdam News, Black Nativity,* which opened at the 41st Street Theatre in New York on 11 December 1961, beginning a four-week run, is essentially a radical treatment of religious iconography because it rewrites the conventional Eurocentric imagery associated with the Nativity. Underlying the basic idea of making Christ relevant to black audiences, the play also implies the historical actuality of a Christ who is of African origin.

Widespread positive responses to *Black Nativity* signaled "the first time gospel singing had ever been reviewed as legitimate Theatre" (Masterson, Lect. #3). Billed as a Christmas song-play, it was directed by Vinnette Carroll and used the gospel singing talents of Marion Williams and the Stars of Faith, Professor Alex Bradford and Singers, Carl Ford, Howard Sanders, Princess Stewart, and dancers Cleo Quitman and Clive Thompson in the roles of Mary and Joseph. Both Carmen De Lavallade and Alvin Ailey, the initial choreographer, had defected, De Lavallade as a result of the name change from "Wasn't That a Mighty Day!" to *Black Nativity,* Ailey "out of loyalty" to De Lavallade (Rampersad 2: 346–347; 396–397).

Though, for the most part, the production was praised in the *Amsterdam News,* especially for its gospel singing and the "continuity" of Hughes's narration, in the first half of the production, the choreography of Louis Johnson and the narration appeared to be "completely devoid of ingenuity or inspiration," but not because they were inherently flawed: "The simple fact is that even the most consummate artists would have trouble standing up to the swelling, surging gospel numbers." The dance segments were also constrained by the small stage (Norford 17).

The success of *Black Nativity* in New York led to international presentations in Copenhagen, Oslo, Rome, Paris, Hamburg, Milan, Brussels and London. The European recognition was launched with the successful performance of *Black Nativity* at the Gian Carlo Menotti Festival of Two Worlds in Spoleto, Italy. Its appearance in the new Coventry Cathedral in England was "the first time a group was ever asked to make a guest appearance" at that location. The play was awarded the Roman Catholic Silver Dove Monte Carlo Award as "the outstanding television program of 1962 in Europe." *Black Nativity* was "recalled to America" for a week-long performance at Lincoln Center's Philharmonic Hall, making it the "first attraction ever to play a full week at Manhattan's most splendid theatre" (Masterson, Lect. #3).

As an international hit, *Black Nativity,* broadcast by WINS Radio from Lincoln Center, was a fitting choice for sponsorship by the Westinghouse Broadcasting Company, which thought that the production would "'enrich the musical fare available to the public'" and would "'further interest'" in an American art form ("'Black Nativity' Will Play" 24). In 1992, the play was revived for a series of annual performances directed by Jesse Wooden, Jr., at St. Paul Community Baptist Church in Brooklyn. Wooden employed unique contemporary urban adaptations.[5]

*Black Nativity* celebrates the Christmas story in an African American folk manner by using nineteenth-century spirituals and original compositions to replicate the "reverence, awe, joy and jubilation" of a black church service. The format of the play is based on structures within the holiness or black Baptist church: the sermon, testifying, quotes from Biblical text, gospel music, spirituals, and call-and-response patterns.[6] Divided into two acts, "The Child Is Born" and "The Word Is Spread," the play contains songs composed by Hughes as well as selections from the gospel, spiritual, and Christian canons: "We Shall Be Changed," "Said I Wasn't Gonna Tell Nobody," "Joy to the World," "O Come, All Ye Faithful," "Go Tell It on the Mountain," and "Get Away Jordan."

The characters are drawn from the Biblical story, particularly, Joseph, Mary, and the "Three Wise Men," Balthazar, Melchior, and Caspar; there is playful humor in the portrayal of the shepherds as Ned, Zed, Jed and Ted. The suggested set for *Black Nativity* is minimal, a "platform of various levels and a star, a single glowing star high over a place that might be a manger." The economical, sparse staging is a reminder of Hughes's borrowings from Russian theatre concepts used in *Don't You Want to Be Free?* (1938) and, in general, the limited sets used by the Harlem Suitcase Theatre (Hughes, "Black Nativity" 1–2).

Hughes continued to employ gospel music in his 1962 production, *The Gospel Glory: From the Manger to the Mountain,* also titled *Gospel Glow,* the first African American Passion play. *The Gospel Glory,* directed by Louis Johnson, opened in Brooklyn at the Washington Temple Church of God in Christ on 25 October 1962, as a benefit for the Eastern Christian Leadership Conference (ECLC) in conjunction with Eastern Seaboard clergymen, who supported Martin Luther King's Southern Christian Leadership Conference (SCLC). (Also in late October, Hughes had been hired as host for a gospel television program aired in twenty-two cities, *The Gospel Time.*) The production of *The Gospel Glory* which used the personnel of the Washington Temple—Alfred Miller, minister of music, and Ernestine Washington, wife of the minister of the Temple—successfully portrayed a church elder, who retells the Christ story. The choir, made up of "wonderfully expressive and dedicated people," including soloists Ernestine Washington, Robert Madison, in the lead role as the elder, and Mildred Bryant, performed such songs as "Can't Sit Down" and "Were You There When They Crucified My Lord?" ("'Gospel Glow,' New Hughes Play" 19; "Producers Make Changes" 19; Gardner 87).

Containing four characters as well as singers and pantomimists, the play, like *Black Nativity,* was designed for minimalist staging, platforms arranged on various levels, benches, and a "simple stand" for the elder. The elder's presentation could be delivered as well from the church rostrum. The play is essentially a sermon punctuated by various responses from the singers, its simplicity suggested in the costuming, basic choir robes and a "Sunday-go-to-meeting suit" for the elder (Hughes, "Gospel").

In its conception, *The Gospel Glory* is a flexible vehicle that could be used to retell either the Nativity or the Passion. The play might be presented in its entirety or in part. Act 1, "Star in the East," might be staged at Christmas time; act 2, "Gospel Glory," could be presented as a Lenten or Easter production. The Pantomimists were optional; their role was to "move in rhythm to the music" (Hughes, "Gospel").[7]

The sources for the play were "traditional Americana religious songs" borrowed from recordings and published texts. "Away in a Manger" was derived from a recording by Marion Williams and the Stars of Faith entitled *O Holy Night,* "Little Boy, How Old Are You?" from the *Art of Roland Hayes,* and "Dry Bones" from a recording by the Delta Rhythm Boys. For act 2, Hughes contributed three originals, most importantly, "Gospel Glory," for which he is credited with both the words and the music (Hughes, "Gospel" act 2, 1–11).[8] "Gospel Glory" is delivered in a call-and-response pattern, suggesting the possibility of interchanges with a chorus, one of the prominent features of the black church service.

Unlike *Black Nativity* and *The Gospel Glory, Tambourines to Glory,* which opened at the Little Theatre on 4lst Street near Broadway on 2 November 1963, is more concerned with the social aspects of Harlem storefront churches. The play, which derived from Hughes's collaboration with gospel singer Jobe Huntley, who scored certain Hughes poems, blended elements of the conventional stage play, which uses a consecutive plot, with gospel song-play patterns (Huntley 9, 15, 40). Panned by New York's prominent drama critics, Taubman and Kerr, it ran for only three weeks—a failed production that "shifts carelessly from comedy to satire to melodrama to piety" (Taubman, *Tambourines* 47). The play had the appropriate number of songs to "declare itself as a light entertainment and to keep you from taking its story line seriously" (Kerr 189).

On the other hand, Candace Womble, writing for the *Amsterdam News,* called the play a "unique experience in religious theatre," though she did identify moments of discontinuity: "at times, the meaning, direction, and characters all seem to be working against each other." These lapses, however, were attributed to the lack of "soul" on the part of director Nikos Psacharopoulos rather than to the play itself (Womble 15). Some critics did not consider that the loose structure was intentional so as to give the singers adequate space for spontaneity, unhampered by theatrical conventions that might lessen the effect of the gospel singing, an "integral part" of the action as designed by Hughes (Hughes, "Gospel Singing" 13).

*Tambourines to Glory* is a social commentary on certain aspects of the black church, a theme that caused negative responses from segments of the

African American community, especially the clergy, who thought it demeaning to the image of the church during a period of involvement in the civil rights struggle. The play tells the story of a Harlem storefront church and its two founders, Laura and Essie. The main conflict involves Laura's use of the church for monetary ends, a reminder of Hughes's criticism of Reverend Becton. For Hughes, storefront churches signified the best and worst intentions:

> Most of them are run by men of good will but there's an occasional bad seed that mars the record. Gospel singing is a feature of the store-front church, and it was with this idea that 'Tambourines' began. ("Langston Hughes Describes" 3)

Originally written as a play, *Tambourines to Glory* was not chosen by the numerous producers to whom Hughes sent the manuscript in the 1950s. After he had rewritten it as a novel, published in 1958, producers such as Lawrence Langner of the Theatre Guild became interested and the play was tried out at Westport, CT, in the summer of 1960. In 1963, it was brought to New York by Joel Schenker and Associates and featured gospel singer Clara Ward as Birdie Lee, Hilda Simms as Laura Wright Reed, Rosetta LeNoire as Essie Belle Johnson, Robert Guillaume as C.J., Micki Grant as Marietta, and Louis Gossett as Big-Eyed Buddy Lomax.

Although Hughes offered his comments at rehearsals, he was primarily in the background during certain stages of the play's preparation. Rosetta LeNoire remembered Hughes's contribution to rehearsals:

> If you gave a suggestion, he would listen. He didn't always agree with you, but he would meet you halfway, and sometimes he would laugh. He'd throw his head back and say, "Oh, Rosie, that's exactly what I'm looking for. That's it." And he'd tell you why, and he'd always relate to something he saw or heard in the streets of Harlem (LeNoire)

*Tambourines to Glory* is a "dramatization of a very old problem—that of good versus evil, God slightly plagued by the Devil, but with God—as He always intends—winning in the end." It was a "folk ballad" and "fable" told in "broad and very simple terms." Hughes wanted the performers themselves to be "sensitive enough to appreciate the complexities of simplicity" (Hughes, *Tambourines* 184).

Like his other Gospel plays, *Tambourines to Glory* reflects patterns of African festival drama in which the audience is directly engaged (a device used by contemporary African playwrights such as Nigerian dramatist Femi Osofisan).

> At certain points in the show audience participation might be
> encouraged—singing, footpatting, hand-clapping, and in the
> program the lyrics of some of the songs might be printed with an
> invitation to sing the refrains along with the chorus of Tambourine
> Temple. (*Tambourines* 184)

The audience is asked to participate in the well-known call-and-response
pattern, when Birdie Lee exhorts them to respond to her *"Amen!"* with their
own shout (*Tambourines* 252–253).

In the play, Big-Eyed Buddy Lomax obviously symbolizes evil, an example of other noted villains of history, folklore, literature, and Biblical text
such as Hitler, Mack-the-Knife, Don Juan, Henry the Eighth, Catherine the
Great, Iago and Cain (Hughes, *Tambourines* 188). Allegory and symbolism
are interwoven with universal themes of trust and love brought out in the
portrayal of Laura, who "believed in God only insofar as it would bring her
what she wanted," and Essie, who "believed in God all the way" (LeNoire).

Another intention of the play is to show the linkages of the secular
and the spiritual, a theme of Baldwin's *The Amen Corner.* One song, "New
York Blues," makes references to jazz scenes and to Charles Mingus, legendary bassist and orchestra leader. The connection between gospel music
and the blues is signified when Buddy claims "it all sounds like blues"
(*Tambourines* 217–218).

One of the social implications is the potential for corruption in the
black church and whether Hughes was intentionally challenging charlatanism, though Rosetta LeNoire did not believe it to be Hughes's goal:

> It was not a ridicule, and if anyone took it that way, they were sadly
> mistaken. He just wanted to show what a big part church played
> in the Harlem community, because the worst person, the numbers
> runner, the gangster, or what not, whether he knew it or not,
> whether he liked it or not, always came back to God. (LeNoire)

The play also concerns black women and the potential for self-destruc-
tion in relationships with men. Laura, trapped in alcoholism and bound by
attraction for Buddy, is somewhat like Zarita of *Simply Heavenly,* who desires male companionship and the security it brings but is unable to establish
a fulfilling relationship. Furthermore, Laura wishes that she were more like
her mother from North Carolina, "who could jive a man back, make him run
and butt his head against the wall, lay down his month's salary at her feet,
and then beg her for a nickel" (*Tambourines* 236–237). A prodigal daughter,
Laura lacks the ability to "protect herself" from the allure of Buddy. Laura's
recognition of her betrayal by those whom she trusted becomes the final

"testifying" of the play, and her robing by the church sisters is a communal salvation accompanied by a crescendo of singing, trumpet playing and tambourine shaking (*Tambourines* 255–258).

In *Jericho-Jim Crow*, Hughes returned to chronicling African American history as in his earlier stage works, *Don't You Want to Be Free?* and *The Sun Do Move* (1942), updating the legacy to include the civil rights era. Using the conventional "morality" play, he portrays Jim Crow as slave trader, policeman, and white Southerner—a multiple character device found in *Scottsboro Limited* (1931). The historical progression is achieved through combining songs with sparse dialogue and poetry to create a "foot tapping" program in which "the rhythm is relentless" (Shephard 25).[9]

Presented by Stella Holt and directed by Alvin Ailey and William Hairston, *Jericho-Jim Crow*, announced in early January in the *Amsterdam News*, opened at the Greenwich Village Sanctuary Theatre on 12 January 1964, when Jean Genet's *The Blacks* was reaching its third year of performances in New York ("'Jerico-Jim Crow' [sic] Set" 11). Hughes collaborated with Hugh Porter on such songs as "Better Leave Segregation Alone," "Is Massa Gwine to Sell Us Tomorrow," "Freedom Land" and "Slavery Chain Done Broke at Last." Featuring William Cain as Jim Crow, Gilbert Price as the Young Man, and Hilda Harris as the Young Girl, the production was praised for its "eloquent and robust" singing. Hughes considered "future exploitation" of the production as a television program, film, or sound recording. The debut led to Crow's Gospel Song Classes, "free to all who can carry a tune," conducted by Clyde Williams at the Greenwich Mews Theatre (Shephard 25; Hughes, "Jericho").[10]

*Jericho-Jim Crow* raises questions concerning the nature of Hughes's political message during a period when moderate civil rights positions were being contested by more militant ones. Jesse Walker, the theatre columnist for the *Amsterdam News*, thought the production to be a "resounding musical play" that promoted the "theme of a desire for equality and brotherhood," and was notable as well for Hughes's original songs, "Such a Little King" and "Freedom Land" (Walker 13). Though protest was the clear message, when the play was revived in 1968 at the Village Presbyterian Church, it was thought to be not militant enough for "a Rap Brown or LeRoi Jones" and "disgracefully obsequious towards the values of white middle-class America" because it emphasized "brotherhood," an indication of Hughes's moderate though assertive political stand (Sullivan 22).

As with *Black Nativity* and *The Gospel Glory*, *Jericho-Jim Crow* relies on the traditional African American religious song canon derived from such sources as Hampton's *Religious Folk Songs of the Negro* ("Jericho"). The final script was achieved through a series of drafts, which demonstrate Hughes's attention to song placement and scene ordering (Hughes, "Jericho," "next to final draft").[11] The set, "any church rostrum, platform or stage with chairs or choir loft," follows the minimalist structure used in certain other Hughes gospel plays. Four chairs and two stools are the only recommended stage furniture, and stage directions encourage "audience participation" in the singing of well-known songs ("Jericho" 1–2).

Though set in the early 1960s, the play uses flashbacks to historical icons from the nineteenth century and the pre-civil rights era, such as Nat Turner, Sojourner Truth, Harriet Tubman, Frederick Douglass, W. E. B. DuBois, Ida B. Wells, and Marcus Garvey. The sixties figures—Martin Luther King, Jr., Fred Shuttleworth, Robert Moses, John Lewis, and John Farmer—suggest the prominent civil rights organizations of the period such as the Southern Christian Leadership Conference (SCLC), the Student Nonviolent Coordinating Committee (SNCC), and the Congress of Racial Equality (CORE). The catalogue also contains those involved in the desegregation of higher education in the early sixties, James Meredith, the University of Mississippi and Charlayne Hunter (Charlayne Hunter-Gault), the University of Georgia.

African American women are well represented by references to Mary Church Terrell, elected president of the National Association of Colored Women in 1896; Mary McLeod Bethune, founder of Bethune-Cookman College; and Rosa Parks, perhaps the preeminent woman icon of the civil rights struggle. Lesser-known women were given credit as well: Autherine Lucy, who, as a student, was involved in the desegregation of the University of Alabama in 1956; Daisy Bates, connected with Little Rock desegregation; and Diane Nash, cofounder of SNCC and president of Black Women for Decent Housing ("Jericho" 2–5).

The play goes beyond national concerns to East-West polarization expressed in a folksy manner by the Old Man, who calls for universal emancipation symbolized in the song "Freedom Land." Colonial and postcolonial issues in Africa emerge in this song, and there is a trace of Hughes's earlier radical idealism in urging unity of the oppressed masses, the theme of a number of his thirties dramas ("Jericho" 19–21). Other political themes are the 1954 Brown Supreme Court decision and support of King's nonviolent strategy. Furthermore, "Freedom" is symbolized as a woman, and there is support for interracial unity through the motif of walking "hand in hand," an emblem of the civil rights movement.

The Jericho trope signifies the victory over Jim Crow through the power of spirit and song; the play supports the nonviolent route to desegregation rather than nationalism or militancy. In the Biblical text, however, Joshua's entrance into Jericho has distinct military implications: "and the armed men went before them, and the rear guard came after the ark of the LORD, while the trumpets blew continually" (Josh. 6:13). The theme of collective action, also an element of the Biblical "march" to Jericho, is echoed in references to A. Philip Randolph and the March on Washington. The play closes with the spiritual "Come and Go with Me," as "all march toward exit," a final indication of support for the political strategies of the SCLC ("Jericho" 29–32). With *Jericho-Jim Crow*, Hughes had given favorable treatment to the black church and its involvement in civil rights protest.

Like *Jericho-Jim Crow*, *The Prodigal Son*, which was scheduled to open in New York on 13 May 1965, at the Greenwich Mews Theatre, located at 141 West 13th Street, also employed dance and song in the spirit of festival drama. (In April, Hughes's *It's a Mighty World*, featuring Odetta, had been aired on Easter Sunday as a "special" news broadcast on CBS.) Directed by Vinnette Carroll—who replaced Sidney Walters—with music by Marion Franklin, *The Prodigal Son* shared billing with Brecht's *The Exception and the Rule* during the same period when Baldwin's *The Amen Corner* was holding forth at the Barrymore Theatre, though by the end of May *The Amen Corner* "received a blood transfusion" from the black community to assist its declining popularity (Taubman, "Double Bill" 19; "Langston Hughes" 22; "Hughes Play Does Casting" 22; Walker, "Theatricals: James Baldwin" 23). For Jesse Walker, writing for the *Amsterdam News*, Hughes's play was more appealing than Brecht's, which was considered "heavy-handed and dogmatic at times." *The Prodigal Son* was a "happy, exuberant song-play" that was "vividly staged," evoking in its conclusion "hand clapping and foot stomping" from the audience (Walker, "Hughes Has Another" 22). Presented by the Greenwich Mews Players, the song-play was produced by Beverly Landau, Stella Holt and Henrietta Stein. The company performed with "rare gusto and elation"; the play moved the audience with its irresistible "pulsating rhythms." Since the production did not rely on spoken dialogue, the merits were in its songs and in the choreography of Syvilla Fort. One of the more "rewarding" productions of the season, it was a "lush, emotional experience" that was "essentially a ballet accompanied by spirituals" (Taubman, "Double Bill" 19; "A Twin Bill" 63).

*The Prodigal Son* was transformed from the original script, making it less of a play and more of a music-dance experience, qualities that might not be appreciated by drama "purists." However, the "marvelous quality of soul" in Dorothy Drake's voice and the "raw power and beauty" of Robert Pinkston's singing overshadowed the unconventional format of the play, for which Hughes was not totally responsible. Hughes's original idea had been changed by director Carroll and choreographer Fort "from a speech-song play to a swinging dance pantomime." However, these changes made it a "novel concoction," no less "delightful"; it contained the same "moral" intended by Hughes. This could not be said for the Paris performance of the play that rendered it as "mostly vaudeville" (Riley 14; Hughes, "Show Biz" 34; Rampersad 2: 396–397).

Hughes had originally conceived the play as a collaborative effort with Alex Bradford that used "traditional gospel hymns illuminating the Bible story." Hughes revised the play a number of times, one of the earliest drafts completed in late November 1961, others in 1962 and 1965 (Hughes, "The Prodigal Son"). He had considered a number of spirituals derived from recordings of prominent vocalists such as Della Reese, Rosetta Tharpe, La Vern Baker, and Marian Anderson as well as a series of songs from the Hampton collection such as 'The Downward Road Is Crowded" and "Standing in the Need of Prayer." Certain Alex Bradford originals were also planned to accompany various scenes: "You Can't Make Me Doubt Him," "You Better Take Time," and "Mother! Mother!" for which Hughes supplied the lyrics.[12]

In *The Prodigal Son*, Hughes explores another of the well-known Biblical stories, using the parable for a modern presentation of good versus evil, redemption, addiction, and the inevitability of sexual attraction. The structure is similar to that of *Black Nativity* and *The Gospel Glory*, songs inserted at appropriate points in the narrative. "I Look Down the Road," for example, sung by Sister Lord, aptly suits the departure of the Prodigal Son with Jezebel, whose place in the narrative is an expansion of the Biblical story to include the Prodigal Son's sexual relations, his having "squandered his property in loose living" or his having consorted with "harlots" (Luke 15:11–32).

The play combines Biblical characters, using the Prodigal Son from the New Testament and Jezebel, the wife of Ahab, from the Old Testament, who has come to symbolize deception and wickedness for having influenced Ahab. Like Ahab, Jezebel is cursed—"'The dogs shall eat Jezebel'" (1 Kings 21:23)—and like Eve and Cleopatra, symbols in Hughes's poem "Jazzonia" (1923), Jezebel is linked to man's downfall. Hughes's Jezebel resembles other Hughes characters associated with nightlife and the secular world, such as Tiny of *Little Ham* (1936), Zarita of *Simply Heavenly* (1957) and Laura of *Tambourines to Glory*, though Laura is deceived by Buddy.

Another intertextual similarity is in the characterization of the Exhorter, who resembles the Elder of *Black Nativity*, the preacher figure who has the power of the word. The Exhorter relates the story of the Prodigal Son, whose journey leads to dissipation through "riotous living." The song "Look at the Prodigal Son" describes his abandonment of his family and uses the "road" as a metaphor of sin. The Exhorter also addresses issues relevant to sixties urban black communities such as Harlem. Although Hughes had briefly touched on the social dilemmas associated with drug use in *Joy to My Soul* (1937), with references to marijuana, he had not dealt to any significant degree with addiction to hard drugs, a problem of increasing concern during the 1960s. The Exhorter's comments expose an often-heard warning regarding the possibility of drug escalation: "a puff leads to a draw and a draw to a pill and a pill to a sniff and a sniff to a pop and a pop to a shot." Sin is personified as the devil in "drag," a rare reference in Hughes's dramas to homosexuality, one other being the portrayal of the effeminate minor character in *Little Ham* (1936).

Appropriately, the song "Done Found My Lost Sheep" is sung by the mother to mark the ultimate return of the son to the Father's house, where "Everything's all right!" To a degree, the script undercuts a conventional moral reading. The final stage directions suggest the return of the Prodigal Son to Jezebel, implying the inevitability of sexual attraction: "But the Prodigal Son breaks away to run smiling off with Jezebel." The farewell song is a call to continue in the path of Jehovah, an ironic closing that seems to foster Biblical moralism tempered by the reality of secular life ("Prodigal" 13–16).

Hughes's gospel plays are not intended as traditional Christian morality works but are soulful celebrations of gospel music, merging conventional stage craft with elements of festival drama—a composite of music, song, and dance. Because gospel music exemplifies the juncture of secular and spiritual music, it is a fitting medium through which to update traditional Christian texts, infusing them with modern soulful energy. By rewriting the Nativity, the Passion, the stories of Jericho and the Prodigal Son, Hughes resembles the youthful character in John Henrik Clarke's short story "The Boy Who Painted Christ Black," who inscribes his own identity. Among Hughes's final dramatic works, the gospel plays, especially *Tambourines to Glory, Jericho-Jim Crow*, and *The Prodigal Son*, contain messages drawn from the body of his creative works: reconciliation within the African American community, fostering the historical record through black iconography, and protest of social injustice. In formalizing the gospel play genre, Hughes had turned to urban folk sources and found in them a vitality that could revise his own portrait of black spirituality.

## Notes

1. See *Black American Literature Forum* 25.1 (1991) special issue, "The Black Church and the Black Theatre," guest editors Michael S. Weaver and James V. Hatch, for an extended discussion of some of these issues.

2. Michael W. Harris's *The Rise of Gospel Blues: The Music of Thomas Andrew Dorsey in the Urban Church* (1952) is a useful social and musical analysis of Dorsey's contribution.

3. See Jeanette Toomer, "Vy Higgensen: Let the Music Play Gospel," *Black Masks* Nov.–Dec. 1996: pp. 5–6+. The novel version of *Mama, I Want to Sing* (New York: Scholastic, 1992) is co-authored with Tonya Bolden.

4. Aimee Semple McPherson, a well-known, controversial white evangelist, was alluded to along with Becton in Hughes's poem "Goodbye Christ," which praised Lenin and mocked the efficacy of Christianity, associating it with corrup-

tion. McPherson launched a protest of a 1940 Hughes reading in Los Angeles, and her exposure of "Goodbye Christ" plagued Hughes for some years thereafter. Hughes, who called Becton "a charlatan if there ever was one," describes in *The Big Sea* the staging of a typical Becton church service, referring to the gospel swing band and Becton's interest in jazz. The theatrical aspects of a Becton church service may have been an inspiration for treatments of the black church in *Tambourines to Glory*. Becton had asked Hughes to join his staff as a writer for a magazine Becton published. Hughes was particularly critical of Becton's "Consecrated Dime–A Dime a Day for God" scheme that drew funds from his congregation.

5. See advertisement in *Black Masks* Nov.–Dec. 1996, St. Paul's production program, and "'Hughes' *Black Nativity*," in *Carribean Life* 10 Dec. 1996: p. 9, for details concerning the St. Paul production. Other versions of *Black Nativity* were staged during the 1996 Christmas season: *Nativity: A Life Story,* based on Hughes's work, at the Schomburg Center for Research in Black Culture; and a version at the Kennedy Center in Washington, DC.

6. The original title, "Wasn't That a Mighty Day!" can be found on the "Final Draft Pre-rehearsal," dated 1961 and containing the author's copyright. The first draft is dated 2 Nov. 1961.

7. Hughes included staging and background notes in certain drafts of this and other plays.

8. Hughes listed the "sources of songs" at the end of the draft used for analysis. Other sources used include recordings by Mahalia Jackson, Odetta, the Weavers, Harry Belafonte, Clara Ward, the Roberta Martin Singers, Sister Tharpe, the Caravans, and Dorothy Maynor. The text sources include *Religious Folk Songs of the Negro,* Hampton Institute; *The Book of American Negro Spirituals,* J. W. Johnson and J. R. Johnson, Vols. 1 & 2; and *The Green Pastures Spirituals,* Hall Johnson.

9. Hughes had considered as possible "backers" Amy Spingarn, Arthur Spingarn, John Hammond, Clara Ward, Ossie Davis, Eartha Kitt, Harry Belafonte and Sidney Poitier.

10. A guest list included Duke Ellington, Ralph Ellison, John Henrik Clarke, Vinnie Burrows, Alice Childress and Katherine Dunham.

11. There were also changes made in the play during the December 1963 and January 1964 rehearsals. Other revisions were made in April of 1964, leading to a "Final Revised Acting Script" sent to Stella Holt on July 14, 1964. This version of thirty-two pages is used for analysis of the play, "Jericho-Jim Crow: A Song Play," ts., LHP-YUBL.

12. These background sources can be found in Hughes's "Drafts of 'The Prodigal Son: A Song-play,'" ts., 30 Nov. 1961, LHP-YUBL.

## WORKS CITED

Berry, Faith. *Langston Hughes: Before and Beyond Harlem.* Westport, CT: Lawrence Hill, 1983.

"'Black Nativity' Will Play Lincoln Center." *New York Amsterdam News,* 8 Dec. 1962: p. 24.

Brooks, Tilford. *America's Black Musical Heritage.* Englewood Cliffs, NJ: Prentice, 1984.

Burdine, Warren. "Let the Theatre Say 'Amen.'" *Black American Literature Forum,* 25.1 (1991): pp. 73–82.

Childress, Alice. Personal Interview. 8 May 1980.

Gardner, Paul. "Brooklyn Church Stages Song Play." *New York Times,* 28 Oct. 1962: p. 87.

"'Gospel Glow:' New Hughes Play to Premiere." *New York Amsterdam News*, 13 Oct. 1962: p. 19.

Harris, Michael W., *The Rise of Gospel Blues: The Music of Thomas Andrew Dorsey in the Urban Church*. New York: Oxford University Press, 1992.

Hepburn, Dave. "Producers Make Changes, Hire Langston for TV Show." *New York Amsterdam News*, 27 Oct. 1962: p. 19.

Hughes, Langston. "The Ballad of the Brown King." ts., 1960. Yale Collection of American Literature, Beinecke Rare Book and Manuscript Library, Yale University, New Haven, CT. Future references to Hughes papers at Yale will appear as LHP-YUBL.

———. *The Big Sea*. New York, Hill and Alang, 1940.

———. "Black Nativity." ts. LHP-YUBL.

———. "The Gospel Glory." ts. 1962. LHP-YUBL.

———. "Gospel Singing: When the Spirit Really Moves." *New York Herald Tribune*, 27 Oct.1963: pp. 12–13.

———. "Jericho-Jim Crow: A Song Play." ts. LHP-YUBL.

———. "The Prodigal Son: A Song Play." ts. 1961. LHP-YUBL.

———. "Show Biz." *New York Post*, 3 Sept. 1965: p. 34.

———. *Tambourines to Glory. Five Plays by Langston Hughes*. Ed. Webster Smalley. Bloomington: Indiana University Press, 1968: pp. 183–258.

"Hughes Play Does Casting." *New York Amsterdam News*, 24 Apr. 1965: p. 22.

Huntley, Jobe. *I Remember Langston Hughes*. New York: Jobe Huntley, 1983.

"'Jericho-Jim Crow' Set to Premiere." *New York Amsterdam News*, 4 Jan. 1964: p. 11.

Kerr, Walter. "Walter Kerr Review: 'Tambourines to Glory.'" *New York Herald Tribune*, 4 Nov. 1963. Rpt. in Edwin Leon Coleman, "Langston Hughes: As American Dramatist." Diss. University of Oregon, 1971: p. 189.

"Langston Hughes Authored the Easter Sunday Special." *New York Amsterdam News*, 24 Apr. 1965: p. 22.

"Langston Hughes Describes the Genesis of His 'Tambourines to Glory.'" *New York Times*, 27 Oct. 1963, sec 2: p. 3.

LeNoire, Rosetta. Personal Interview. 25 March 1980.

"Margaret Bonds, Composer." *New York Amsterdam News*, 23 Dec. 1961: p. 17.

Masterson, Daniel E. "Black Nativity School Kit: Lecture Notes on Gospel Singing." Lectures 1–3. LHP-YUBL.

Norford, Thomasina. "Gospel Songs Top 'Black Nativity.'" *New York Amsterdam News*, 16 Dec. 1961: p. 17.

Rampersad, Arnold. *The Life of Langston Hughes*. 2 Vols, New York: Oxford University Press, 1986–1988.

Riley, Clayton, *Liberator,* 5:10 (Oct. 1965): p. 14.

Sanders, Leslie Catherine. *The Development of Black Theater in America: From Shadows to Selves*. Baton Rouge: Louisiana State University Press, 1988.

Shephard, Richard F. "Langston Hughes' Play with Music Opens." *New York Times*, 13 Jan. 1964: p. 25.

Sullivan, Dan. Rev. of *Jericho-Jim Crow. New York Times*, 23 March 1968; p. 22.

"A Twin Bill." *America* 113:2 (10 July 1965): p. 63.

———. "'Tambourines' Is Unique Experience in Theatre." *New York Amsterdam News*, 9 Nov. 1963: p. 15.

Taubman, Howard. "Double Bill Opens at Greenwich Mews." *New York Times*, 21 May 1965: p. 19.

———. Rev. of *Tambourines to Glory. New York Times*, 4 Nov. 1963: p. 47

Walker, Jesse H., " Hughes Has Another Show Off-Broadway." *New York Amsterdam News,* 29 May 1965: p. 22.

———. "Theatricals: James Baldwin." *New York Amsterdam News,* 22 May 1965: p. 23.

———. "They Might Hear 'Jerico' All the Way Up on 113th St." *New York Amsterdam News,* 18 Jan. 1964: p. 13.

Weaver, Michael S., "Makers and Redeemers: The Theatricality of the Black Church." *Black American Literature Forum,* 25:1 (1991): pp. 53–61.

Womble, Candice. "'Tambourines' Is Unique Experience in Theatre." *New York Amsterdam News,* 9 Nov. 1963: p. 15.

H. NIGEL THOMAS

# Patronage and the Writing of Langston Hughes's Not Without Laughter: *A Paradoxical Case*

As Cathy Davidson and other scholars of American literature have observed, the work of literature in the United States has been from the very beginning a commodity almost like any other, with suppliers and consumers.[1] The writer who wishes to earn a living from his work must invariably produce according to the demands of the literary marketplace. Langston Hughes rudely discovered this in 1928 while creating *Not Without Laughter*. In 1926 he had declared that black writers (at least those for whom he spoke) would create works that reflected their personal visions and would be indifferent to the reactions of both their black and white readers.[2] But Hughes soon discovered that what one wrote was subject to the vagaries of the literary marketplace: the first challenge was to have enough readers to make publishing the work commercially viable; to this effect, publishers placed restrictions on the kinds of characters black writers created; and for those African American writers fortunate or unfortunate enough to have them, there were the whims of patrons.

Intent on creating from an African American worldview, Hughes found himself trapped in the spaces that Western ideology and economics had already assigned blacks. They were ensconced in the confines of what Raymond Williams terms "use" and "superstructure."[3] And although Hughes wished his writing to belong to the challenging or "emergent" category of art—the

*CLA Journal*, 42 (1); 1998 Sept.: pp. 48–70. © The College Language Association.

sorts of texts James Weldon Johnson argued for in black American writing—[4] Hughes soon discovered the limits beyond which his expressivity and ideology would not be tolerated. The macrocosmic base and superstructure (at the heart of Marxist literary theory) became microcosmically replicated in the Hughes-Mason relationship. Mrs. Mason, Hughes's patron, had accorded him a role: articulator of the gospel of the primitive, and Hughes, always wanting to be the unfettered creator, found himself manacled.

There is some irony in the fact that while Mrs. Mason saw herself as revolting against Western civilization and donated portions of her wealth to make it possible for the "primitive" voice to be heard, she simultaneously censored the utterances of those voices. Moreover, by the time Mrs. Mason and Hughes began their patronage relationship, "primitivism" had already been co-opted by the superstructure. It was a concept created and defined by the West. And, reading Margaret Mead's introduction to *Coming of Age in Samoa* (1928), her rationale for that study, we see that "primitivism" had already been accorded a function: that of documenting the process of acculturation.[5] Suffice it to say, that evidence is now available for us to believe that Mead either distorted her material or was duped by the Samoan youngsters from whose statements she theorized.[6]

What follows is an analysis of the Mason-Hughes patronage relationship as it affected the writing of *Not Without Laughter*. Because several analyses already exist on the patronage relationship between Mrs. Mason and those whom she subsidized—Alain Locke, Langston Hughes, Zora Neale Hurston, Aaron Douglas, Hall Johnson—[7] it is not worthwhile to repeat this information here. The following statement by Arnold Rampersad is worth citing, however, for it effectively summarizes Mrs. Mason's relationships with the beneficiaries of her patronage: "Fearless almost to the point of fantasy, Mrs. Mason could be a terror to those who crossed her. And whenever the force of her personality or her logic began to fail, her cash usually got what she wanted" (148). While Faith Barry and Rampersad have extensively documented the freedom from pecuniary cares that Mrs. Mason's stipends allowed Hughes while he wrote *Not Without Laughter,* neither biographer analyzes the definite changes wrought by Mrs. Mason's critiques of the manuscript in its embryonic and later stages. I hope to show in this essay how extensive her influence was on the writing of the novel, an influence which she exerted because she was subsidizing Hughes, and one which Hughes would have curtailed had he been less dependent on her money.

The note signed by Hughes that accompanies the drafts of *Not Without Laughter* in the James Weldon Johnson Collection implies that Robert Labaree and Alain Locke were the only persons who read and criticized the manuscript before it was submitted to the publisher.[8] Far more influential than either of these men in the writing and shaping of the manuscript was Mrs. Mason. Hughes's account in *The Big Sea* of the novel's conception and realization excludes any mention of Mrs. Mason's role.[9] This was probably due to her insistence that their dealings remain strictly confidential. His confession, however, that he did not accomplish what he had envisaged for the novel (*Big Sea* 306) is probably a cryptic reference to the concessions he made to Mrs. Mason as regards the novel's content.

Shortly after the publication of *Not Without Laughter*, Hughes told Mrs. Mason:

> I never read a letter in praise of the novel—what they call its simplicity and lack of propaganda—but that I think, "They do not know who helped me write it—Godmother[;]" and every criticism in the papers must inevitably bear comparison with the superior and flaming criticism that you wrote long ago when the book was only half-finished.[10]

This statement contains more than the customary sycophancy that Mrs. Mason demanded from the recipients of her patronage. By all indications, *Not Without Laughter* should have formally resembled Claude McKay's *Home to Harlem*.[11] That is to say, it should have been freighted with several discrete passages explaining the circumstances of African American existence, and melodrama as well as humour for its own sake should have predominated in Hughes's presentation of its incidents. But between the first and final drafts of the novel most of the excrescent passages disappeared and much of the melodrama was muted, to such an extent that in his review of it Wallace Thurman contrasted it with *Home to Harlem*.[12] Moreover, a comparison of *Not Without Laughter* with *Tambourines to Glory*, Hughes's other novel, and some of his short fiction will reveal a greater preponderance of melodrama and distracting humour in the latter. Besides, it was Hughes's view that good fiction had to be dramatic.[13] *Not Without Laughter*, in its relative lack of melodrama and its muted humour, is therefore uncharacteristic Hughes's fiction.

That this is so is paradoxical, for it was largely Mrs. Mason's criticism of the manuscript that saved the novel from such a fate; and this is somewhat aberrant, considering that Mrs. Mason was herself the epitome of melodrama: she expressed her dogmatic views in superlatives and hyperboles; she perceived Native Americans and Africans as the eventual redeemers of a world sick from the disease of civilization;[14] her patronage to artists she saw as her contribution to the redemption of civilization. Naming herself Godmother (in the sense of a mother who could show her children the way to God—Zora Neale Hurston addressed her once as the "Guard-mother who sits in the twelfth heaven and shapes the destinies of primitives"),[15] and the

recipients of her patronage her children—and literally treating the patronized as children, exerting what was tantamount to tyranny over them—it is
thus an enigma that she was able to curb Hughes's tendency to melodrama
and discursiveness in the overall conception and creation of *Not Without
Laughter.*

The varying components of Mrs. Mason's strategy while she encouraged Hughes to actualize *Not Without Laughter* are best highlighted by the
contrast in the laudatory praise she gave the various episodes Hughes sent
her right after he wrote them[16] and the trenchant criticism to which she subjected the first draft.[17] In the latter case, her advice was in some cases very
helpful and could have been—and was—in others very inept.

In her twenty-five-page critique of the novel's first draft, dated May
1929, she informs Hughes that

> when it becomes possible to separate one's mind from the vivid
> characterization of Hager, Harriet and little Sandy, one sees that
> the whole book needs literary welding together. There are many
> good separate events, but no real sense of juxtaposition in the
> action.
>
> One realizes in the reading that you have ideas about people,
> about your race [,] about the differences in character, but, though
> beauty flashes through the pages, in all your writing, it is apparent
> that you had no training in literary expression in your home life
> as a little child, and in college, no fundamental literary training
> to give you a useful background to have at your command so that
> your own thought might rise for free flight and carry their clear
> message unhampered.
>
> You must he careful, Langston, in both your novel and your play
> that you really write a novel and really write a play which no critic
> can dismiss as propaganda. (JWJ)

This was the first time that Mrs. Mason informed him so bluntly about
the limitations of his literary training. Rampersad, probably with Mrs.
Mason's effulgent personality in mind, interprets her remark about the lack
of literary training to mean that she was finding fault "with the childlike
honesty [and] absence of inflated rhetoric in the text," qualities that reflect
Hughes's best style (172). Her critique, which I shall discuss below, both
supports and contradicts Rampersad's interpretations.

It is worth remembering that Hughes, even though he was already
the author of two volumes of poetry and had travelled widely, was still

only twenty-six when he began working on this manuscript; moreover, he worked on it while undertaking full-time studies at Lincoln University; and those studies, which covered a very general curriculum, probably taught him little as regards literary form. But good writing was not necessarily what the publishers of the period wanted. On this matter, Mrs. Mason gave Hughes a crucial bit of advice: that publishing houses and editors were looking uniquely for salable material "in order that they can make their bread. Your business is to smash this great wall . . . and set the members of your audience free." Setting aside her tumid rhetoric, she was alluding to the "Nigger Heaven"/"Home to Harlem" phenomenon, which Amrijit Singh notes, "exalt[ed] the exotic, the sensual, and the primitive . . ." and "black writers who were willing to describe the exotic scene 'had no trouble finding sponsors, publishers and immediate popularity,'"[18] and of which Arna Bontemps, in the writing of his first novel, *God Sends Sunday,* was a victim.[19] But Hughes had already noted this phenomenon in "The Negro Artist and the Racial Mountain": "'Be stereotyped, don't go too far, don't shatter our illusions about you, don't amuse us too seriously. We will pay you,' say the whites" (170). At this point it is worth noting that as art, McKay's *Home to Harlem* is very deficient; notwithstanding, its "prurient" content (the reviewers' terminology) had established it as a touchstone of the salable in fiction by and about African Americans. Still, on the one hand, Hughes's most immediate models as regards form in the African American novel were *Home to Harlem* and (James Weldon Johnson's) *The Autobiography of an Ex-Colored Man.* Hughes was attracted to the former because of its iconoclastic themes—the lifestyles of the uninhibited, unlettered poor—themes he remained passionate about throughout his life. Moreover, Hughes's texts written in defense of McKay never distinguished between McKay's iconoclastic, anti-bourgeois themes and McKay's tone; essentially, Hughes loved and defended *Home to Harlem* for extra-literary reasons.[20]

As regards one formal requirement of the novel, that all ideology should be implicit rather than explicit (less rigid in the 1920s than a decade or two later), both of Hughes's models were seriously flawed, although, on this count, *The Autobiography of an Ex-Colored Man* was worse, for Johnson's long discursive passages explaining the historical and moral circumstances of blacks make of his novel something of an illustrated essay.

Because of the foregoing reality, Mrs. Mason's suggestion that Hughes expunge those passages that furnish mere sociological data (this is what her use of the word "propaganda" appears to mean) was excellent advice, for it forced Hughes to confront the formal properties of novel writing. The consequences of her advice on the final form of the manuscript will be evident following my analysis of her opinions on the chapters "Work," "White Folks," "Revival," "Stanton," and "Tempy's House."

Regarding "Work," she wrote, "Good points brought out are Hager's working herself to death and Jimboy's not only going off fishing but teaching Sandy. Excellent picture of the difficulties of Negro work-a-day existence (sic) without any hint of propagandic (sic) writing." The printed text shows that Hughes changed very little in this chapter, an indication that he agreed with her. The reader, too, agrees with her: the tensions between Hager and Jimboy are convincingly shown to be their *modus vivendi,* perfected long before the novel begins; Sandy's relationship with his father is intensive, affectionate, and convincing. Undoubtedly, the urge on Hughes's part to apologize for Jimboy's refusal to submit to the humiliating practices of Jim Crow employment must have been extremely powerful. But Hughes accomplishes this implicitly rather than explicitly elsewhere: in "White Folks," and far more effectively than if he had simply made the reader privy to Jimboy's thoughts on the subject. Moreover, to have heard Jimboy reflecting on what would have then become his victim status would have destroyed a significant aspect of his portrait—the fact that Jimboy is too naive to ever perceive himself as a victim of Jim Crow practices. Instead, in ways analogous to Hager's use of religion, he employs blues metaphors and rhythms to mediate the abuse stemming from racism and thus saves himself any conscious analysis of their effects.

But one could easily argue that this chapter was pleasing to Mrs. Mason because it reflects, in Jimboy's and Hager's accommodation of existence—i.e., in their fatalistic abandonment to their particular predilections and the fate reserved for them by their environment (highly irresponsible in Jimboy's case)—the contemporary opinions about the "primitive," especially the oft-repeated belief that the behaviour of primitive peoples lacks complexity.[21] Between Carl Vechten, Hughes's other mentor, and Mrs. Mason, Hughes would have certainly imbibed such doctrines. Moreover, in the initial foreword which Hughes wrote to his sociological study about relations between students and faculty at Lincoln University, he echoes Mrs. Mason's views about 'primitive' peoples, indicating an eagerness on his part to have his writing reflect Mrs. Mason's views.[22] With this in mind, one could conjecture that Hughes's characterization of Hager and Jimboy was influenced by Mrs. Mason's views on primitive peoples. Hughes's frequent attempts to reassure Mrs. Mason of his desire to please her as well as the humorous stories he sometimes sent her also lend credence to this hypothesis.[23]

Hughes and Mrs. Mason differed on the "White Folks" chapter, which, in both the first draft and printed text, follows "Work." According to Mrs. Mason,

> this chapter needs working over. Mrs. Johnson's story, while true to life, is out of proportion and should be shortened so that it will

be looked on as part of the substance and not as a digression. For the first time, in this chapter, you do not live with the people, you begin to be an on looker (sic).

These observations derived from Mrs. Mason's own ideology—*her* propaganda, so to speak—for this chapter is about African American response to the brutality of Jim Crow practices. It is significant that Mrs. Mason focuses on Sister Johnson, the character through whom Hughes effectively inscribes an essential component for the reader's understanding of the multifaceted responses by African Americans to racial oppression. Essentially, Sister Johnson's narrative is a concise and effectively rendered, even humorous, account of the fiery brutality that African Americans endured at the hands of white Southerners in the post-Construction years. Sister Johnson specifically states that it was the material prosperity of blacks that enraged Southerners into destroying black property; beyond that she shows that she and all the blacks in Vicksburg refused to submit to white tyranny; most of all, she embodies a character trait that could not but jar Mrs. Mason's concept of "primitive" peoples: she neither has nor desires any rituals to contain her hatred for white people; her earnest wish, expressed here and in the "Children's Day" chapter, is that they will all burn in hell. In essence, then, Sister Johnson challenges the "superstructure," and Mrs. Mason, despite what she considered to be her liberalism toward "primitives," felt targeted. The superstructure's role for blacks can be deduced from the fact that the American Senate before and after the time of Hughes's novel refused to pass a bill that would outlaw lynching.

Also significant, because it escapes Mrs. Mason's commentary, are Hager's cheek-turning love for white people and her apologies for their cruelty. Mrs. Mason found this reassuring, for in several places she lauds the character of Hager. More will be said of the Hager-Sister Johnson dichotomy when the suppressed chapter "Revival" is discussed.

Wisely Hughes kept the "White Folks" chapter, for, contrary to what Mrs. Mason felt, this chapter is pivotal to the worldview that unifies the novel, since, to a considerable degree, the characters are determined by white racism, regardless of whether they choose to deal with it consciously. This chapter is needed to orient the audience, to give it information useful in analyzing the degree of the characters' awareness of the world by which they are circumscribed. Hughes's major change was to insert humour into Sister Johnson's speech and thus soften the brutal acts with transient comic relief.

It was one of the few chapters where he overtly disagreed with her. Although his letter to her is not available, one can infer the nature of his objection from Mrs. Mason's reply:

Of course I knew it must be written from an onlooker's point of view, because Sandy is only a child looking on at a world he could not understand. What I object to is not that it is detached but that the quality of the writing at that point becomes self-conscious, and has the air of the author's propaganda. (Letter of 11 July 1929)

Fortunately, Hughes did not succumb to her criticism. Unfortunately, it may have influenced Mrs. Mason's decision to terminate her patronage even before the novel's publication; it probably underlies Hughes's statement in *The Big Sea* that he was not sufficiently primitive for her (325).

On the subject of Mrs. Mason's own propaganda, her positive response to the chapter "Tempy's House" is very revealing. Among the worse-written chapters in the first draft, it remained so even after Locke read the final draft and insisted that Hughes remove many of the verbose passages he employed to deflate the "Black bourgeoisie." The passages that follow exemplify Hughes's method for dramatizing Tempy and her class. The narrator reveals that Tempy's husband, Mr. Siles, shared Tempy's views:

The whites had the money, and if Negroes wanted any of it, the quicker they learned to be like the whites the better. Stop being lazy, stop attending revivals and dances, and learn to get the dollar because money buys everything, even the respect of white people.

Other passages read as follows:

Blues and spirituals Tempy and her husband hated because they were too typically Negro. In their house Sandy dared not sing a word of "Swing Low, Sweet Chariot," for what had darkie slave songs to do with respectable people? And Ragtime belonged in the Bottoms with the sinners. (It was ironically strange that the Bottoms was the only section of Stanton where Negroes and whites mingled freely on equal terms.) But according to Tempy, that part of town was lost to God, and the fact that she had a sister living there burned like a hidden cancer in her breast. She never mentioned Harriett to anyone.

It was better to try to forget your blackness by doing everything possible to be like white folks, Tempy thought, and in order to accomplish this, she believed that one had to act reserved toward persons below one's social station, especially toward servants, so the porter in Duval's Drug store, who had been Tempy's classmate for eight years, was no longer her friend. . . .

White folks thought most Negroes were porters. But she would show them that in Stanton there were some coloured people of dignity who did not associate with servants, and who were not themselves servants.

Tempy's Friends were all people of standing in the darker world—doctors, school teachers, a dentist, a lawyer, a hair dresser. And she moved among these friends as importantly as Mrs. Barr-Grant had moved among a similar group in the white race. Of course, many of the ladies in Tempy's circle had had washer-women for mothers and day-labourers for fathers, but none of them ever spoke of that. And while Aunt Hager lived, Tempy, after getting her position with Mrs. Grant-Barr, was seldom seen near the old woman. After her marriage she was even more ashamed of her family connections—a little sister running wild, and another sister married for the sake of love—for Tempy could never abide Jimboy, or understand why Annjee had taken up with such a rounder from the South. One's family as a topic of conversation, however, was not popular in high circles, for too many dark society folks in Stanton had sprung from humble family trees and low black bottoms.

These excerpts, characteristic of "Tempy's House" in the first draft and only somewhat less so in the published version, differ from McKay's expository passages in *Home to Harlem* in tone only, and are but a slight improvement on Johnson's exposition and narration. However, because the chapter expressed many of Mrs. Mason's own biases against white civilization and her belief that it destroys those "primitives" who embrace it, her comments on it are the following:

Very good to have this other angle. You will [,] of course [,] go over this—shorten it a little and thereby make it more succinct. Good piece of writing. Tempy's attitude toward Mrs. Barr-Grant shows she is entirely a slave to white civilization in both body and soul. This is a psychological aftermath of slavery [,] a point to accent (sic) for your "Three Generations." Excellent to have put in, "It was ironically strange that the bottoms were the only place that Negroes and Whites [mingled] on equal terms."

Such advice reveals the superficiality of Mrs. Mason's own knowledge of literary technique, that what she considered good fiction was not necessarily writing that employs a diverse number of techniques but rather writing that dramatized her own ideology. That Hughes made few alterations to the chapter, even after Locke had pointed out in detail its excesses, suggests at one level the extent to which he sometimes trusted Mrs. Mason's judgement and at another level the intensity of his need to flay the black bourgeoisie.[24] Sterling Brown's otherwise laudatory review of *Not Without Laughter* points to the caricatured portrait of Tempy as the novel's principal weakness,[25] and so does Wallace Thurman's review.[26]

Hughes removed two entire chapters from the manuscript because of Mrs. Mason's negative reactions: "Revival" and "The Town of Stanton." Most of "Revival" Hughes later incorporated into the short story "Big Meeting." "Revival" brims with drama (even if Mrs. Mason wanted to see its drama heightened). When she received the chapter separately, before the first draft of the novel was completed, she praised it (letter of 12 December 1928). This chapter, had it been included, would have modified Hager's character; for as the chapter is written, it represents Hager as part of the chorus of a communal ritual which enables pain-ridden blacks to exorcise their hurt. Its presence in the novel would have diffused the focus somewhat, away from Hager's calm, accommodating manner, and shift it slightly from the major characters to the community as a whole. In this chapter, too, Sister Johnson plays an excellent, analytic, dissenting role as she strips the preacher of his oratorical masks to reveal his mercenary motives. Thus her ideology and perceptive approach to phenomena would have contrasted more graphically with Hager's more faith-reliant acceptance of the events of her life, and would have strengthened the argument that Hager's holiness and self-sacrifice result partly from docility and poor judgement.

Elsewhere, I note that because the reader witnesses the secular rituals by which the nonreligious characters periodically dissipate the pain engendered by bigotry, the reader feels cheated because the text, other than for fleeting comments, never shows the rituals by which the religious characters exorcise theirs.[27] Nevertheless, because Hager is present, as part of the chorus, in the atmosphere of white heat that the revival sermon creates, the quietness of her character (a quietness that can only manage to break out in song when bigotry bruises her grandson) would have undergone some mutation. This reader would have felt that her religion had oversedated her.

One familiar with Mrs. Mason's views—that "primitives" could invoke the power of the sun, and conjure their enemies—[28] could suspect that subliminally, at least, this chapter disturbed her, for it is as much a presentation of black Baptist revival rituals as it is a comment on the racket that such revival rituals had/could become. The chapter also undermines Mrs. Mason's ideology, insofar as Hager, a pure "primitive," is among those gulled by the revival preacher, while Sister Johnson (a potential "bad nigger," to whom Mrs. Mason is antipathic) quickly intuits and articulates the preacher's dishonesty. Such intuition should have been Hager's. The purity of her primitive instincts should have alerted her to the evil in the preacher.

Whether or not Hughes felt that he could not rewrite the chapter in a way pleasing to Mrs. Mason and to himself, we do not know. But his decision to exclude it lessens Sister Johnson's role in the story and leaves the non-African American uninformed about why upcoming revivals excite Hager and Sister Whiteside. Significantly, it removes an implicit criticism of Hager and a highly melodramatic episode, which would have tilted the novel's calm, joyous, gently humorous and ironic tone toward a more ebullient one, especially if Hughes had followed Mrs. Mason's advice to make the chapter more dramatic.

"The Town of Stanton," Mrs. Mason informed Hughes, was a misplaced chapter. Her suggestion that it should be placed much earlier "before the story gets underway, so that it becomes an unconscious part of [the reader's] understanding of the whole," was good literary advice. She also felt that the "chapter loses in effectiveness because it is too much like propaganda in the way it is written." In this, too, she was right, for Hughes did not seem to understand, initially at any rate, that his choice of characters restricted the themes he could dramatize; consequently, he provided the material he could not dramatize in the narrator's voice (as Melville did in *Billy Budd*, which was published with great fanfare in 1924, just a few years before Hughes began writing *Not Without Laughter*). Mrs. Mason must have had in mind passages like the following:

> Nobody seemed to know how many colored people there were, since they didn't matter anyway and weren't really counted until the war came and captured them in the draft. . . .

> There were some foreigners in town, Italians, Greeks, Mexicans, and Jews [,] but by the natives, they were classed as little less than white, although still considerably more than Negro since they were not denied admittance to the newest motion picture house nor were shutted (sic) into the back rows at the older and cheaper temples of Dustin Farnum and Pearl White. And they could drink ice cream sodas in any drug store.

> A few natural Indians had, by some miracle [,] remained to generate their weak and palid (sic) progeny, but they were fast dying out and were of less importance than the negroes—unless they owned oil lands—and the only Indian who possessed oil had

mistakenly gone to Washington for protection. But, sometimes, in the nearby meadows you could still find scattered Indian arrow heads buried in the grassy earth.

Responding to such passages, Mrs. Mason advised Hughes, "This passage loses in effectiveness because it is too much like propaganda in the way it is written. You make your points best where you state them without comments [,] as they are clear and well handled." The expository quality of these passages, however, is identical to that in "Tempy's House," which Mrs. Mason commended. In spite of the contradiction, it was nevertheless good advice, and Hughes heeded it, retaining only the Bottoms section, which Mrs. Mason had approved. But like much of the writing used to characterize Tempy that made it into the final text, the Bottoms passage, too, although rendered graphically and concisely, is overwhelmingly discursive.

When one considers the numerous dramatic and humorous but excrescent episodes that Hughes expunged from several of the chapters, and the clearer focus that the story consequently assumed, it is evident that Hughes heeded Mrs. Mason's advice to provide greater coherence to his story. A great deal of the social commentary that he could not incorporate into the character's interactions disappeared.

Hughes's judgment could be questioned, however, in the case of one passage removed from "Children's Day." The passage is highly relevant in revealing Hughes's dilemma as regards the degree of militancy he wanted his characters to reflect. The excised passage reads:

> Reverend Butler, Madam de Carter, and all the leading Negroes of Stanton, including Tempy, wrote letters to the paper about it, [the turning away of African American children who had been led to believe they could participate in the activities at the park on Children's Day] and went to see the white people in charge. None of these letters were ever published, however. The park officials placed the blame on the paper, while the editor of *The Daily Leader* said, on the contrary, that it was the policy of the park to bar Negroes and he could do nothing about it. The mayor of Stanton said he wasn't running for office again so it wasn't his business to say anything. Nobody apologized, and nobody cared—except the colored folks. But Willa-Mae and Sandy never clipped coupons from the *Leader* again.

This, admittedly, is closer to journalism than fiction, but rendered in dialogue among Hager, Sister Whiteside, and Sister Johnson with Sandy present and reflecting on what he hears (as Hughes does in "White Folks"), it could have been easily incorporated into the story. Instead, Hughes replaced the passage with the following, one he rewrote several times:

> "I guess Kansas is getting like the South, isn't it, ma?" Sandy said to his grandmother as they came out on the porch that evening after supper. They don't like us here, either, do they?"
>
> But Hager gave him no answer. In silence they watched the sunset fade from the sky. Slowly the evening star grew bright, and looking at the stars Hager began to sing, very softly at first:
>> From this world o' trouble free,
>>> Stars beyond!
>>> Stars beyond!
>
> And Sandy as he stood beside his grandmother on the porch, heard a great chorus out of the black past—singing generations of toil-worn Negroes, echoing Hager's voice as it deepened and grew in volume:
>> There's a star fo' you an' me,
>>> Stars beyond!

No one will dispute the artistry of this passage: it is lyrical and subtle and quietly dramatic. But while it cements the consistency of Hager's character, it forebodes ill for the black struggle against bigotry; it connotes resignation to such bigotry. Undoubtedly it is a passage more reassuring to the white reader than the one it replaced; Mrs. Mason would have called the former propaganda and the latter art; but this reader finds it to be art for its own sake, which Hughes was never comfortable creating (1965).

Mrs. Mason continued to influence Hughes's rewriting of the manuscript beyond the first draft, as is evident in her letters of 2 August 1929 and 24 September 1929. In the former she suggests changes in the wording of certain passages, approves the rearrangement of the chapters, enthuses over some passages, like Sandy's overhearing black religious worship in Chicago, and rejects Hughes's working title. Her thoughts on this last are worth quoting:

> About the title. I do not feel that "So Moves This Swift World" is characteristic enough of your writing, which is always original and arresting. Somehow to my mind [,] Langston [,] the title should suggest the sum of Hager, and be prophetic of Sandy's flaming spirit. And here I become excited, realizing that the title is flying in space, just out of range of our vision. But you will get it [,]

Langston. And at the same time your strange Godmother hears again the tramp of those thousand men winding their way up the mountain in the Singing Play. . . .

In the 24 September 1929 letter, she castigates him for "adding details that do not help the stream of the story but turn it instead to propaganda." On the whole this letter states her dissatisfaction with the changes he had made to the manuscript, pointing out Annjee's preparations for the Lodge meeting and the supper scene at the Rice's as digressions that detract from the story's integrity (Hughes kept them). She concluded this critique by informing Hughes that "adding controversial detail does not make for strength. . . . So far the thing is not lifted to an art, which it must be. We do not get above the events, so to speak." Her objections here are predictable: all her critiques of the manuscripts reveal a pattern of discomfort with most of the scenes that deal with white bigotry. If Hughes had followed her advice slavishly, he would have excised all references to white bigotry from his novel (something that Hurston, who benefitted from Mason's patronage longer than Hughes, consciously did in her novels and books on black folklore).

From the foregoing we can confidently assert that Mrs. Mason influenced every stage of the creation of *Not Without Laughter*, and that much that is commendable and even undesirable in the novel can be attributed to her. *Not Without Laughter*, compared with Hughes's other novel and short stories, emerges as the superior work. It is more nuanced, more subtle, and more complex, less distractingly histrionic. It would be difficult not to credit Mrs. Mason for at least goading Hughes into achieving some of these effects and into reflecting on the function and characteristics of the episodes that comprise the final text. Given Mrs. Mason's dogmatic views, mercurial personality, and dramatic proclivities, it is paradoxical that on balance her advice and interventions could have been as valuable.

On the other hand, it was not the novel Hughes wanted to write. The fact is, however, that his two earlier books as well as the poems and short stories sold to various magazines had not provided him with a viable living,[29] largely, one suspects, because his works depicted African American as opposed to Euro-American reality, and in ways that many influential African Americans opposed. Consequently, he was forced to accept Mrs. Mason's patronage and to create works that reified her worldview, a worldview centered in the "superstructure" that had already relegated African Americans to the "base." Hughes did not tell the historical truth in his account of why the patronage relationship with Mrs. Mason foundered; however, in equating her with the patrons of the Waldorf Astoria and the class that clips coupons, while his art incites challenges to this class (*Big Sea* 320–324), he ideologically understood how firmly rooted Mrs. Mason was in the "super-structure," even if on occasion she leaned away from it.

## NOTES

1. Cathy N. Davidson, *Revolution and the Word: The Rise of the Novel in America* (New York: Oxford University Press, 1986): pp. 14–27.

2. Langston Hughes, "The Negro Artist and the Racial Mountain," *The Black Aesthetic*, ed. Addison Gayle, Jr. (Garden. City, NY: Anchor, 1972): p. 172. (Originally appeared in the *Nation* in 1926.) Hereafter cited parenthetically in the text.

3. Raymond Williams, *Problems in Materialism and Culture* (London: Verso, 1980): pp. 32–34.

4. See Johnson's preface to the first edition of *The Book of Negro Poetry* (40–41) and his continued defense of his position in the revised edition (3) in which he pleads with black writers to avoid writing in the black American dialect. He argues that black American vernacular speech, because of its long use to demean black characters, evokes such demeaning characteristics even when the writer does not intend them (rev. ed. [1931; New York: Harcourt, 1959]). Hughes found Johnson's suggestion preposterous, and a letter from Mrs. Mason to him on the subject implies that he had shared his views on the subject with her.

5. Margaret Mead, *Coming of Age in Samoa: A Psychological Study of Primitive Youth for Western Civilization* (1928; New York: William Morrow, 1975): pp. 1–14.

6. See, for example, chapter 16, "Refutation of Mead's Conclusions: Sexual Mores and Behaviour," of Derek Freeman's *Margaret Mead and Samoa: The Making and Unmaking of an Anthropological Myth* (Cambridge, MA: Harvard University Press, 1983): pp. 226–257. Several anthropologists have since tried to salvage Mead's reputation by nuancing Freeman's charges and by challenging Freeman's methods. The consensus—a representative sampling of which is to be found in the essays comprising *Confronting the Margaret Mead Legacy: Scholarship, Empire and the South Pacific*, ed. Lenora Foestel and Angela Gilliam (Philadelphia: Temple University Press, 1992)—is that Mead made several false claims, condescended to the people she studied, was silent about the forced labour the US Navy subjected Samoans to and, in fact, cooperated with and defended the navy's methods, and did not always verify the bigoted information her informers gave her about people living in other communities. An interesting fact is that Mead's defenders do not challenge Freeman's claim that Mead distorted Samoan adolescent sexual practices to fit her thesis promoting freer adolescent sexuality and to accord with the views of those who charged themselves with "The White Man's Burden."

7. For some of the analyses, see Faith Berry, *Langston Hughes: Before and Beyond Harlem* (Westport, CT: Lawrence Hill, 1953): pp. 69–109; Arnold Rampersad, *The Life of Langston Hughes—Volume 1: 1902–1941: I, Too, Sing America* (New York & Oxford: Oxford University Press, 1986): pp. 146–188; and Ralph D. Story, "Patronage and the Harlem Renaissance: You Get What You Pay For," *CLA Journal* 32.3 (March 1989): pp. 284–295, hereafter cited parenthetically in the text. See also most of the recent book-length works on the Harlem Renaissance.

8. Based on information in Hughes's papers in the James Weldon Johnson Collection, Beinecke Library of Rare Books and Manuscripts, Yale University. Hughes lists the dates between which he wrote each draft, made revisions, and corrected the galley proofs as well as the persons who typed each copy of the manuscript.

9. Langston Hughes, *The Big Sea* (1940; New York: Thunder's Mouth Press, 1986): pp. 303–306. Hereafter cited parenthetically in the text.

10. Langston Hughes, Langston Hughes Papers, James Weldon Johnson Collection, Beinecke Library of Rare Books and Manuscripts, Yale University. All references to correspondence between Hughes and Mrs. Mason are to this collection, cited in the text as JWJ.

11. Hughes defended McKay's writing in several places but the most passionate example of this is in the copy of a speech (in Hughes's Papers, James Weldon Johnson Collection) he gave in New York on 24 October 1931 as part of the series "Negro Art and Its Audience." Part of the speech states the following:

> In his novels (McKay) writes about the life he knew here, the way he lived. He writes about it truthfully, beautifully, in swiftly moving prose, passionate and warm.

> *Home to Harlem* exposes the terrible conditions under which certain classes of Negroes must live and work today. It should have awakened sympathy and pity instead of the scorn which the Negro press gave it. True, it was not about "the best people." But, why is it that, with all their pretensions to culture, their money, and their degrees the best Negroes have not yet produced a writer remotely approaching the artistry of Claude McKay. (JWJ)

It needs to be said, however, that similarity of technique aside, *Not Without Laughter* was from its earliest conception a very different novel from *Home to Harlem*. Its emphasis is on stable families. Tom Johnson and Mr. Siles are family men; Bro. Logan is a widower; Buster's mother and father are married and so are the Lanes; even Maude has a father who is married to her mother. The major focus of the novel is on the struggle for material survival among the black working class. See Hughes's *Not Without Laughter* (1930; New York: Collier, 1969) and McKay's *Home to Harlem* (1928; Boston: Northeastern University Press, 1972); excerpts from this edition of *Not Without Laughter* will be cited parenthetically in the text.

12. Wallace Thurman, "Entire Family Circle," rev. of *Not Without Laughter*, by Langston Hughes, *New York Evening Post* 28 July 1930: p. 7.

13. In a letter to Arna Bontemps, dated 18 February 1953, Hughes states that he had read Baldwin's *Go Tell It on the Mountain* and considered it a failure because Baldwin lacks the feel for the folk idiom; written by Zora Neale Hurston it would be a wonderful book. But it is mostly Baldwin's subtlety and complex narration that most frustrates him. "The too frequent use of flashbacks (a la Lilian Smith's 'Strange Fruit') slows the book down to a sleepy pace each time the story seems to be about to start to go somewhere. . . . If it is meant to show the futility of religion, then it should be sharper and clearer and not so muddy and pretty and poetic and exalted without being exalting" (Charles H. Nichols, ed., *Arna Bontemps—Langston Hughes Letters: 1925–1967* [New York: Dodd, 1980]: p. 302).

14. See, for example, her letter to Hughes dated 5 June 1927: "My winged poet child who as he flies through my mind is a noble silent Indian chief, a shining messenger of hope for his people and then again a previous simple precious child with his pockets full of bright, colored marbles looking up at me with his dear [,] blessing eyes" (JWJ). See as well her 19 June 1927 letter: "Godmother prays to the sun to keep her boy free from any germs and dry up the foul air. You see, Langston, you

will forget about yourself while you are absorbing the colors of all kinds and types. And all I have to depend upon to have my boy preserved are those great Gods that sit in space, who, while they set his spirit free to absorb must protect his body from harm. And so, Langston, find in your make-up the Indian song that preserves you from all evil and disease, and sing it with your whole heart. Surely [,] Godmother's great love and belief in you she hopes may be a little protection too" (JWJ).

15. See, for example, the text of Hughes's letter of 15 August 1930 to Mrs. Mason, following the cessation of her patronage, particularly this passage: "I ask you to help the gods to make me good, to make me clean, to make me strong and fine that I might stand aflame before my people, powerful and wise, with eyes that can discern the ways of truth. I am nothing now, no more than a body of dust without wisdom, having no sight to see" (JWJ). See also Hurston's letter to Mrs. Mason, 10 March 1931, in the Alain Locke Papers, Moorland-Spingarn Collection, Howard University; hereafter cited as Moorland-Spingarn in the text and notes.

16. With few exceptions, letter after letter during the writing of the first draft praises the writing. The following excerpt from a letter to Hughes dated 11 November 1928 is characteristic of her tone during this period:

> I had the joy of reading to Catherine your chapter on The Dance. She was thrilled by it. This chapter of your novel is a living thing, so perfectly done that one never loses the brilliancy of the evolution of any of the characters who move through that evening. My dear child [,] it is an amazing piece of writing. I am wondering if Revival is on its way. (JWJ)

17. Mrs. Mason did not like being perceived as a strategist (letter to Hughes, 12 February 1931 [JWJ]); yet her advice to Hughes, to keep his work in utmost secrecy (letter of 26 June 1927 [JWJ]), and her prolix praise to McKay—for his *Home to Harlem* (letter to McKay 11 March 1928 [Moorland-Spingarn]) while holding it up to Hughes as epitomizing the weaknesses of black writing (letter of 26 August 1928 [JWJ]): "Of course, it *[Not Without Laughter]* will not be like *Home to Harlem* or Fisher's *Walls of Jericho* because my Langston is not made to catch the applause of the world")—indicate that a strategist is exactly what she was.

18. Amrijit Singh, *The Novels of the Harlem Renaissance: Twelve Black Writers—1923–1933* (University Park, PA: Pennsylvania University Press, 1976): p. 25.

19. Singh, pp. 25–26.

20. See Note 6.

21. See Margaret Mead's *Coming of Age* 7–8 and her *Margaret Mead: My Earlier Years* (New York: Pocket Books, 1972): p. 181. It must also be noted that the roustabout was already considered a stock character even before the publication of *Not Without Laughter*. See, for example, Theophilus Lewis, "If This Be Puritanism: (Review of) 'Harlem,' a Melodrama by William Jourdan Rapp and William Thurman," *Opportunity* Apr. 1929: p. 32.

22. The foreword reads: "In the primitive world, where people live closer to the earth and much nearer to the stars, every inner and outer act combines to form the single harmony, life. Not just the tribal lore then, but every movement of life becomes a part of their education. They do not, as many civilized people do, neglect the truth of the physical for the sake of the mind. Nor do they teach with speech alone, but rather with all the acts of life. There are no books, so the barrier between words and reality is not so great as with us. The earth is right under their feet. The

stars are never far away. The strength of the surest dream is the strength of the primitive world."

23. See (1) Hughes's letters of 23 February 1929 that repeatedly state how much he loves and wants to please Mrs. Mason; their tone is at times self-deprecatory: "I must have been terribly stupid to have hurt you so, terribly lacking in understanding, terribly blind to what you have wanted me to see. . . . I know well that I am dull and slow, but I do not want to remain that way. I don't know what to say except that I am sorry that I have not changed rapidly enough into what you would have me be;" (2) the "Sea Letters" to Mrs. Mason which contain a few "darky" jokes (JWJ).

24. See, for example, his remarks about the "Black Bourgeoisie" in *The Big Sea*, pp. 201–209, in "The Negro Artist and the Racial Mountain" pp. 167–172, as well as in the lecture "Negro Art and Its Audience" 24 October 1931; see note 6 for additional details.

25. Sterling Brown, rev. of *Not Without Laughter*, by Langston Hughes, *Opportunity*, Sept. 1930, rpt. in *Langston Hughes: Critical Perspectives Past and Present*, ed. Henry Louis Gates, Jr., and K. A. Appiah (New York: Amistad, 1993): p. 17.

26. Thurman 7.

27. H. Nigel Thomas, *From Folklore to Fiction: A Study of Folk Heroes and Rituals in the Black American Novel* (Westport, CT: Greenwood, 1988): p. 188.

28. Her letter to Hughes dated 13 February 1928 terms Paul Radin a highway robber because with money deposited at Fisk University for Negro work he investigated some "Indian things that he personally wanted to add to his collection, which shows him to be dumb to the truth and honesty of primitive people. Zora, Alain, you and I must checkmate this robbery. 'Help Godmother to try voodhoo on him' to protect Cudjoe Lewis and Africa'" (JWJ).

29. Hughes, despite the publication of the very popular *The Weary Blues* and the soon-to-follow controversial *Fine Clothes to the Jew*, was able to return to Lincoln University in the fall of 1926 for a second year only because of a $400 loan from Amy Spingarn (Rampersad 131). In January 1927, he was so broke he had to ask Locke to loan him ten dollars (Rampersad 139). In terms of sales *Fine Clothes to the Jew*, despite the controversy it generated in the black press, was the Langston Hughes's book that probably sold the fewest copies (Rampersad 141). In Rampersad's words, "Undoubtedly, [Mrs. Mason's] money also attracted Langston. . . . Even now, his continuance at college depended almost entirely on Amy Spingarn's goodwill" (148–149).

ROBERT O'BRIEN HOKANSON

# *Jazzing It Up: The Be-Bop Modernism of Langston Hughes*

Although few topics in literary studies these days are more complex and contested than the concept of "modernism," it would seem that there remains a consensus that its dominant note is, "Make it new!" Similarly, critics tend to agree that modernist innovation entails breaking down boundaries between the arts, so that musical terms like "canto" and pictorial terms like "imagism" have come to be seen as synonymous with the literary modes of the movement. What seems in turn to have initiated the current revisioning of modernism is the way that the notion of barrier-crossing has also come to include breaking down racial and ethnic boundaries, challenging modernism's exclusive association with Euro-American writers and placing renewed emphasis on other voices, especially the African American writers of the Harlem Renaissance. With such revisioning, perhaps even occasioning it, there also came the recognition of the need to broaden the music/literary interaction to include African American musical traditions, particularly jazz.

Within this context, what still needs more attention is the work of Langston Hughes, for it could be argued that no other African American writer is quite so central to an understanding of how jazz dynamics might operate in poetry and that none so daringly enacts and extends the modernist challenge to "make it new." What distinguishes Hughes is not merely his

*Mosaic (Winnipeg)* 31.4 (Dec 1998): p. 61(2). Copyright © 1998 University of Manitoba, *Mosaic.*

departures from the Euro-American modernist tradition but also the extent
to which his practice differs from other African American modernists. The
unofficial poet laureate of black America, Hughes's life and work spanned
more than a half-century of the modern African American experience,
ranging from the great urban migration and the Harlem Renaissance of the
1920s through the stirrings of the Civil Rights and Black Arts movements
of the 1960s. A prolific and versatile writer, Hughes published more than
12 volumes of poetry, as well as fiction, drama, essays, and historical studies
for adults and children. Across decades and genres, he maintained a commitment to expressing the richness and diversity of African American life
in (and on) its own terms, building a body of work that was both artistically
innovative and decidedly "popular" (that is, of and for the people).

In keeping with Hughes's own daring, in this essay I wish to focus
not on his early work with African American musical forms in his already
much-discussed first published volume, *The Weary Blues* (1926), but on his
less well known long poem, *Montage of a Dream Deferred* (1951), which in
itself departs from mainstream jazz and taps into the more rebellious mode
known as "be-bop." Although the essence of this work lies in Hughes's intricate blending of a variety of cultural issues and music-literary techniques,
for the purpose of analysis I will discuss its major component features in
the following manner. First, after a brief overview of the musico-cultural
context, I will examine the aesthetic principles that Hughes drew from the
jazz tradition generally and be-bop in particular, tracing the impact of this
interaction on the structure and style of the poem. I will then consider how
Hughes's jazz aesthetic plays out in the nature of the poetic voice of *Montage*
(both in terms of the multiplicity of speakers the poem presents and the
stance and status of the poet's voice among them). Finally, I will return to
Hughes's relation to modernism, exploring the way that his work constitutes
a distinctively "popular" modernism, one that uses jazz to ground its poetic
experimentation in the vernacular tradition of African American culture.

Before I proceed, however, I should clarify some important concepts
that are fundamental to my approach to Hughes and his work in *Montage of
a Dream Deferred*. First, in referring to the vernacular tradition of African
American culture I mean primarily the oral and musical expressive practices
of a cultural tradition that for centuries was largely non-written. I also mean
to suggest the extent to which these cultural practices have maintained a popular base in "the folk," even as African American artistic and literary production has grown increasingly professionalized in the 20th century. Second, my
understanding of Hughes's adaptation of African American musical forms in
*Montage* has been profoundly influenced by Henry Louis Gates's notion of a
"black Signifyin(g) difference" in which one finds the distinctively "black"
quality of African American literature (xxiv). "Signifyin(g)" is the master

trope of Gates's theory of African American literature, standing for the black revision of standard English signification, intertextual relationships among African American texts, and an indigenously African American interpretive approach. I will concentrate on the first dimension of this concept—the sense of signifying as an array of distinctively black expressive practices—in my analysis of the ways *Montage* draws on jazz for its literary innovations.

The blues, gospel, and jazz are generally regarded as some of the richest manifestations of African American culture, and it is from black music and the larger black vernacular tradition that *Montage* draws its boldest experiments in language and form, as Hughes himself explicitly stated in his introductory note to the text:

> In terms of current Afro-American popular music and the sources from which it has progressed—jazz, ragtime, swing, blues, boogie-woogie, and be-bop—this poem on contemporary Harlem, like be-bop, is marked by conflicting changes, sudden nuances, sharp and impudent interjections, broken rhythms, and passages sometimes in the manner of the jam session, sometimes the popular song, punctuated by the riffs, runs, breaks, and disctortions of the music of a community in transition. (387)[1]

The significance of this adaptation of musical forms in the poem can hardly be overstated. Be-bop, the most immediate and pervasive embodiment of the jazz tradition in *Montage,* began in the early 1940s as a revolt against more commercialized forms of jazz, like big-band swing, on the part of such musicians as Dizzy Gillespie, Thelonius Monk, and Charlie Parker, who gathered for jam sessions outside their regular work with swing orchestras. The new music was rooted in the tradition of improvisational jazz, but its dramatic extensions of and departures from jazz conventions soon established be-bop as a "radical" jazz form. Ross Russell, who worked with the legendary saxophonist Charlie Parker as head of Dial Records, described be-bop in terms of a rebellion against the musical status quo in a series of articles written in 1948–1949. As he defined it:

> Be-bop is music of revolt: revolt against big bands, arrangers, vertical harmonies, soggy rhythms, non-playing orchestra leaders, Tin-Pan Alley—against commercialized music in general. It reasserts the individuality of the jazz musician as a creative artist, playing spontaneous and melodic music within the framework of jazz, but with new tools, sounds, and concepts. (202)

Moreover, in its relation to "traditional" jazz, be-bop can itself be thought of as an African American modernist form comparable to the Euro-American modernist forms of collage and *Montage*. Russell sensed this, perhaps, in comparing the sometimes hostile reactions against be-bop with the initial response to the work of James Joyce and Arnold Schonberg (188). Similarly, looking back on the be-bop era, in a 1964 essay, novelist and cultural critic Ralph Ellison recalled the impact of the new sound:

> It was itself a texture of fragments, repetitive, nervous, not fully formed; its melodic lines underground, secret and taunting; its riffs jeering—"Salt peanuts! Salt peanuts!" Its timbres flat or shrill, with a minimum of thrilling vibrato. Its rhythms were out of stride and seemingly arbitrary, its drummers frozen-faced introverts dedicated to chaos. And in it the steady flow of memory, desire and defined experience summed up by the traditional jazz beat and blues mood seemed swept like a great river from its old, deep bed. We know better now, and recognize the old moods in the new sounds, but what we know is that which was then becoming. (203)

In drawing on be-bop, then, Hughes was not only tapping into the rich vein of the jazz tradition but also registering a moment of tumultuous change in that tradition. This tumult in the world of jazz corresponded with unrest in the wider world, and according to his biographer Arnold Rampersad, Hughes saw in be-bop "the growing fissures in Afro-American culture, the myth of integration and American social harmony jarred by a message of deep discord" (*Life* 2:151).

Specifically placing *Montage* in its musical and social context of 1940s Harlem, Walter Farrell and Patricia Johnson have suggested that be-bop offered Hughes not only a mood but also a form: a way of building a long poem out of a number of shorter poems or phrases (61). According to Steven Tracy, however, the idea of building a long poem from a sequence of shorter pieces did not originate with Hughes, and he attempts to show how the structure of *Montage* responds in a similar fashion to some of the same kinds of problems confronted by a number of modernist poets in trying to make a long poem that corresponded to their experience (224–225). Agreeing in principle, I would nevertheless argue that the specific experience that Hughes's poem attempts to convey and the particulars of its aesthetic principles do set it apart from the work of "traditional" modernists, whereby it truly breaks new ground for modern poetry. As a key element of what makes *Montage* a distinctively modernist *and* African American text, the nature and extent of its use of aesthetic principles drawn from be-bop and the larger jazz tradition clearly merits more detailed examination.

Originally recorded in 1945, a composition by Charlie Parker entitled "KoKo" demonstrates how be-bop radically departed from the big-band swing that had become the dominant jazz style of the 1940s, and the piece can also serve as an illustration of the aesthetic principles that Hughes employs in *Montage*. In keeping with the way that Hughes described be-bop in the introduction to his poem, "KoKo" is marked by abrupt, sometimes rapid, shifts in direction, tone, rhythm, and melody. The piece is largely a showcase for Parker's work on alto saxophone, with Dizzy Gillespie playing trumpet in a supporting role along with a bassist, pianist, and drummer. The ensemble opens with a brief passage that suggests a theme or melody which reappears in varied forms throughout the piece. Short solos by Gillespie and Parker and another brief passage by the ensemble follows. Next comes Parker's extended solo—the heart of the piece. He plays fast and faster, looping up and down the scale as the bass keeps up a quick, faint undertone and the cymbals shimmer. Jazz critic Martin Williams aptly describes Parker's rhythmic innovations in this solo that helped define be-bop: "Following a pause, notes fall over and between this beat and that beat: breaking them asunder, robbing them of any vestige of monotony; rests fall where heavy beats once came, now 'heavy' beats come between beats and on weak beats" (134). A bombastic drum solo and a longer ensemble passage, which ends abruptly with two notes that sound like a "be-bop," conclude the number. All this happens in two minutes and 50 seconds. "KoKo," it turns out, is in part a variation on the jazz standard "Cherokee," but Parker's "KoKo" is unmistakably original.

As the example of "KoKo" suggests, one may think of be-bop in terms of a set of principles of formal revision and performative improvisation. Like more traditional forms of jazz, be-bop is an eclectic composite of earlier African American musical forms and styles. Even more significant, be-bop musicians took the jazz tradition of devising variations on standard tunes to lengths that tested the limits of what other musicians and jazz audiences would accept. Jazz critic Marshall Stearns explains that the new music's harmonies sounded like mistakes to a typical Dixieland jazz musician and that its melodies seemed deliberately confusing. But he also notes that many be-bop numbers were in fact based on the chord progressions of standard jazz tunes, such as "I've Got Rhythm," "Indiana," and "How High the Moon": "The piano, guitar, and bass would play the same accompaniment to "Indiana" as they might ordinarily, for example, and the soloist would improvise as usual—but nobody would play the tune. It wasn't exactly new to jazz, but bop made a practice of featuring variations upon melodies that were never stated" (229). This kind of virtuosity—itself a form of signifying—would seem to be based on the assumption that the "original" melody is understood and that the piece can therefore proceed from it. Distinctive instrumental styles and techniques also contributed to be-bop's revision of more traditional music. For example, after stating that Charlie Parker was jazz's "greatest *inventor* of melodies," Williams is quick to add that a "typical" Parker phrase is likely to be much the same as one that had been employed by previous generations of jazz musicians. "The secret," Williams explains, "is of course that Parker inflects, accents, and pronounces that phrase so differently that one simply may not recognize it" (127).

Such distinctive inflections, accents, and changes in "pronunciation" of black vernacular forms are characteristic of Hughes's writing as well—particularly in *Montage*. Like be-bop, the poem reworks "standards" from the African American musical and broader expressive traditions, pushing them farther than previous poetic practice had allowed in its composite of diverse poetic modes and styles and its variations on standard musical and linguistic forms, such as blues lyrics and the dozens. Similarly, the poem replicates other be-bop departures from improvisational and performative conventions, such as the foregrounding of the individual performer/artist in relation to the group and its emphasis on the detached, "cool" approach to performance that defied stereotypes of the black entertainer. In all this, be-bop provided Hughes with a way of organizing a nonlinear, multiple-voiced long poem that was grounded in African American culture and offered a distinctively African American means of disrupting conventional poetic language and form.

If we look at *Montage of a Dream Deferred* in the context of be-bop and the larger black vernacular tradition, its innovative force also comes into sharper focus. As its title suggests, the poem presents a rapid sequence of scenes and images that reiterate "The boogie-woogie rumble / Of a dream deferred" (*Collected Poems* 388). In myriad ways *Montage* records, explains, and enacts the undercurrent of frustrated hopes that runs through the lives of black Americans in the aftermath of World War II. This disparity between the ideal and the reality is the central thread of the poem, and it is underscored throughout the text by the repetition of the phrases "dream deferred" and "ain't you heard," which insist that the reader recognize this fact of African American life.

The original 1951 edition of the poem is 75 pages long and consists of 91 pieces set off from each other by individual headings or subtitles. An aural and visual montage, the poem shifts, sometimes abruptly, sometimes by thematic transition, from one image, voice, or vignette to the next through six unnumbered sections of varying length. Ranging from one line to three pages, the distinct pieces can be called "poems" for convenience, but they clearly function as parts of a larger whole. It is particularly important to note the structure and format of the first edition of the poem because the versions of it published in *The Langston Hughes Reader* (1958) and the *Selected Poems of Langston Hughes* (1959) tend to "normalize" its typography and format, making it appear more like a series of independent poems and less like a single long poem. Although in the recently published *Collected Poems of Langston Hughes* the typography and format are much the same as that of the *Selected Poems*, this edition does reaffirm the status of *Montage* as a single poem by shading the edges of the pages of this section.

One striking parallel with the composite form and revisionary approach of be-bop is the way that the poem itself includes specific adaptations of standard African American musical forms. These standard forms, rather than, as in jazz, specific standard tunes, serve as the basis for new compositions in the poem. *Montage* includes both pieces that work within the conventions of particular forms, such as the traditional blues stanza form of "Blues at Dawn," and pieces that qualify or expand on the forms themselves, such as "Same in Blues" and what Tracy calls the "boogie poems" of *Montage*—a set of pieces scattered throughout the poem that play off the conventions of boogie-woogie. As Tracy describes it, "Same in Blues" modifies a traditional blues stanza by changing a key word in the refrain (165–166). Consider here the opening stanzas:

Same in Blues

> I said to my baby,
> Baby, take it slow.
> I can't, she said, I can't!
> I got to go!
>
> *There's a certain*
> *amount of traveling*
> *in a dream deferred.*
>
> Lulu said to Leonard,
> I want a diamond ring.
> Leonard said to Lulu,
> You won't get a goddam thing!
>
> *A certain*
> *amount of nothing*
> *in a dream deferred.* (427)

The refrain pattern not only encourages the "audience" to repeat the refrain with the "singer" in the traditional manner but also provides more detached generalizations on the situations depicted. By separating the refrains from the body of the piece and highlighting judgments and summations of the episodes in the stanzas with key words (*traveling, nothing*), the poem works inside and outside of the blues tradition, just as a be-bop composition plays off traditional jazz forms.

In a similar fashion, the boogie poems bring the forms and rhythms of boogie-woogie into the poem's composite structure. A driving, blues-based piano style that emerged in the 1920s and remained popular into the 1940s, boogie-woogie is marked by the interplay between improvisations played on the treble keys with the right hand and repeated phrases played on the bass keys with the left hand. Tracy suggests that the boogie poems replicate the playing of a boogie-woogie pianist, "combining the rumbling infectious bass beat and rhythm with treble variations and improvisations" (234). "Dream Boogie," the opening piece of the poem, sets up this juxtaposition in its first stanza:

Dream Boogie

> Good morning, daddy!
> Ain't you heard
> The boogie-woogie rumble
> Of a dream deferred?
>
> Listen closely:
> You'll hear their feet
> Beating out and beating out a—
>
> *You think*
> *It's a happy beat?* (388)

This use of a "boogie-woogie rumble" to convey the deferred dreams and double consciousness of African Americans echoes throughout the poem in the repetition of the phrases "ain't you heard" and "dream deferred" in and beyond the "boogie poems" themselves. In its manipulation of the blues form and its adaptation of the interplay between the rumbling bass and tingling treble of boogie-woogie, *Montage* clearly demonstrates the creative revision and manipulation of standard forms that be-bop allows for, and, in fact, demands.

As the pervasiveness of the "boogie-woogie rumble" in *Montage* suggests, the dynamics of jazz and signifying inform the poem's overall structure and aesthetic principles in ways that go far beyond specific adaptations of musical forms in particular passages. The piece "What? So Soon!" is a short but striking example of the be-bop aesthetic that runs throughout the entire poem:

What? So Soon!

> I believe my old lady's
> pregnant again!
> Fate must have
> some kind of trickeration
> to populate the
> cullud nation!

> *Comment against Lamp Post*
> *You call it fate?*

> *Figurette*
> *De-daddle-dy!*
> *De-dop!* (398)

The format, spacing, and typography of this piece and others like it adds to the dynamism and fluidity of the poem's form, underscoring the role of distinctive individual pieces as parts of a larger whole. Like jazz solos, these pieces are often in dialogue with each other, as in the ironic commentary that the two-line phrase of *"Comment against Lamp Post"* provides on the speaker's opening exclamations in "What? So Soon!" This short reply both serves as a signifying retort and puts the speaker's complaint into a broader, more profound context. The multiple dimensions of this simple exchange—as overheard speech, statement on the circumstances of black life, and comment on individual responsibility (or the lack of it)—is typical of Hughes's vernacular style throughout *Montage*.

Lines like the *"Figurette"* section of "What? So Soon!" punctuate the shift from one piece or sequence of pieces to the next in the same way brief "tags" signal the end of jazz or blues numbers. Yet, as in improvised jazz, the connections between one voice and the next are often tight enough in *Montage* that despite abrupt changes in the speaker and tone it is difficult to say exactly where one sequence definitely ends and another begins. "What? So Soon!" for example, is preceded by a section entitled "Numbers," the ambiguous pledge of a gambler to go straight once he (or she) hits it big, and followed by the "Motto" of a cool be-bop cat. Although distinct, these other voices are not so different from those of "What? So Soon!" just as the way Hughes knits them together underscores what they share: hopes and concerns about money, living to get the most out of the

moment, and a signifying sensibility that is evident in a sense of irony and
a gift for turning a phrase.

As the "What? So Soon!" sequence illustrates, the overall structure of the
poem recalls the organization of such earlier modernist long poems as *The Waste
Land* and *Hugh Selwyn Mauberley*, which also aspire to the form of collage or
montage. Like these poems, *Montage* depends more on thematic and associative
connections than narrative or chronology for its structure. In *Montage*, however,
it is jazz and the signifying voices of the African American tradition that provide Hughes with the kind of broad and deep collective foundation that T. S.
Eliot and Ezra Pound aimed for in their references to classical mythology and
the monuments of Western culture. The collective and open-ended improvisatory quality that *Montage* gains from the black vernacular is significantly different from the associative leaps of the "traditional" modernist long poems of
writers like Eliot and Pound, which continue to evoke notions of formal closure
even as they pursue more individualized and subjective associative connections.

The discontinuous, nonlinear form of *Montage* not only mirrors the
musical and social dissonance of the be-bop years but also reflects the deeper
structures of the jazz tradition. In terms of jazz, the poem can be thought
of as a sequence of distinctive voices that play off each other while building
a freeform, improvisational whole. The sequence of pieces "Evening Song,"
"Chord," and "Fact" is a further illustration of this dynamic:

Evening Song

> A woman standing in the doorway
> Trying to make her where-with-all:
> *Come here, baby, darlin'!*
> *Don't you hear me call?*
>
> If I was anybody's sister,
> I'd tell her, *Gimme a place to sleep.*
> But I ain't nobody's sister.
> I'm just a poor lost sheep.
>
> Mary, Mary, Mary,
> Had a little lamb.
> Well, I hope that lamb of Mary's
> Don't turn out like I am.

Chord

> Shadow faces
> In the shadow night

> Before the early dawn
> Bops bright.

Fact

> There's been an eagle on a nickel,
> An eagle on a quarter, too,
> But there ain't no eagle
> On a dime. (422–423)

In the space of one page, the poem shifts from the opening juxtaposition of the voices of a prostitute and a more reflective speaker to the imagistic lines of "Chord" and then to the signifying aphorism "Fact." Again and again throughout the poem, individual voices come forward to highlight distinctive nuances and perspectives from the Harlem that the poem represents, but the individual voices (and the poet's voice) remain rooted in a communal context, resulting in a poetic version of the collective improvisations of jazz.

It is in the process of this interplay—a signifying practice of repetition and revision—that what Charles Hartman calls the "dialogic understanding" of a jazz aesthetic is most evident. Hartman explains that the key principles of jazz that relate to poetry include not only voice and improvisation but also ideas about performance and the kind of conversational call-and-response that jazz's language of repetition and revision entails (146). Similarly, William Harris underscores the crucial role of revision and parody in jazz (particularly through repetition and inversion) in outlining the "jazz aesthetic" of Amiri Baraka, one of a younger generation of African American poets who returned to jazz forms in the 1960s. Such perspectives on jazz and poetry remind us that even more than images and stanza structures, what be-bop jazz offered Hughes was an array of aesthetic principles rooted in the black vernacular. Concepts like these can help us make more substantive connections between jazz and the poetry of *Montage,* and they enable us to pursue the implications of this relationship more fully.

Much of *Montage* consists of dramatic monologues and dialogues spoken by a crosssection of Harlem blacks, and the poem's foregrounding of individual voices in a communal context is a major manifestation of the dynamics of jazz in *Montage.* Yet the multitude of African American voices represented in the poem, and Hughes's handling of them, also demonstrates the poem's engagement with the signifying tradition of the black vernacular, which includes and extends beyond the realm of music. The signifying voices of *Montage* illustrate the verbal dexterity and rhetorical skill of its African American speakers, and Hughes's commitment to this "collective improvisation" has important implications for the poem's relation to the vernacular and the poet's relation to his people. The depth and breadth of Hughes's commitment to rendering distinctive African American voices indicate that he, too, is engaged in what Gates has described as the "search of the black subject for a textual voice" in the African American literary tradition (169). The multiple speakers, monologues, and dialogues of *Montage* play off each other like the solos in a be-bop performance, but they also swell into a larger, communal voice. Like its manipulation of black musical forms, this play of voices itself disrupts conventional literary form, adding another layer to Hughes's African American modernism.

The varied voices of *Montage* quite literally make it what Gates has called a "speakerly text." For Gates, Zora Neale Hurston's *Their Eyes Were Watching God* is a prime example of a text that "enable[s] a multiplicity of narrative voices to assume control of the text" in its pursuit of a black textual voice (196). As a non-narrative poem, *Montage* is free from the strictures of a narrator, protagonist, or plot and can concentrate more exclusively on a "speakerly" play of voices. These voices also represent the black subject's quest for a textual voice on a broader, more fully communal scale rather than in individual terms. While Hurston's novel centers on Janie's gaining her own voice, Hughes's poem focuses on amplifying the voices that the black community of Harlem already has.

The way that *Montage* presents not only the variations of a single voice or persona but also the speakerly play of a variety of voices in a communal context is clear from sequences like the following:

Warning

        Daddy,
        don't let your dog
        curb you!

Croon

        I don't give a damn
        For Alabam'
        Even if it is my home.

New Yorkers

        I was born here,
        that's no lie, he said,
        right here beneath God's sky.

*I wasn't born here, she said,*
*I come—and why?*
*Where I come from*
*folks work hard*
*all their lives*
*until they die*
*and never own no parts*
*of earth nor sky.*
*So I come up here.*
*Now what've I got?*
    *You!*
She lifted up her lips
in the dark:
The same old spark! (393–394)

Five distinct speakers make up this passage and only the last of them corresponds to what might be considered the authorial or "poetic" voice of the poem. A sense of the depth and texture of Harlem life, particularly the contrast between Harlem natives and migrants from the South, emerges from the interaction of these five voices. The hip, aphoristic "Warning" about self-effacement and the blunt "Croon" of the native of Alabama stake out what in "New Yorkers" becomes the opposition between the apparently autonomous, Whitmanian "I" of the male speaker and the more materially grounded, ironic female voice that responds to him. Typical of *Montage*, the authorial voice concludes the piece with a signifying punch line, which at once celebrates and calls attention to the superficiality of such a resolution given the profound differences in outlook among Harlem blacks.

The monologues and dialogues of *Montage* function like improvised solos and duets, emphasizing the distinctiveness and particularity of individual voices against a collective background. In this, they also can be thought of in terms of what Houston Baker calls "blues moments"—moments when African American voices "achieve a resonant, improvisational, expressive dignity" in a communal context (*Blues* 13). By presenting African American voices in dialogue and then making dialogues out of monologues, the poem insists on both the "expressive dignity" of the individual voices that it represents and their larger communal context. Again, this quality may bring to mind canonical modernist texts that experiment with multiple voices, but in *Montage* the sound and the structure of these voices is distinctively black.

In its theme, scope, and style, *Montage* epitomizes the work of a self-described "social poet" whose ear was finely tuned to the interplay of voices that make up a larger, communal voice, and the play of black voices represented in *Montage* demonstrates the poem's aspirations toward orchestrating a collective black voice that maintains the differences among its speakers. In the tradition of the black vernacular and jazz, *Montage* calls up and calls on a communal voice (a *literary* collective improvisation) but remains committed to the diversity of discrete, particular voices rather than attempting to totalize or generalize from them. In this way, *Montage* defies conventions that tie poetry to a single, central consciousness and would have it aspire to a single, unitary voice.

A direct and fundamentally important result of the role of jazz and the black vernacular in Hughes's work is the implications it has for the stance and status of the author in the text. Throughout the poem, what might be considered the poet's voice is muted, and the poem's wider play of voices dominates the text. The difference between the poet's voice and the other voices in the poem is registered dramatically in passages like these:

Street Song

>          Jack, if you got to be a rounder
>          Be a rounder right—
>          Just don't let mama catch you
>          Makin' rounds at night.

125th Street

>          Face like a chocolate bar
>          full of nuts and sweet.
>
>          Face like a jack-o'-lantern,
>          candle inside.
>
>          Face like a slice of melon,
>          grin that wide. (407)

In these consecutive pieces, the poem shifts abruptly from what could be overheard speech (perhaps that of a woman) to an imagistic, "poetic" treatment of faces on the street.

The speech rendered in "Street Song," with its colloquial terms ("Jack," "rounder," "mama") and signifying rhyme, seems to be the opposite of the detached poetic perspective of "125th Street," which consists of a string of similes that recall the imagism of poems like Pound's "In a Station of the Metro." Yet within the difference in style and point of view between "Street Song" and "125th Street," continuities remain. The terms of Hughes's "imagism" are thoroughly popular, evoking even the stereotype of watermelon-eating blacks and concluding with a rhyme that echoes the rhyme scheme of "Street Song." Another poem, "Wonder," combines this popular imagism with a "folk" voice:

> Wonder
>
> Early blue evening.
>
> Lights ain't come on yet.
> *Looky yonder!*
> *They come on now!* (394)

Characteristic of *Montage*, "125th Street" and "Wonder" indulge in what may be clichéd or even stereotypical expressions and transform such material into something more. As "125th Street" shows, the poet's voice is distinct from the multitude of other voices in the poem but not divorced from or condescending toward them. Hughes brings a poetic perspective to Harlem, but even his most poetic rendering of it is steeped in folk images and language.

The stance and status of the poet's voice in *Montage* also relates back to be-bop's emphasis on a "cool" attitude and approach to performance. Consistent with the "cool" style, the poet's voice in the poem, when present, has a detached quality. Arthur Davis has examined this stance in Hughes's work generally, and nowhere is it more apparent than in *Montage*, where Hughes maintains this "cool" even when the voice that seems to be the poet's conveys anger or bitterness. For example, in "Movies" the speaker concludes:

> Movies
>
> (Hollywood
> laughs at me,
> black—
> so I laugh
> back.) (395)

The companion piece, "Not a Movie," matter-of-factly summarizes the brutality that drove a man from the South to Harlem. He arrives with six knots on his head, but "there ain't no Ku Klux / on a 133rd" (396). The poem returns to a critical perspective, with touches of humor, in "Shame on You," which concludes:

> Shame on You
>
> A movie house in Harlem named after Lincoln,
> Nothing at all named after John Brown.

Black people don't remember
any better than white.

If you're not alive and kicking,
*shame on you!* (415)

When the poet's voice emerges from the chorus of Harlem voices, it is most
often in this ironic and sadly comic vein, providing a critical commentary on
life in Harlem and the United States at large. The varying distance between
author and speaker throughout the poem—and such other variations as
shifts between first and third person, degrees of self-consciousness, uses of
folk material, and episodes of ironic commentary—show the breadth of the
range of voices that comprise *Montage*.

Instead of an omnipotent, Whitmanian "I" or shorer of fragments like
Eliot's speaker, *Montage* presents the poet's voice(s) as a pervasive but not a
commanding presence in a chorus of diverse voices. This may in part reflect
the ironies of the relationship between a black speaker/author and the "white"
language that he/she must employ, since, as Gates asks, "how can the black
subject posit a full and sufficient self in a language in which blackness is a
sign of absence?" (169). Hughes may to some extent be "unable" to project
the voice of a central subject—in a post-structuralist sense—in *Montage*. Yet
the lack of a strong, central "I" in the text seems to be as much a positive as
a negative quality. The poem can be understood as positively refraining from
projecting a single authoritative voice in favor of the communal play of voices
it presents. In this respect, *Montage* points toward a sense of identity that is
not necessarily predicated on the individual self. By defining and nurturing
a communal sense of identity, the poem wrests a measure of agency from a
history of objectification and victimization.

A key aspect of the authorial stance in the poem is Hughes's handling
of what are sometimes called "folk materials," which is also a point on which
he has been criticized, both in regard to *Montage* specifically and his work
in general. Initially, there were objections to the allegedly sordid and un-
flattering image of blacks, his choice of themes and use of black vernacular
language, and more recently it has been argued or implied that Hughes's use
of popular forms displays a lack of artistic seriousness or depth. What one
needs to understand, however, is that Hughes's use of folk material not only
makes sense in terms of what his poetry aims to accomplish but is in fact
essential. Further, it can be argued that Hughes is particularly successful in
representing "the folk" because of the extent to which he lets the vernacular
shape his writing. Hazel Carby notes that Hughes avoids the pitfalls of ob-
jectifying or romanticizing the folk because of the way he uses the blues to
convey a communal sensibility in social rather than individual terms. Simi-

larly, David Chinitz has argued that Hughes's "primitivism" is a much more complex—and much richer—matter than has been previously acknowledged. In *Montage* in particular, Hughes's manipulation of folk language and forms is integral to the logic of the poem. Like its diverse voices, the poem employs folk material in a variety of ways, ranging from relatively direct, unmediated representations to subtle adaptations of and commentaries on it. In this way, the poem also reflects back on the complex relationship between jazz and the vernacular sources from which it arose.

Rather than using Euro-American poetic models, Hughes turned to the tradition of black music and speech for aesthetic principles and expressive forms, and nothing so well suggests the relationship between identity and writing that shapes *Montage* as the words of the black student in "Theme for English B":

Theme for English B

> It's not easy to know what is true for you or me
> at twenty-two, my age. But I guess I'm what
> I feel and see and hear. Harlem, I hear you:
> hear you, hear me—we two—you, me, talk on this page.
> (I hear New York, too.) Me—who? (409–410)

Here Hughes suggests the problematic nature of the ideal of universality for a "Harlem" writer and presents an image of that "writing subject" as being constituted by and in dialogue with the world—particularly the black voices—around him. It is in this way that the black student's page is "colored" by his identity and social context. *Montage* is thus a prime example of how, as Jean Wagner aptly puts it, Hughes lived "in terms of the external world and in unison with it, making himself one with the community and refusing to stand apart as an individual" (393). This quality is a crucial element of Hughes's popular modernism, and it also suggests what the relationship between jazz and poetry in his work still has to offer contemporary poets and readers.

*M*ontage *of a Dream Deferred* figures the relationship between author and text differently than most "traditional" modernist works at the same time that it pursues an alternative language, structure, and theme rooted in African American traditions. Not only does the poem "make it new" in terms of African American culture, it also offers a representation of the author as one among many voices—constituted by and reconstituting the culture from which and for which he speaks. The absence of a strong personal or individual identity is a given in the poem, and the poet neither despairs over its loss or projects its return or fulfillment. Instead, Hughes engages in a dialogue with the African American culture that provides his sense of identity, both celebrating and critiquing it.

The relationship between jazz and Hughes's poetry has profound implications for our understanding not only of his work in isolation but also of the aesthetic and cultural phenomena of modernism and the Harlem Renaissance. Like the other great innovators of the Harlem Renaissance, Hughes blends the black vernacular with modernist experimentation. As yet, however, the nature and value of Hughes's contribution to an African American modernism has been underappreciated. His unique combination of a jazz aesthetic and an unreservedly popular orientation—seen in the extent to which he allows vernacular voices and forms to shape his poetry—suggests powerful ways of bringing the individual and the communal, the poet and his people, together. In this, Hughes's voice is one that still needs to be heard by literary historians who aim to understand modernism and the Harlem Renaissance and by poets who aim to speak to, for, and with their people, whoever they might be.

Such a "modernizing" of Hughes may at first seem willful, but a careful reading of his work reveals that he was engaged in a modernist enterprise of his own. Although Hughes was indeed critical of the high-modernist style of Melvin Tolson, with its "foreign words and footnotes" (Nielsen 242), rather than being anti-modernist, Hughes's work represents a distinct version of African American modernism. Tolson and of course Ellison brilliantly assert their place in the modern tradition, transforming it from "within" through their mastery of a high-modernist style *and* the black vernacular. Although Hughes also knew the work of Pound and James Joyce, in his own writing he was almost always the populist "outsider," and his work relates to the idea of "Literature" differently than most canonical modernist texts. He described himself as a "literary sharecropper," for whom writing was a job and an art (*Bontemps-Hughes Letters* 292), and in a text like *Montage of a Dream Deferred* Hughes draws less on the centuries of literary tradition behind him than on the vivid life around him. Overall, his work is marked by what Karen Jackson Ford calls an "aesthetic of simplicity"—one which puts aside the complex conventions of Poetry in order to get his message across with directness, humor, and signifying wit (454). This "unliterary" quality may be a reason Hughes's work has not figured prominently in the sophisticated theories of black literature developed by critics like Gates and Baker. Yet with the central role that these scholars ascribe to the black vernacular, the popular orientation of texts like *Montage* suggests that Hughes's writing should be all the more important. In his own way, Hughes certainly engages in what Nielsen calls the "deterritorialization" of modernism by "rearticulat[ing] modernism as a virtuoso African American form" (250) and in the "deformation of mastery" that Baker finds in the work of the African American modernists who appropriated the black vernacular in their effort to re-make "white" language (*Modernism* 50). If he himself had been inclined to such theoretical musings, Hughes would no doubt have found simpler terms for his take on modernism, perhaps something like "jazzing it up."

Those critics who have examined Hughes's relation to modernism locate his particular contribution in his ability to combine a modern consciousness with an abiding racial consciousness. Rampersad, for example, finds this quality in the blues poems of *The Weary Blues* (1926) and *Fine Clothes to the Jew* (1927) ("Langston Hughes"), and R. Baxter Miller has written of Hughes's attempts to fuse the individual and the collective in the long poem *Ask Your Mama: Twelve Moods for Jazz* (1961) ("Framing"). A major text from the middle of Hughes's career, *Montage* goes beyond the earlier blues poems in scope and anticipates the ways that *Ask Your Mama* conveys the images and energies of a historical moment. Like other writers of the Harlem Renaissance and since, Hughes uses black linguistic and musical forms to convey a sense of the collective memory and voice of African Americans. But it is his thoroughly popular orientation—the extent to which he allows vernacular voices and forms to shape his poetry—that makes Hughes's work distinctively his own. If we are to move toward a three-dimensional image of Hughes, today's continuing re-examination of the ideas about "literariness" and aesthetic value—handed down from Euro-American modernism and the New Criticism—needs to account fully for the ways he brings poetry and jazz together.

In *Montage* Hughes brings the dynamics of jazz and the black vernacular tradition to the broad canvas of the long poem—the form that became the ultimate measure of poetic achievement for a generation of modernist poets. He also demonstrates how he kept his ear for the vernacular current, drawing on the sounds of a particular moment in the history of Harlem and black America. The be-bop era of the 1940s was a time when it became clear that the "dream revived" by the war effort would once again be "deferred," and, as James de Jongh notes, *Montage* captures the sea-change of Harlem's transition from black cultural capital to urban ghetto (100). In *Montage*, Hughes's engagement with the black vernacular—both in terms of expressive forms and lived experience—results in a text that is shaped by the dynamics of jazz and its play of signifying black voices. The poem thus differs from some more "traditional" modernist long poems (such as *The Waste Land*, Pound's *Cantos*, or William Carlos Williams's *Paterson*) in the particular structure it adopts and in the governing aesthetic principles of that structure. The African American musical tradition (and be-bop in particular) provides *Montage* with a form that challenges conventional Euro-American ideas about aesthetic unity, the status of the text, and the role of the author—ideas that linger even in some modernist revisions of received forms.

The poetic stance that Hughes adopts in *Montage* is also crucial to his particular contribution to an African American modernism. His willingness (and ability) to let the sounds and shapes of jazz and the black vernacular guide his poetry results in modernist experimentation that maintains a popular grounding. In this way, the jazz aesthetic and signifying voices of *Montage* succeed in meaningfully engaging the vernacular on its own terms. This unreservedly popular orientation is a valuable complement to the more self-consciously intellectual writing of such African American modernists as Ellison and Tolson. Beyond this, Hughes's work continues to offer a vibrant model for all contemporary poets who would aspire to "popular" poetry— poetry that speaks *with* a broader community in its own language and about its deepest concerns—and it testifies to the rich possibilities of interarts relationships. When Hughes brings the "boogie-woogie rumble" of jazz to the poetry of *Montage*, the black vernacular sounds through literary tradition, a sound that continues to reverberate for us today.

## NOTE

1. Unless otherwise indicated, all quotations from *Montage* will refer to the version published in *Collected Poems*. In these quotations, all italics are Hughes's own.

## WORKS CITED

Baker, Houston A., Jr. *Blues, Ideology, and Afro-American Literature: A Vernacular Theory.* Chicago: University of Chicago Press, 1984.
———. *Modernism and the Harlem Renaissance.* Chicago: University of Chicago Press, 1987.
Carby, Hazel. "The Politics of Fiction, Anthropology, and the Folk: Zora Neale Hurston." *History and Memory in African American Culture.* Eds. Genevieve Fabre and Robert O'Meally. New York: Oxford University Press, 1994: pp. 28–44.
Chinitz, David. "Rejuvenation through Joy: Langston Hughes, Primitivism, and Jazz." *American Literary History* 9.1 (1997): pp. 60–78.
Davis, Arthur P. "Langston Hughes: Cool Poet." *Langston Hughes: Black Genius.* Ed. Therman B. O'Daniel. New York: Morrow, 1971: pp. 18–38.
de Jongh, James. *Vicious Modernism: Black Harlem and the Literary Imagination.* Cambridge: Cambridge University Press, 1990.
Ellison, Ralph. "The Golden Age, Time Past." *Shadow and Act.* New York: Random House, 1964: pp. 199–213.
Farrell, Walter C., Jr., and Patricia A. Johnson. "Poetic Interpretations of Urban Black Folk Culture: Langston Hughes and the 'Bebop' Era." *MELUS*, 8.3 (1981): pp. 57–72.
Ford, Karen Jackson. "Do Right to Write Right: Langston Hughes's Aesthetics of Simplicity." *Twentieth-Century Literature* 38.4 (1992): pp. 436–456.
Gates, Henry Louis, Jr. *The Signifying Monkey: A Theory of Afro-American Literary Criticism.* New York: Oxford University Press, 1988.

Harris, William J., *The Poetry and Poetics of Amiri Baraka: The Jazz Aesthetic*. Columbia: University of Missouri Press, 1985.

Hartman, Charles O., *Jazz Text: Voice and Improvisation in Poetry, Jazz, and Song*. Princeton, NJ: Princeton University Press, 1991.

Hughes, Langston. *The Collected Poems of Langston Hughes*. Eds. Arnold Rampersad and David Roessel. New York: Knopf, 1994.

———. *Montage of a Dream Deferred*. New York: Holt, 1951.

———. "My Adventures as a Social Poet." *Good Morning Revolution: Uncollected Social Protest Writings by Langston Hughes*. Ed. with Intro. by Faith Berry. New York: Hill, 1973: pp. 135–143.

———, and Arna Bontemps. *Arna Bontemps–Langston Hughes Letters: 1925–1967*. Ed. Charles H. Nichols. New York: Paragon, 1990.

Miller, R. Baxter. "Framing and Framed Languages in Hughes's *Ask Your Mama: 12 Moods for Jazz*." *MELUS* 17.4 (1991–1992): pp. 3–13.

Nielsen, Aldon L. "Melvin B. Tolson and the Deterritorialization of Modernism." *African American Review* 26.2 (1992): pp. 241–255.

Rampersad, Arnold. "Langston Hughes and Approaches to Modernism in the Harlem Renaissance." *The Harlem Renaissance: Revaluations*. Eds. Amritjit Singh, William S. Shiver, and Stanley Brodwin. New York: Garland, 1989: pp. 49–71.

———. *The Life of Langston Hughes*. 2 Vols. New York: Oxford University Press, 1986, 1988.

Russell, Ross. "Bebop." *The Art of Jazz: Essays on the Nature and Development of Jazz*. Ed. Martin T. Williams. New York: Oxford University Press, 1959: pp. 187–213.

Stearns, Marshall W., *The Story of Jazz*. 1956. New York: Oxford University Press, 1972.

Tracy, Steven C., *Langston Hughes and the Blues*. Urbana: University of Illinois Press, 1988.

Wagner, Jean. *Black Poets of the United States from Paul Laurence Dunbar to Langston Hughes*. Trans. Kenneth Douglas. Urbana: University of Illinois Press, 1973.

Williams, Martin. *The Jazz Tradition*. New York: Oxford University Press, 1970.

ANITA PATTERSON

# Jazz, Realism, and the Modernist Lyric: The Poetry of Langston Hughes

In 1940 Richard Wright, praising Langston Hughes's contribution to the development of modern American literature, observed that Hughes's "realistic position" had become the "dominant outlook of all those Negro writers who have something to say."[1] Nineteen years later James Baldwin faulted Hughes for failing to follow through consistently on the artistic premises laid out in his early verse. The problem with his unsuccessful poems, Baldwin said, was that they "take refuge, finally, in a fake simplicity in order to avoid the very difficult simplicity of experience." In succumbing to the idiomatic demands of a sociological perspective—the pressure, that is, to "hold the experience outside him"—they did not fulfill an essential criterion of Baldwin's realism, namely, the evocation of a point of view that stands "within the experience and outside it at the same time." To argue his point, Baldwin cited the last line of a jazz poem by Hughes called "Dream Boogie," which first appeared as part of *Montage of a Dream Deferred* in 1951. "Hughes," said Baldwin, "knows the bitter truth behind these hieroglyphics, what they are designed to protect, what they are designed to convey. But he has not forced them into the realm of art where their meaning would become clear and overwhelming. 'Hey, pop! / Re-bop! / Mop!' conveys much more on Lenox Avenue than it does in this book, which is not the way it ought to be."[2]

*MLQ: Modern Language Quarterly* 61:4; 2000: pp. 651–682. Copyright © 2000 University of Washington.

The main criticism Baldwin raises against jazz poems like "Dream Boogie" is that they do not offer a clearly recognizable, accurate record of experience that calls attention to their embeddedness in history. Such summary judgment has hampered further exploration of how Hughes's jazz poetics contributed to twentieth-century realism or to the development of the modernist lyric.

This essay situates Hughes's jazz poetics within the arc of his entire career to show how modernist experiments in poems like "Dream Boogie" are in keeping with his earlier attempts at lyric realism. I will focus on two main ideas. The first is that Hughes's poems challenge the critical distinction between "realism" and the "avant-garde": even his simplest, most documentary, and most historically engaged poems evince a characteristically modernist preoccupation with the figurative implications of form. Second, Hughes's realist approach to the lyric offers a fresh perspective on some central tendencies in transatlantic modernism: his repudiation of racial separatism, his interest in the relationship between poetry and American music, and his experiments with a jazz poetics are, in many ways, comparable to the critique of romantic cultural nationalism undertaken by Ezra Pound, Hart Crane, T. S. Eliot, and other modernists writing in the aftermath of the Great War. The convergence between Hughes's techniques and those of the American avant-garde highlights the importance of metonymic style, and of the historical knowledge that underlies the impulse toward formal experiment and improvisation, as a relatively neglected feature of the modernist lyric.

It is by now almost a commonplace to say that Hughes revised and extended the populist angle of vision explored in the previous decade by Edwin Arlington Robinson, Vachel Lindsay, Carl Sandburg, and others. But we have yet to understand the series of formal experiments he executed within the lyric that show his engagement with questions shared by his high modernist contemporaries.

### Realism and Form in Hughes's Poetry

As a rubric, realism has been subject to heated debate and casual dismissal in the history of American criticism. "American realism virtually has no school; its most dominating and influential advocate, William Dean Howells, often seems to ride along in a strange vacuum, nearly unheeded in his continual insistence on the proprieties of the everyday, stable characterization, and moral certainty, while almost every other important author of the period simply refused, on these terms, to become a realist."[3] Whereas in Europe the great period of realism occurred throughout the second half of the nineteenth century, in North America the movement emerged in full force only with Howells's advocacy in the nineties.[4]

Partly in response to Erich Auerbach's *Mimesis,* theoretical descriptions of realism in modern American fiction have proliferated in recent decades.[5] Yet little sustained, systematic analysis has been done on the formal development of realism in the modern lyric.[6] Such neglect may be explained in part by the fact that the realist movement was long excluded from accounts of twentieth-century American poetry, because it was considered formally without interest—a servile, transparent copying of the world.[7] *The New Princeton Encyclopedia of Poetry and Poetics,* for example, defines realism solely in contradistinction to the intensified perception, densely metaphorical style, and artificiality of the lyric and adds that, "in a general sense, realistic poetry may result from any down-to-earth opposition to what seem artificial rules of versification or arbitrary restrictions on matter or diction. . . . The precepts of realism are often considered inimical to the spirit of lyric poetry."[8]

The latent critical bias against realism was memorably addressed by Georg Lukács, who in the late 1950s offered a surprising and useful theoretical reappraisal that paid special attention to formal issues. In *The Meaning of Contemporary Realism* Lukács arrived at a description of literary realism that helped readers bracket ideological content and focus instead on innovations in language and method. One objection he raised to current critical approaches to realism was that the political message of literature was fast becoming the overriding preoccupation of reviewers; as a result, literary standards were falling precipitously.[9] Another pressing concern was that modernist tastes in the 1920s had led critics to neglect works that exhibited the traditional mimetic techniques of realism. Criticism, according to Lukács, was hindered by the unexamined belief that realism was always, by definition, antithetical to modernism:

> Let us begin by examining two prejudices. The first is typical of much present-day bourgeois criticism. It is contained in the proposition that the literature of "modernism," of the *avant-garde,* is the essentially modern literature. The traditional techniques of realism, these critics assert, are inadequate, because too superficial, to deal with the realities of our age. (13)

Hughes's poems raise questions about stultifying critical binarisms that for years have pitted modern realism against modernist antirealism, tradition against the avant-garde, political content against artistic form. As a poet, Hughes constantly tries to illustrate how formal qualities may assist an act of engaged social criticism. Instead of using words that deceive us into seeing only their "transparency" and make us believe that we are taking an unmediated look through a windowpane to a world outside the poem, Hughes offers historical knowledge by directing our attention to his careful arrangement of words on the page. His style often dramatizes how language shapes the poem's social perspectives.

"Flight," which first appeared in the June 1930 issue of *Opportunity*, demonstrates how Hughes's realist poetics meets modernist formal expectations. The poem is set in a swamp, during the postemancipation period: a black man, accused of raping a white woman, is trying to escape from a lynch mob. The pursuit of hounds recalls the history of slavery and suggests that rituals of racial violence in the South continued, and even escalated, after emancipation. Hughes's speaker assumes two points of view: observer and victim. The poem begins by giving the victim, who initially occupies the same position as the reader, the impossible task of stepping in mud without leaving tracks:

> Plant your toes in the cool swamp mud.
> Step and leave no track.
> Hurry, sweating runner!
> The hounds are at your back.
>
> *No I didn't touch her*
> *White flesh ain't for me.*
>
> Hurry! Black boy, hurry!
> They'll swing you to a tree.[10]

In "Flight" Hughes uses a short lyric form to present a splintered aspect of a reality too vast and horrifying to comprehend in its entirety. Instead the speaker describes, analyzes, and orders a tragic, swiftly unfolding moment. The lyric evokes a tension between Hughes's artistic suspension of time and the time-bound social realities that are the subject of his poem. But despite his reliance on the temporal restrictions of the genre, Hughes refuses to rest content with the familiar consolations of lyric transcendence and disengagement. Distrustful of such forced integrities and closures, he builds in a narrative structure that implies a larger, sociohistorical context, giving disquieting openness to the exigencies that lend the poem shape and significance.

The reign of terror in the wake of emancipation generated the special conditions in which modern African American poetry emerged. In the postbellum South slavery was replaced by other forms of racial subjection: indentured servitude, black codes, the contract system, vagrancy statutes, and lynching.[11] Between 1900 and 1930 massive numbers of African Americans fled the rural South and traveled to northern cities like Chicago, Detroit, and New York. During the time that Hughes wrote, many of his contemporaries started the long process of coming to grips with his lyric's main subject, namely, the violent causes of this exodus, now known as the "Great Migration."[12] "Flight" documents how, for many southern freedmen, migration had become more than a necessary socioeconomic resource; it was a way of life, a means of preserving their safety, sanity, and dignity.

In "Flight," however, realist verisimilitude coexists with modernist formal innovation. In this respect Hughes's style fits an essential criterion that Hugo Friedrich proposes for the modernist lyric.[13] The preoccupation with expressive freedom makes sense inasmuch as the plight of the lynched man described in "Flight" forces us to question a fundamental tenet of nineteenth-century realism: that a realist work should depict a form of social life in which the individual can act with "autonomous motivation" (Preminger and Brogan, 1016).

The guiding metaphor in the poem's title also works to correct popular misconceptions of the causes of the Great Migration, misconceptions exacerbated by the constant use of the trope in journalistic analyses by Hughes's black contemporaries. In *Opportunity*, the same journal in which Hughes's poem appeared, Charles S. Johnson asked, "How much is migration a flight from persecution?"[14] Black public intellectuals such as Alain Locke, portraying the social formation of the "New Negro" in 1925, tried to play down the violent causes of migration by using the image of "deliberate flight" to suggest that African Americans were engaged in a mythic, quintessentially American quest for opportunity.[15]

Lynching was, in certain respects, similar to the experience that the Great War offered transatlantic modernists, since its moral horrors spurred Hughes and other African American poets to discover formalist freedoms that were wholly new. But although Hughes's passion for freedom resembles that of the avant-garde, his practices as a modern lyricist are distinctive insofar as they dramatize his effort to bridge a cultural divide between a folkloric African American tradition that is largely oral and the privileged arena of "literature." Thus the lyric's opening line may be read as an apt allegory of Hughes's predicament as a modern African American poet. It compares his effort to fashion enduring metrical feet that fit the rhythms of an oral tradition with a fleeing man's attempt to "plant" his "toes" in the mud.

Because self-referentiality penetrates a privileged arena, there is also the suggestion of trespass: the poet's act is described in terms that bring to mind a man in flight, a man accused of rape. Hughes's exhilarating discovery of freedom through formal modes of expression—metaphors rich in ambiguity, the distancing effects and pleasures of rhyme and writerly italicization, the metrical swing of his verse—is counterpointed by an awareness that such freedom implicates him in the history he relates. Hughes's use of italics, for example, makes the victim's words echo, as if lifted from a realist novel about a lynching that was written for a mass audience.[16]

The device reminds us that, by adopting the lyric as his preferred genre, Hughes has aligned himself with other avant-garde artists in refusing to satisfy the raging market demand for sensationalist fiction that exacerbated a mass audience's tendency toward escapism. Even as his poem resists such a flight from reality, however, Hughes also insists on his freedom as an artist: the freedom, that is, to work continually at formal experimentation and to transcend the all-determining, muddy historical contingencies that fatally distort perception.

Hughes's gesture toward modernist innovation—his veiled reference to an avant-garde flight from verisimilitude—ultimately serves the ends of his realism, insofar as it raises the reader's awareness of the postemancipation context of the lyric. The violent historical developments that caused the Great Migration and spurred Hughes's engagement with formal questions are linked to the rhythmic cadences of "Flight" by the verb *swing*, at the end of the poem: the neat succession of rhythms that fall ("Hurry! Black boy, hurry!") and rise again ("They'll swing you to a tree") ominously dramatizes the swinging motion of the hanged man's body.

"Flight" questions familiar definitions of literary realism, as well as the idea that Hughes's realist commitments foreclose the possibility of modernism. At the same time that he tries to document the violent conditions that shaped the emergence of modern African American poetry, Hughes also invites us to consider how, and why, the poet's manipulation of his medium expresses artistic freedom from the contingencies he depicts. In the end he shows us that the nineteenth-century realist goal of transparent verisimilitude is unattainable in the modern lyric. Such figurative complexity highlights a modernist tendency in Hughes's realism.

## "The Weary Blues": Hughes's Critique of Black Cultural Nationalism

To confer shape on what Eliot described as the "immense panorama of futility and anarchy which is contemporary history," Hughes turned not to classical myths but to a poetics of migration that had been used to impose order on and give significance to the traumatic postemancipation experience of African Americans, and that figured in many ballads, reels, and blues and ragtime songs Hughes remembered hearing during his childhood in Lawrence, Kansas.[17] A great deal has already been said about the "modernity" of African American music and, in particular, about the centrality of the blues to Hughes's lyric practice.[18] Arnold Rampersad's suggestion that the blues poems in *Fine Clothes to the Jew* are some of Hughes's most important works has prompted a critical reassessment of his project and legacy.[19] There is, however, much to be learned about how his blues and jazz poetics fit in the development of the modernist lyric, both in the United States and in

Europe, and, conversely, how his engagement with modernism contributed to his technique as a realist poet.

In his autobiography Hughes, appealing to the strength, humor, and "rooted power" of the blues, tries to change the derogatory view of folk culture that prevailed among the African American middle class and Euro-Americans.[20] Ralph Ellison once described the blues as a "chronicle of personal catastrophe expressed lyrically," a mode of remembrance that keeps the experience alive and also transcends it, "not by the consolations of philosophy, but by squeezing from it a near-tragic, near-comic lyricism."[21] The artistic possibilities of traditional blues are examined in "Red Clay Blues," a poem Hughes wrote in collaboration with Richard Wright. The lyric states, with eloquent simplicity, a near-tragic vision of history that is tempered by a strong belief in the sanctity of knowledge. The first premise of the opening stanza is that "knowing" history means knowing what it feels like to long for the red clay of Georgia:

> I miss that red clay, Lawd, I
> Need to feel it in my shoes.
> Says miss that red clay, Lawd, I
> Need to feel it in my shoes.
> I want to get to Georgia cause I
> Got them red clay blues.
> (*CP*, 212)

These lines suggest, with remarkable precision, the transition from spiritual to blues, and from sacred to secular idioms, that took place during the late nineteenth century. For instance, the syntax subsumes the act of praying in an ornamental cadence ("Lawd") designed to enhance the expression of personal, daily needs. Despite the starkly conventional form, the lyric's style affirms the individuality of both speaker and poet. The line breaks rhythmically emphasize the importance of human desire and possession ("miss," "need," "want," "got"), Hughes's unabashed embrace of the oral tradition and a vernacular blues syntax ("Says miss that red clay"), and the metrical freedom discovered through repeated pronominal self-naming ("I").

Hughes broke new ground in his poetry, partly because he saw that his engagement with canonical texts and his interest in traditional English and American prosody would provide a much-needed, clarifying distance from the rich but potentially formulaic idioms he borrowed from African American folk culture. Ellison made a comment that seems to encapsulate Hughes's efforts to establish a critical, intellectual perspective on the folk tradition as a poetic resource:

> The Negro American writer is also an heir of the human experience which is literature, and this might well be more important to him than his living folk tradition. For me, at least . . . the stability of the Negro American folk tradition became precious as a result of an act of literary discovery. . . . For those who are able to translate its meanings into wider, more precise vocabularies it has much to offer indeed.[22]

Hughes was well aware that, as a poet, he needed to come to terms with the fundamental difference between blues language and poetic language. Despite his devotion to the traditional African American folk idiom, in a number of poems written during the 1920s he took a serious look at the artistic costs and devastating emotional consequences of the strict expressive constraints imposed by the blues.

In "The Weary Blues," first published in 1925, Hughes expresses his desire to encounter the idiomatic options raised by the blues as possibilities that he was free to choose, not as habitual motions that he was compelled to reiterate. The blues song has been framed by the mediating perspective of the lyric speaker, who describes the "moan" of the "poor piano." In contrast to the speaker, who tries to put the meaning of the music into words, the blues player conveys his feelings not so much with words as with the "lazy sway" of his body:[23]

> Droning a drowsy syncopated tune,
> Rocking back and forth to a mellow croon,
>     I heard a Negro play.
> Down on Lenox Avenue the other night
> By the pale dull pallor of an old gas light
>     He did a lazy sway. . . .
>     He did a lazy sway. . . .
> To the tune o' those Weary Blues.
> With his ebony hands on each ivory key
> He made that poor piano moan with melody.
>     O Blues!
> Swaying to and fro on his rickety stool
> He played that sad raggy tune like a musical fool.
>     Sweet Blues!
> Coming from a black man's soul.
>     . . . . . . . . . . . .
> Thump, thump, thump, went his foot on the floor.
> He played a few chords then he sang some more—
>     "I got the Weary Blues

> And I can't be satisfied.
> Got the Weary Blues
> And can't be satisfied—
> I ain't happy no mo'
> And I wish that I had died."
> And far into the night he crooned that tune.
> The stars went out and so did the moon.
> The singer stopped playing and went to bed
> While the Weary Blues echoed through his head.
> He slept like a rock or a man that's dead.
> (*CP*, 50)

Hughes expected many readers to think that poems such as "The Weary Blues" were not about anything more than a piano player playing blues. In fact, he often invited and validated such interpretations.[24] The poem may be seen to enact, however, a renunciation of metaphor—a despairing gesture suggesting that imaginative dreamlike escapes from the "outer" world do nothing to change social conditions. In another poem the romantic images of the stars and moon going out would be richly evocative and metaphorical, signifying unfulfilled desire or desolation over a dream deferred. But here their figurative weight is offset by a context that leads us to believe that Hughes merely wants to indicate the passage of time. The latent metaphorical meaning of his idiom is suppressed. Whereas in "Flight" Hughes acknowledges his passion for figuration as a mode of transcendence, in this lyric he dramatizes how having the blues may undermine a poet's belief in the modernist freedom to trope. The stars and moon going out and the player going to bed illustrate the action of lulling metaphorical language to the dead sleep of verisimilitude.

In "The Weary Blues" Hughes implies that the conventional blues idiom is so compelling, and so limited, as to threaten his imaginative freedom. In addition, the mechanical objects that occupy the poem's setting—the gas light, the rickety stool, the piano parts, and so on—evoke another modern development that imperils artistic freedom. Like many of his contemporaries, both in the United States and abroad, Hughes was aware of the cultural crisis caused by mechanization. In 1933 F. R. Leavis, quoting H. G. Wells, would vividly condemn the "vast and increasing inattention" resulting from new forms of mechanical reproduction: "The machine . . . has brought about changes in habit and the circumstances of life at a rate for which we have no parallel. . . . When we consider, for instance, the processes of mass-production and standardisation in the form represented by the Press, it becomes obviously of sinister significance that they should be accompanied by a process of levelling-down." Two years before Hughes published "The Weary Blues,"

Eliot warned against the insidious effects of gramophones, motorcars, loud-speakers, and cinemas in which the mind was "lulled by continuous senseless music and continuous action too rapid . . . to act upon."[25]

Hughes's concern about the leveling-down effects of technology, which are barely hinted at in "The Weary Blues," becomes a point of focus in "Summer Night," which first appeared in the December 1925 issue of *Crisis*. Like the typist in Eliot's *Waste Land*, who paces about her room, her brain allowing only a "half-formed thought," and who "smoothes her hair with automatic hand" as she puts a record on the gramophone, Hughes's lyric speaker is left virtually without words once the player piano, the Victrola, and the other "sounds" of Harlem fall silent in the still night.[26] He can only toss restlessly, muttering ineffective generalities:

> The sounds
> Of the Harlem night
> Drop one by one into stillness.
> The last player-piano is closed.
> The last victrola ceases with the
> "Jazz-Boy Blues."
> The last crying baby sleeps
> And the night becomes
> Still as a whispering heartbeat.
> I toss
> Without rest in the darkness,
> Weary as the tired night,
> My soul
> Empty as the silence,
> Empty with a vague,
> Aching emptiness,
> Desiring,
> Needing someone,
> Something. (*CP*, 59)

The passage demonstrates the high stakes of Hughes's project as a poet who deals in words, and it implies his effort, as Pound might say, to "modernize" his perspective by distancing himself from the nonverbal expressiveness of the blues.

Together, "Summer Night" and "The Weary Blues" scrutinize the view that the blues is an essentially "black" musical emotion that can never be individuated for Euro-American readers. By raising this question, Hughes anticipates Paul Gilroy's proposition, in his recent study of music and the black diaspora, that a "topos of unsayability"—a habitual invocation of truths that cannot be put into words—lies at the heart of black musical culture.[27]

Gilroy's discussion follows in large part from W. E. B. DuBois's analysis of African American spirituals in *The Souls of Black Folk*. DuBois was one of the first to notice that many things were conventionally left unsaid in the folk lyrics. Such "omissions and silences," and the lack of reference to social conditions, testify to the violent subjugation of enslavement and reflect the "shadow of fear" that hung over the slaves. DuBois concludes that, in this crucial respect, the folk idiom imposed constraints on "allowable thought" and confined poetry "for the most part to single or double lines":

> Over the inner thoughts of the slaves and their relations one with another the shadow of fear ever hung, so that we get but glimpses here and there, and also with them, eloquent omissions and silences. Mother and child are sung, but seldom father; fugitive and weary wanderer call for pity and affection, but there is little of wooing and wedding; the rocks and the mountains are well known, but home is unknown. . . . Of deep successful love there is ominous silence. . . . [The] rhythm of the songs, and the limitations of allowable thought, confined the poetry for the most part to single or double lines, and they seldom were expanded to quatrains or longer tales.[28]

Gilroy argues that the "topos of unsayability" is an outgrowth of the experience of slavery, and no doubt DuBois and Hughes would agree. But whereas Gilroy celebrates this topos, which can be used "to challenge the privileged conceptions of both language and writing as preeminent expressions of human consciousness" (74), Hughes considered it part of the debilitating legacy of slavery and was deeply concerned about the "silences" that structure thought and expression in the blues. True, in the short lyric "Hey!" Hughes jokes about the curious effects of unsayability by drawing our attention to the alluring ambiguity of the blues singer's sustained note, "hey":

> Sun's a settin',
> This is what I'm gonna sing.
> Sun's a settin',
> This is what I'm gonna sing:
> I feels de blues a comin',
> Wonder what de blues'll bring?
> (*CP*, 112)

But Hughes also understood how severely limiting such a convention was. In "The Weary Blues" he suggests that unsayability cannot be a topos so long as it is forced on African Americans by the memory of "racial terror" (Gilroy, 74).

As we have seen, the stylistic complexity of many of the poems Hughes wrote during the 1920s and early 1930s creates a clarifying perspective on the folk tradition and distances him from racial separatist explanations of culture.[29] Although Hughes was noted as one of the first poets to celebrate the beauty of the blues as an American art form, he was not a "black nationalist," in Amiri Baraka's sense of the term.[30] In *Blues People: Negro Music in White America* (1963) Baraka began to advance a separatist line of argument:

> Blues as an autonomous music had been in a sense inviolable. There was no clear way into it . . . except as concomitant with what seems to me to be the peculiar social, cultural, economic, and emotional experience of a black man in America. . . . The materials of blues were not available to the white American. . . . It was as if these materials were secret and obscure, and blues a kind of ethno-historic rite as basic as blood.[31]

Forty years before the Black Arts movement Hughes was writing poems that examined the tragic implications of racial separatist logic. As "The Weary Blues" shows, it would have been impossible for him to write completely in accordance with the verbal constraints of the folk tradition: to do so would have resulted in an endlessly mechanical recapitulation of the racial terror of slavery. Viewed in these terms, Hughes's repudiation of racialist ideas about culture in poems written during the 1920s anticipates the positions he explored in his so-called radical poetry, written between 1932 and 1938.[32]

### Hughes and the Modernist Critique of Romantic Nationalism

Hughes's resistance to separatist descriptions of African American culture is, in certain respects, strikingly similar to the critique of romantic nationalism undertaken by many of his modernist contemporaries, both in the United States and in Europe. D. H. Lawrence, T. S. Eliot, Ezra Pound, Wallace Stevens, Hart Crane, and others wrote poems in which they tried to come to terms with the difficult necessity of cross-cultural identification. Many of these poems centered on the changing nature of musical experience and the devastating, far-reaching consequences of European nationalism that culminated in the Great War.

An early draft of Lawrence's "Piano," which first appeared in *New Poems* in 1918, explores how the speaker's response to Hungarian music reflects the historical causes of the war. Like Hughes, Lawrence tried to show

how traces of history were ceaselessly echoed in nineteenth-century musical forms. But whereas Hughes was primarily concerned with illustrating the American legacy of racial violence that shaped musical forms such as swing and the blues, Lawrence confronted the legacy of romanticism in Europe:

Somewhere beneath that piano's superb sleek black
Must hide my mother's piano, little and brown, with the back
That stood close to the wall, and the front's faded silk, both torn,
And the keys with little hollows, that my mother's fingers had worn.

Softly, in the shadows, a woman is singing to me
Quietly, through the years I have crept back to see
A child sitting under the piano, in the boom of the shaking strings
Pressing the little poised feet of the mother who smiles as she sings.

The full throated woman has chosen a winning, living song
And surely the heart that is in me must belong
To the old Sunday evenings, when darkness wandered outside
And hymns gleamed on our warm lips, as we watched mother's fingers glide.

Or this is my sister at home in the old front room
Singing love's first surprised gladness, alone in the gloom.
She will start when she sees me, and blushing, spread out her hands
To cover my mouth's raillery, till I'm bound in her shame's heart-spun bands.

A woman is singing me a wild Hungarian air
And her arms, and her bosom, and the whole of her soul is bare,
And the great black piano is clamouring as my mother's never could clamour
And my mother's tunes are devoured of this music's ravaging glamour. [33]

"Piano" is as much about the creative hunger to absorb different cultural influences, and the threat it poses to the cherished individuality of regions, as it is about the fateful vying for dominance among the major European powers in the decades preceding the Great War. The "wild Hungarian air" (a phrase Lawrence omitted in the final version of the poem) recalls the intensification of European nationalist rivalries during this period.[34] The poem is built on a perceived contrast between, on the one hand, the speaker's present experience of the "clamouring" sound of a sleek black concert hall piano and a song that bares a woman's soul to the public; and, on the other, his secretly erotic childhood memories of his mother and sister performing hymns and love songs at home. By searching for hidden continuities between the raging, devouring glamour associated with Hungarian music and the speaker's fond memories of British middle-class musical culture, Lawrence discloses the speaker's painful ambivalence toward the sentiment awakened in him by the song.[35]

"Piano" also refers, more broadly, to the changing of European musical experience and sensibility from the early nineteenth to the early twentieth century. Concert life and musical tastes were dramatically transformed in the Allied countries during and after the Great War. Fewer keyboard battle pieces, for example, were written then than at the height of romantic nationalism during the nineteenth century, and composers began to turn their attention to serious vocal and orchestral laments. In the Allied countries there was a growing tendency to ban concert performances of German music; in England, France, and America musicians were encouraged to perform the works of "native" composers.[36] In the first half of the nineteenth century chamber music had gradually been moved out of domestic spaces and salons into public performance halls. "Personality," observes James H. Johnson, "thrust itself to center stage in the romantic decades."[37]

Lawrence and Hughes both questioned popular notions of racial authenticity in music. Like Hughes's "Weary Blues," Lawrence's "Piano" expresses ambivalence toward the expressive and perceptual constraints of the "polarization" of peoples in "particular localit[ies]."[38] Hughes was concerned to stand, as it were, both inside and outside the blues and figuratively to imply his own motives for moving away from the rich but ultimately constraining formulas of traditional blues lyrics. Lawrence's stance is similar, insofar as his speaker affirms, with great affection, the distinctive musical heritages of nations while he conveys the horrifying irony that such seemingly benign cultural distinctions would, in the end, be used as a justification for war. By upholding both the distinctiveness and the universality of musical experience, both poets suggest that music, in the words of Theodor Adorno, "more than any other artistic medium, expresses the national principle's antinomies" (quoted in Gilroy, 72).

Hughes's technically self-conscious approach to realism in the lyric, his prosodic resistance to separatist paradigms, and his interest in the history and irreducible hybridity of African American culture are aspects of his lyric practice that he shared with his American modernist contemporaries. Pound's 1920 poem *Hugh Selwyn Mauberley*, for example, may be said to anticipate Hughes's "Weary Blues," since it also confronts the problem of realism in the lyric. Although Pound keeps references to social setting and details to a bare minimum in the poem, his interest in finding a modern poetic equivalent to Henry James's realism is evident in a 1922 letter to Felix Schelling, in which Pound calls his poem "an attempt to condense the James novel."[39] Morever, like Hughes, Pound uses the image of a piano to explore how modern art has come dangerously close to the mass-produced conformity, planned obsolescence, and rapid replacement associated with fashion. The pianola metonymically represents the forces of mass production:

> The tea-rose tea-gown, etc.
> supplants the mousseline of Cos,
> The pianola "replaces"
> Sappho's barbitos.[40]

Another American modernist, Hart Crane, examined how the violent history that gave rise to African American music ultimately shaped the imagery and cadence of his own idiom:

> "what do you want? getting weak on the links?
> fandaddle daddy don't ask for change—is this
> FOURTEENTH? it's half past six she said—if
> you don't like my gate why did you
> swing on it, why *didja*
> swing on it
> anyhow—"
>
> And somehow anyhow swing—
>
> The phonographs of hades in the brain
> Are tunnels that re-wind themselves, and love
> A burnt match skating in a urinal—
> Somewhere above Fourteenth TAKE THE EXPRESS
> To brush some new presentiment of pain—[41]

In 1948, in *The Auroras of Autumn,* Wallace Stevens vividly probed the sources of his ambivalent love of and animosity toward primitivist decadence: the mind's eye first summons up a festive scene of "negresses" dancing and then suddenly becomes cruelly analytic, mocking the whole party for their brutish disorderliness:

The father fetches negresses to dance,
Among the children, like curious ripenesses
Of pattern in the dance's ripening.

For these the musicians make insidious tones,
Clawing the sing-song of their instruments.
The children laugh and jangle a tinny time.
. . . . . . . . . . . . . . .
What festival? This loud, disordered mooch?
These hospitaliers? These brute-like guests? [42]

Of Hughes's modernist contemporaries, however, the poet whose interest in realism, racial cross-identification, and American music comes
closest to his own is not Pound, Crane, or Stevens but Eliot. In many
of the early poems collected in the leather-bound notebook begun in
1909—some, such as "Opera," "First Caprice in North Cambridge," and
"The Burnt Dancer," which were unpublished until 1996, and others, such
as "Rhapsody on a Windy Night" and "Portrait of a Lady," which appeared
in *Prufrock and Other Observations* in 1917—Eliot shares Hughes's preoccupation with realism and the analogy between musical and poetic
forms.[43] But whereas Hughes's poems more often than not call attention
to the African American folk origins of the blues as an American musical
form, Eliot takes the occasion of these early poems to explore the hybrid
European origins of modern American music by adapting the idea of the
"caprice" or the "rhapsody": pieces that were written out, not improvised,
most likely for the piano.

In *The Dialect of Modernism* Michael North offers a groundbreaking,
provocative analysis of how Eliot adapted techniques such as linguistic
mimicry and racial masquerade to make the language new and to resist in-
stitutional forces of standardization. In 1921 Eliot "was laboring to put his
knowledge of black music to work in *The Waste Land,* which contained at
one time references to a number of rag and minstrel songs."[44] The musical allusions cut from the final text are of particular interest, since many of
them—for example, Eliot's reference to a song ("I'm proud of all the Irish
blood that's in me") from a musical play called *Fifty Miles from Boston* and
his adaptation of lines from minstrel shows ("By the Watermelon Vine,"
"My Evaline," and "The Cubanola Glide")—cryptically encode the composite regional landscapes and irreducibly hybrid cultures evoked by American
popular music.[45]

Eliot's fascination with ragtime is best understood in light of his effort to understand the idea of "purity" in poetry, that is, the peculiar effect
of works that direct the reader's attention primarily to style and virtually

exclude consideration of their subject matter. In "From Poe to Valéry," for example, he discusses poems in which words have been chosen for the right sounds while the poet has been deliberately "irresponsible" toward their meaning.[46] In "The Music of Poetry" Eliot singles out Edward Lear's "nonsense verse," whose reader is moved by the music and enjoys, again, a "feeling of irresponsibility towards the sense." In these instances, however, the source of enjoyment is not a "vacuity of sense," or the poet's total escape from meaningful representation. Rather, Lear's "non-sense . . . is a parody of sense, and that is the sense of it." [47]

In *The Waste Land* Eliot illustrates the rich senses of nonsense by alluding to a popular ragtime song that hit the charts in 1912, called "That Shakespearian Rag":

> That Shakespearian rag,—
> Most intelligent, very elegant,
> That old classical drag,
> Has the proper stuff, the line "Lay on Macduff,"
> Desdemona was the colored pet,
> Romeo loved his Juliet—
> And they were some lovers, you can bet, and yet,
> I know if they were here today,
> They'd Grizzly Bear in a diff'rent way,
> And you'd hear old Hamlet say,
> "To be or not to be,"
> That Shakespearian Rag.[48]

Eliot adapted lines from the original chorus by adding the "O O O O" and a syncopated syllable in "Shakespeherian" (McElderry, 185–186):

> O O O O that Shakespeherian Rag—
> It's so elegant
> So intelligent
> "What shall I do now? What shall I do?"
> (*WL*, 57)

The poem's miming of ragtime gives both the speaker and the reader a brief reprieve from the burdensome duty to convey meaning truthfully. But the "vacuity of sense" brought about by the repetition of the apostrophe "O"—a repetition that reduces the trope, quite literally, to a series of zeroes on the page—also signals the tragic lack of continuity, as well as a tragic lack of engagement with the sense of Shakespeare's vibrant words, evidenced by American popular music. Eliot's allusion to ragtime, followed by the listless, bored, near-hysterical line "What shall I do now? What shall I do?" evokes apocalyptic dread. The passage implies that, taken to an extreme, such fleeting moments of enjoyable irresponsibility toward sense may promote an increasingly automated, vast inattention in American society. By pursuing the analogies between music and poetry in *The Waste Land*, Eliot's "Shakespeherian Rag" responds stylistically to conditions that imperiled artistic freedom and anticipated Hughes's experiments with a jazz poetics.[49]

*The Waste Land* calls attention to the danger of popular ragtime songs, in which words have been torn away from their traditional contexts. In "The Music of Poetry," however, Eliot proposes that nonsense verse also has profoundly restorative powers, as in Lear's work. "*The Jumblies*," for example, "is a poem of adventure, and of nostalgia for the romance of foreign voyage and exploration; *The Yongy-Bongy Bo* and *The Dong with a Luminous Nose* are poems of unrequited passion—'blues' in fact. We enjoy the music, which is of a high order, and we enjoy the feeling of irresponsibility towards the sense" (*PP*, 21). In "Fragment of an Agon," part of the unfinished jazz play *Sweeney Agonistes*, Eliot illustrates the poetic vitality and beauty of nonsense. The poem includes the following text, adapted from a popular song written by the African American poet James Weldon Johnson, called "Under the Bamboo Tree":

> *Under the bamboo*
> *Bamboo bamboo*
> *Under the bamboo tree*
> *Two live as one*
> *One live as two*
> *Two live as three*
> *Under the bam*
> *Under the boo*
> *Under the bamboo tree.*
>
> *Where the breadfruit fall*
> *And the penguin call*
> *And the sound is the sound of the sea*
> *Under the bam*
> *Under the boo*
> *Under the bamboo tree.*
>
> *Where the Gauguin maids*
> *In the banyan shades*
> *Wear palmleaf drapery*

*Under the bam*
*Under the boo*
*Under the bamboo tree.*[50]

That the other personages in the play are ludicrous, materialistic, and superficial does not suggest that Eliot's allusion to Johnson's lyric "imprisons the song once again in the minstrel tradition" (North, 88).[51] The sense of adventure and the nostalgia for exotic romance that Eliot identifies in Lear's poems are beautifully highlighted in the passage he borrows from Johnson's artful rendering of the African American vernacular.[52] The enjoyable irresponsibility toward sense that the poem dramatizes enhances the meaning: it is a poem of "unrequited passion— 'blues' in fact." The provocatively playful nonsense of "Two live as one / One live as two / Two live as three" expresses the speaker's yearning to transform the social fragmentation of American society and hints at Eliot's deeper motive for incorporating Johnson's lyric. Two poets—one Euro-American, the other African American—in effect "live as one" in Eliot's poem and intimately share a sensibility embodied by the blues. The poem's outlook is hopeful and forward-looking: after all, as Eliot has shown, the hope of perpetuating any given culture lies in the creative action of exchanging ideas and influences with others.[53]

### Conclusion: Jazz and Modern Realism

Many, if not all, of Hughes's late jazz poems highlight the freedom of improvisation and formal innovation. In "The Trumpet Player: 57th Street," published in 1947, the freedom of choice Hughes himself exercises in creating a metonymic style opens new expressive possibilities.[54] The lyric not only educates the reader to hear his writing as trumpetlike, an instrument with voiced inflection and phrasing. It also dramatically illustrates the advantages of metonymy:

The Negro
With the trumpet at his lips
Has dark moons of weariness
Beneath his eyes
Where the smoldering memory
Of slave ships
Blazed to the crack of whips
About his thighs.
. . . . . .
The music
From the trumpet at his lips

Is honey
Mixed with liquid fire.
The rhythm
From the trumpet at his lips
Is ecstasy
Distilled from old desire—

The Negro
With the trumpet at his lips
Whose jacket
Has a *fine* one-button roll,
Does not know
Upon what riff the music slips
Its hypodermic needle
To his soul. (*CP,* 338)

Even as the lyric speaker refers to the uses of metaphor in describing the "ecstasy / Distilled from old desire" expressed in the trumpet's rhythm, he ends up showing us the profound artistic satisfactions and referential range of metonymy, the depiction of the body's surface and the temporal and spatial relatedness of everyday objects in the room. As an expression of weariness, traces of a personal and collective history of oppression, the "thump, thump, thump" of "The Weary Blues" is here inscribed on the body as "dark moons of weariness" beneath the trumpet player's eyes. The relatively obscure meaning of the moon going out as an image of thwarted desire and a dream deferred in "The Weary Blues" is considered and then freely cast off in "The Trumpet Player" in favor of hybrid tropes that hover somewhere between metonymy and metaphor:

Desire
That is longing for the moon
Where the moonlight's but a spotlight
In his eyes,
Desire
That is longing for the sea
Where the sea's a bar-glass
Sucker size. (*CP,* 338)

Like a held chord, the romantic, sentimental idiom of "longing for the moon" is sustained and, at the same time, transmuted into a "spotlight / In his eyes." As an evocation of desire, the sea is condensed into a "bar-glass, / Sucker size."

Insofar as Hughes's later poems mime the improvisatory action of jazz to discover emancipatory techniques, they are stylistically similar to works written by the American avant-gardes of the interwar period. In *Spring and All*, for example, William Carlos Williams praises the freedoms of improvisation, while he laments the dangers of incomprehensibility:

> The Improvisations—coming at a time when I was trying to remain firm at great cost—I had recourse to the expedient of letting life go completely in order to live in the world of my choice. . . .
>
> The virtue of the improvisations is their placement in a world of new values—
> their fault is their dislocation of
> sense, often complete.[55]

The convergence between Hughes's techniques and those of Williams, Eliot, and others discloses the historical knowledge that informs the impulse toward formal experiment and improvisation in the modernist lyric.

At the beginning of this essay we saw Baldwin criticize Hughes's late jazz poem, "Dream Boogie," for falling short of the standards of realism. I want to conclude by suggesting that, Baldwin's criticisms notwithstanding, the spirit of formal innovation in "Dream Boogie" is entirely in keeping with Hughes's earlier realism in poems such as "Flight."

"Dream Boogie" is far more modernist than "Flight," since it manifests a sustained, figurative effort to move away from the realist duties of verisimilitude. It avoids familiar reference to historical contexts; it twists away from language toward abstract sequences of sound; and it brings us into a discursive world in which speech and perception have been broken down into fragments. Insofar as the speaker touches on realities, his treatment of them is almost wholly nondescriptive:

> Good morning, daddy!
> Ain't you heard
> The boogie-woogie rumble
> Of a dream deferred?
>
> Listen closely:
> You'll hear their feet
> Beating out and beating out a—
>
> > *You think*
> > *It's a happy beat?*

Listen to it closely:
Ain't you heard
something underneath
like a—

*What did I say?*

Sure,
I'm happy!
Take it away!

*Hey, pop!*
*Re-bop!*
*Mop!*

*Y-e-a-h!* (*CP,* 388)

Like many works written by his avant-garde contemporaries, Hughes's poem is not designed to meet our interpretive expectations; it contains no meaning that, as Eliot says, would readily satisfy a "habit" of the reader (*UP,* 151). According to Eliot, modern poems are sometimes intended primarily to amplify the reader's experience of the intensity of feeling that results from the poet's movement toward ideas at the "frontiers of consciousness," where meanings have not yet been put into words. In "The Music of Poetry" he writes: "We can be deeply stirred by hearing the recitation of a poem in a language of which we understand no word. . . . If, as we are aware, only a part of the meaning can be conveyed by paraphrase, that is because the poet is occupied with frontiers of consciousness beyond which words fail, though meanings still exist" (*PP,* 22).

In "Dream Boogie" Hughes's idiom is modernist in Eliot's sense: the lyric's form embodies an effort to move beyond the frontiers of social consciousness and expression. The line breaks; the arrangement of words on the page, flush left and flush right; and the use of italics are stylistic elements that show the ambivalence and animosity of an African American speaker trying to explain the meaning of the music to a Euro-American listener. The rhetorical question *"You think / It's a happy beat?"* has the visual effect of stretching, tonally inflecting, and thereby extending the meaning of the trope to include its own correct response. The poem pauses, calling attention to its own act of figuration and to the poet's act of writing. Hughes's modernist predilection for experimental forms that allegorize the struggle for and against verisimilitude, and his constant awareness of the constraints of language as an artistic medium, is central to his practice as a realist poet.

Although "Dream Boogie" is modernist insofar as it illustrates an effort to escape from historical referentiality and refuses to state explicitly the bitter social truths encoded in what Baldwin calls the "hieroglyphics" of African American music, it also remains anchored in the particularities of its own time and place, since it is essentially about the dangers posed to American society as a whole when these truths are not brought to light in the realm of art. The speaker's ambivalence toward the project of meaningful representation makes sense only when we realize that the poem takes on a subject that Adorno systematically elaborated in his celebrated diatribe against the popular culture industry: the poem figuratively suggests a deplorable lack of conscious perception on the part of many Euro-Americans who considered themselves avid jazz fans.

Like Adorno, Hughes in "Dream Boogie" suggests that too many people who listened to jazz did not hear the seriousness of its emotional message and were not aware of the violent historical conditions out of which the impulse to formal innovation emerged. Instead many Americans regarded jazz merely as a pleasant background for conversation or a happy accompaniment to dancing.[56] The italicized question addressed to the Euro-American reader marks a crucial transition from the lyric's effort to mime violence (that is, from its performance of a nonrepresentational, violent motion of beating measured feet) to an all-out confrontation with meanings on the verge of verbal explicitness. The italics themselves highlight the social and emotional pressure exerted on the speaker when he tries to say that the historical implications of jazz as an art form—a form rooted in the traumatic postemancipation history of lynching and migration—were anything but happy; they express the speaker's frustration at the listener's inability to hear the social and emotional truths conveyed by the music.[57]

Hughes's experiments with realism in the lyric help us question the distinction between realism and the avant-garde in accounts of transatlantic modernism. Like Eliot, Crane, Stevens, and other twentieth-century American poets, Hughes demonstrated that certain modernist styles were created in response to historical conditions and addressed the danger posed by modernity to artistic freedom. Leo Bersani once said that "the realistic novel gives us an image of social fragmentation contained within the order of significant form—and it thereby suggests that the chaotic fragments are somehow socially viable and morally redeemable" (quoted in Anesko, 83), and this claim also seems an apt description of Hughes's poetic evocation of jazz. Insofar as his lyrics transcend frontiers of consciousness and culture, they fulfill a cherished criterion of modernism, and this modernism, in turn, serves the moral ends of realism by allowing him to encompass, order, and preserve fragments of history.

## Notes

1. Wright, "The Big Sea," in *Langston Hughes: Critical Perspectives Past and Present*, eds. Henry Louis Gates Jr. and K. A. Appiah (New York: Amistad, 1993): p. 21. Comparing Hughes to Theodore Dreiser, Wright observed that both writers undertook the crucial task of "freeing American literary expression from the restrictions of Puritanism" (21).

2. Baldwin, "Sermons and Blues," review of *Selected Poems*, by Langston Hughes, *New York Times Book Review*, 29 March 1959, p. 6.

3. Eric J. Sundquist, ed., *American Realism: New Essays* (Baltimore, Md.: Johns Hopkins University Press, 1982): p. 4.

4. Louis Budd, "The American Background," in *The Cambridge Companion to American Realism and Naturalism: Howells to London*, ed. Donald Pizer (Cambridge: Cambridge University Press, 1995): pp. 21–46. The concept of realism surfaced again in the 1920s, when a generation of journalists—H. L. Mencken, John Macy, Van Wyck Brooks, Ludwig Lewisohn, Lewis Mumford, and Randolph Bourne, to name a few—probed the social purpose of literature and lavished praise on previously neglected artists, such as Mark Twain, Stephen Crane, and the late Howells, who had been critical of America's social and economic values. In 1930 Vernon Louis Parrington published *The Beginnings of Critical Realism in America: 1860–1920*, an influential analysis that roundly criticized writers who were too committed to narrowly "belletristic" aspects of literature. Parrington was, in turn, condemned to obscurity by critics like Lionel Trilling, who sharply criticized his literary nationalism and his insistence that literature should appeal to a popular constituency. More recently, at least since the publication of Warner Berthoff's *Ferment of Realism: American Literature, 1884–1919* in 1965, a number of revisionary studies have explored the social construction of American realism: Sundquist; Amy Kaplan, *The Social Construction of American Realism* (Chicago: University of Chicago Press, 1988); and Michael Anesko, "Recent Critical Approaches," in Pizer, pp. 77–94.

5. Auerbach, *Mimesis: The Representation of Reality in Western Literature*, trans. Willard R. Trask (Princeton, N.J.: Princeton University Press, 1953). Auerbach's helpful, systematic account of the emergence of modern realist fiction identifies four criteria of realism as a literary method: detailed description of everyday occurrences; serious treatment of "socially inferior groups" as subject matter for existential representation (491); belief in the capacity of language to reveal truths about the phenomenal world; and portrayal of the individual's destiny in both a particular social hierarchy and a broader historical context.

6. In a useful account of the diverse approaches undertaken by modern American poets, Cary Nelson discusses "partly forgotten poetry—including black poetry, poetry by women, the poetry of popular song, and the poetry of social mass movements—thereby giving those texts new connotations appropriate to our time" (*Repression and Recovery: Modern American Poetry and the Politics of Cultural Memory, 1910–1945* [Madison: University of Wisconsin Press, 1989]: pp. 22–23). But his study is primarily historical: he gives no extended formal analyses and—aside from

remarking that "traditional forms continued to do vital cultural work" throughout the modern period (23)—tells us little about the poetics of realism.

7. See Jonathan Arac, "Rhetoric and Realism; or, Marxism, Deconstruction, and the Novel," in *Criticism without Boundaries: Directions and Crosscurrents in Postmodern Critical Theory,* ed. Joseph A. Buttigieg (Notre Dame, Ind.: University of Notre Dame Press, 1987): p. 161.

8. Alex Preminger and T. V. F. Brogan, eds., *The New Princeton Encyclopedia of Poetry and Poetics* (Princeton, N.J.: Princeton University Press, 1993): p. 1016.

9. "If every mediocre product of socialist realism is to be hailed as a masterpiece," Lukács writes, "confusion will be worse confounded. My *tertium datur* is an objective critical appraisal of the very real innovations which we owe to socialist realism. In exposing literary mediocrity, and criticizing theoretical dogmatism, I am trying to ensure that the creative aspects of this new realism will be more clearly understood" (*The Meaning of Contemporary Realism,* trans. John Mander and Necke Mander [London: Merlin, 1963]: p. 11).

10. *The Collected Poems of Langston Hughes,* ed. Arnold Rampersad and David Roessel (New York: Knopf, 1994): p. 127; hereafter cited as *CP.*

11. See Saidiya V. Hartman, *Scenes of Subjection: Terror, Slavery, and Self-Making in Nineteenth-Century America* (New York: Oxford University Press, 1997).

12. See, e.g., W. E. B. DuBois, *The Philadelphia Negro: A Social Study* (1899; rpt. New York: Schocken, 1967); Carter G. Woodson, *A Century of Negro Migration* (1918; rpt. New York: Russell and Russell, 1969); Emmett J. Scott, *Negro Migration during the War* (1920; rpt. New York: Arno, 1969); Louise Kennedy, *The Negro Peasant Turns Cityward: Effects of Recent Migrations to Northern Cities* (New York: Columbia University Press; London: King and Son, 1930); E. Franklin Frazier, *The Negro Family in Chicago* (Chicago: University of Chicago Press, 1932); St. Clair Drake and Horace R. Cayton, *Black Metropolis: A Study of Negro Life in a Northern City* (1945; rpt. New York: Harcourt, Brace and World, 1962); and Gunnar Myrdal, *An American Dilemma: The Negro Problem and Modern Democracy,* 2 vols. (1945; rpt. New York: Harper and Row, 1962). For a useful overview of the vast literature on the Great Migration see Joe Trotter, "Black Migration in Historical Perspective: A Review of the Literature," in *The Great Migration in Historical Perspective: New Dimensions of Race, Class, and Gender,* ed. Joe William Trotter Jr. (Bloomington: Indiana University Press, 1991): pp. 1–21.

13. Friedrich argues, on the evidence of poems by Baudelaire, Rimbaud, Mallarmé, and others, that "modern poetry, in its dissonances, is obeying a law of its style. And this law . . . is, in turn, obeying the historical situation of the modern mind, which, because of the excessive imperiling of its freedom, has an excessive passion for freedom" (*The Structure of Modern Poetry: From the Mid-Nineteenth to the Mid-Twentieth Century,* trans. Joachim Neugroschel [Evanston, Ill.: Northwestern University Press, 1974]: p. 168). Cf. Paul de Man's claim that a definitively "modern" poet must reject the burdensome assumption that artists convey meaning, since it poses a limit on expressive freedom and denies "the conception of language as the act of an autonomous self" ("Lyric and Modernity," in *Blindness and Insight: Essays in the Rhetoric of Contemporary Criticism* [Minneapolis: University of Minnesota Press, 1971]: p. 171).

14. Johnson, "How Much Is Migration a Flight from Persecution?" *Opportunity,* September 1923: pp. 272–275.

15. Whereas in 1930 Hughes used the image of flight ironically, juxtaposing the poem's title with the closing image of a hanged black man swinging in a tree,

in 1925 Locke had used a similar image to mythologize the modernizing effects of migration: "The wash and rush of this human tide on the beach line of the northern city centers is to be explained primarily in terms of a new vision of opportunity, of social and economic freedom. . . . With each successive wave of it, the movement of the Negro becomes more and more a mass movement toward the larger and the more democratic chance—in the Negro's case a deliberate flight not only from countryside to city, but from medieval America to modern" ("The New Negro," in *The New Negro* [New York: Atheneum, 1992]: p. 6).

16. Hughes did not use these italics until 1949, when the poem appeared in the collection *One-Way Ticket*. But he did use quotation marks in 1931, when it was published in *Dear Lovely Death*.

17. "'Ulysses,' Order, and Myth," in *Selected Prose of T. S. Eliot*, ed. Frank Kermode (New York: Harcourt Brace Jovanovich, 1975): p. 177. For a discussion of Hughes's early exposure to black music see Steven Tracy, "To the Tune of Those Weary Blues," in Gates, pp. 69–93. Tracy observes that during his childhood (from about 1902 to 1915) Hughes would have heard ballads, reels, and the "crude blues" of an older man like Henry Thomas; that the blues shouter Big Joe Turner led blues singers through the streets of Kansas City during the late 1910s and early 1920s; and that, although early blues was often accompanied by crude homemade instruments, orchestral-type blues was already emerging during the 1910s.

18. For a discussion of Hughes's folk sources and references to blues structure, themes, and imagery, and for a useful bibliography on jazz and blues, see Steven Tracy, *Langston Hughes and the Blues* (Urbana: University of Illinois Press, 1988). For other insights into Hughes's use of the blues idiom see Patricia E. Bonner, "Cryin' the Jazzy Blues and Livin' Blue Jazz: Analyzing the Blues and Jazz Poetry of Langston Hughes," *West Georgia College Review*, 20 (1990): pp. 15–28; Patricia Johns and Walter Farrell, "How Langston Hughes Used the Blues," *MELUS*, 6 (1979): pp. 55–63; and Edward E. Waldron, "The Blues Poetry of Langston Hughes," *Negro American Literature Forum*, 5 (1971): pp. 140–149.

19. Rampersad insists that we take a revisionary look at Hughes's aesthetic as having been shaped by his recognition of a link between poetry and black music; he claims that *Fine Clothes to the Jew*, Hughes's least successful volume, marks the height of his creative originality ("Hughes's *Fine Clothes to the Jew*," in Gates, 54). Rampersad's monumental biography of Hughes, as well as his and Roessel's recent edition of the *Collected Poems*, has also contributed to the renewed interest in Hughes's poetry. For an illuminating review of the *Collected Poems* that characterizes Hughes's poems in light of four main attributes—his poetics of "announced . . . [but] cryptic reciprocity," his "idiosyncrasy of personal identity," his inveterate sociality, and his humorous irony—see Helen Vendler, "The Unweary Blues," *New Republic*, 6 March 1995: pp. 37–42.

20. "I tried," Hughes observes, "to write poems like the songs they sang on Seventh Street—gay songs, because you had to be gay or die; sad songs, because you couldn't help being sad sometimes. But gay or sad, you kept on living and you kept on going. . . . Like the waves of the sea coming one after another, always one after another, like the earth moving around the sun, night, day—night, day-night, day—forever, so is the undertow of Black music with its rhythm that never betrays you, its strength like the beat of the human heart, its humor, and its rooted power" (*The Big Sea*, 2d ed. [New York: Hill and Wang, 1993]: p. 215).

21. Quoted in Shelby Steele, "The Content of His Character," *New Republic*, 1 March 1999: p. 30.

22. Ellison, *Shadow and Act* (New York: Vintage, 1995): pp. 58–59.

23. R. Baxter Miller argues that the blues performance in "The Weary Blues" dramatizes several actions, including black self-affirmation, a remaking of the black self-image, and Hughes's transcendence of racial stereotypes through lyric discourse (*The Art and Imagination of Langston Hughes* [Lexington: University Press of Kentucky, 1989]: p. 55). My discussion suggests, on the contrary, that the figurative complexity of Hughes's poem helps him arrive at a clarifying, critical perspective on the folk tradition.

24. Hughes remarked that "it was a poem about a working man who sang the blues all night and then went to bed and slept like a rock. That was all" (*Big Sea,* 215).

25. Leavis, "Mass Civilization and Minority Culture," in *For Continuity* (Cambridge: Minority, 1933): pp. 16–18; Eliot, "Marie Lloyd," in *Selected Essays* (New York: Harcourt, Brace and World, 1960): p. 407. "In an interesting essay in the volume of *Essays on the Depopulation of Melanesia,*" Eliot writes, "the psychologist W. H. R. Rivers adduced evidence which has led him to believe that the natives of that unfortunate archipelago are dying out principally for the reason that 'Civilization' forced upon them has deprived them of all interest in life. They are dying from pure boredom. When every theatre has been replaced by 100 cinemas, when every musical instrument has been replaced by 100 gramophones, when every horse has been replaced by 100 cheap motor cars, when electrical ingenuity has made it possible for every child to hear its bedtime stories from a loud-speaker, when applied science has done everything possible with the materials on this earth to make life as interesting as possible, it will not be surprising if the population of the entire civilized world rapidly follows the fate of the Melanesians" (407–408).

26. Eliot, *The Waste Land,* in *Collected Poems, 1909–1962* (New York: Harcourt Brace, 1963): p. 62; hereafter cited as *WL.*

27. "The question of racial terror," Gilroy suggests, "always remains in view when these modernisms are discussed because their imaginative proximity to terror is their inaugural experience. . . . Though they were unspeakable, these terrors were not inexpressible, and . . . residual traces of their necessarily painful expression still contribute to historical memories inscribed and incorporated into the volatile core of Afro-Atlantic cultural creation. . . . The topos of unsayability produced from the slaves' experiences of racial terror . . . can be used to challenge the privileged conceptions of both language and writing as preeminent expressions of human consciousness" (*The Black Atlantic: Modernity and Double Consciousness* [Cambridge, Mass.: Harvard University Press, 1993]: pp. 73–74).

28. DuBois, *The Souls of Black Folk,* in *Writings,* ed. Nathan Huggins (New York: Library of America, 1986): pp. 542–543.

29. In "The Negro Artist and the Racial Mountain," a polemical essay published in the *Nation* in 1926, Hughes emphasizes his "racial individuality" as a poet. But even here he implies that knowledge of traditional prosody would have helped him acquire an interpretive, distanced perspective on folk resources: the African American artist, he says, must learn to "interest himself in *interpreting* the beauty of his own people" (*Within the Circle: An Anthology of African American Literary Criticism from the Harlem Renaissance to the Present,* ed. Angelyn Mitchell [Durham, N.C.: Duke University Press, 1994]: pp. 55–56).

30. In the 1960s Baraka advocated a racial separatist approach to African American music. Many of his essays written in 1965, for example, affirm nine-

teenth-century racialist ideas of black manifest destiny and propose the formation of a black nation through a cultural consciousness flowing from the soul of the artist: "The Black Man must realize himself as Black. And idealize and aspire to that. . . . The Black Artist's role in America is to aid the destruction of America as we know it" (*Home: Social Essays* [New York: Morrow, 1966]: pp. 248, 252).

31. Although at this point in his career Baraka's position is not entirely separatist, insofar as he concedes that the blues can be "appreciated" by non-African Americans, what comes across here is the inaccessibility of the blues to a Euro-American audience (*The Leroi Jones/Amiri Baraka Reader*, ed. William J. Harris [New York: Thunder's Mouth, 1991]: p. 37).

32. For a discussion of Hughes's repudiation of racial separatist accounts of African American culture during the 1930s see Anthony Dawahare, "Langston Hughes's Radical Poetry and the End of Race," *MELUS*, 23, no. 3 (1998): pp. 21–41.

33. Lawrence, *Complete Poems*, ed. Vivian de Sola Pinto and Warren Roberts (New York: Penguin, 1994): p. 943.

34. For a discussion of the themes and figurative resources used to remember, mythologize, and represent the war see Paul Fussell, *The Great War and Modern Memory* (New York: Oxford University Press, 1975).

35. In the final, frequently anthologized version of the poem, the speaker recognizes that the sentiments inspired by the "insidious mastery" of music betray him even as he helplessly yields to them, "till the heart of me weeps to belong / To the old Sunday evenings at home" (Lawrence, *Complete Poems*, 148).

36. Ben Arnold, *Music and War: A Research and Information Guide* (New York: Garland, 1993): p. 135. Arnold writes that "the concert life naturally changed, particularly in the Allied countries, where German music had been so widespread. In Great Britain, all German music was at first banned outright. . . . Musicians performed more music by native composers in France, England, and America than before the war" (135). See also Barbara L. Tischler, "World War I and the Challenge of 100% Americanism," in *An American Music: The Search for an American Musical Identity* (New York: Oxford University Press, 1986): pp. 68–91.

37. Johnson, *Listening in Paris: A Cultural History* (Berkeley: University of California Press, 1995): p. 267.

38. Lawrence's statement sheds some light on "Piano": "Every people is polarized in some particular locality, which is home, the homeland. . . . The Island of Great Britain had a wonderful terrestrial magnetism or polarity of its own, which made the British people. For the moment, this polarity seems to be breaking. Can England die? And what if England dies?" (*Studies in Classic American Literature* [New York: Doubleday, 1953]: p. 16).

39. *The Letters of Ezra Pound, 1907-1941*, ed. D. D. Paige (New York: Harcourt Brace, 1950): p. 180.

40. Pound, *Diptych Rome-London* (New York: New Directions, 1994): p. 40.

41. *The Bridge*, in *The Complete Poems of Hart Crane*, ed. Marc Simon (New York: Liveright, 1993): pp. 98–99.

42. *The Auroras of Autumn*, in *The Collected Poems of Wallace Stevens* (New York: Vintage, 1982): p. 415. Helen Vendler suggests that "the source of the disgust for the father-impresario seems to be Stevens' revulsion against that deliberate primitivism of his own . . . which sets itself to conjure up negresses, guitarists, and the 'unherded herds' of oxlike freed men, all in a vain attempt to reproduce

on an ignorant and one-stringed instrument the sophisticated chaos of the self" (*On Extended Wings: Wallace Stevens' Longer Poems* [Cambridge, Mass.: Harvard University Press, 1969]: p. 252).

43. Eliot, *Inventions of the March Hare: Poems, 1909–1917*, ed. Christopher Ricks (New York: Harcourt Brace, 1996): pp. 13, 17, 62.

44. North, *The Dialect of Modernism: Race, Language, and Twentieth-Century Literature* (New York: Oxford University Press, 1994): p. 10.

45. Eliot, *The Waste Land: A Facsimile and Transcript of the Original Drafts Including the Annotations of Ezra Pound*, ed. Valerie Eliot (San Diego: Harcourt Brace, 1994): p. 125 nn. 2–3.

46. Eliot, "From Poe to Valéry," in *To Criticize the Critic, and Other Writings* (London: Faber & Faber, 1965): p. 32.

47. Eliot, "The Music of Poetry," in *On Poetry and Poets* (New York: Farrar, Straus & Cudahy, 1957): p. 21; hereafter cited as *PP*.

48. Quoted in Bruce McElderry, "Eliot's Shakespeherian Rag," *American Quarterly*, 9 (1957): pp. 185.

49. For a discussion of Eliot's pursuit of analogies between musical and poetic procedures, which situates his engagement with symbolism within the context of Stravinsky's *Shakespeare Songs* and works by other twentieth-century composers, see James Anderson Winn, *Unsuspected Eloquence: A History of the Relations between Poetry and Music* (New Haven, Conn.: Yale University Press, 1981): pp. 295–299.

50. Eliot, "Fragment of an Agon," in *Collected Poems, 1909–1962*, pp. 119–120.

51. Referring to the nature of his "experiment" in writing *Sweeney Agonistes*, Eliot recalled: "I once designed, and drafted a couple of scenes, of a verse play. My intention was to have one character whose sensibility and intelligence should be on the plane of the most sensitive and intelligent members of the audience; his speeches should be addressed to them as much as the other personages in the play—or rather, should be addressed to the latter, who were to be material, literal-minded and visionless, with the consciousness of being overheard by the former. There was to be an understanding between this protagonist and a small number of the audience, while the rest of the audience would share the responses of the other characters in the play. Perhaps this is all too deliberate, but one must experiment as one can" (*The Use of Poetry and the Use of Criticism: Studies in the Relation of Criticism to Poetry in England* [London: Faber & Faber, 1933]: pp. 153–154; hereafter cited as *UP*).

52. Henry Louis Gates Jr. observes, "We are forced to wonder aloud where in dialect poetry, with the notable exception of Sterling Brown, a black poet used his medium as effectively as did Eliot in *Sweeney Agonistes*" (*Figures in Black: Words, Signs, and the "Racial" Self* [New York: Oxford University Press, 1987]: p. 289 n. 17).

53. See, e.g., Eliot, *Notes towards the Definition of Culture* (London: Faber & Faber, 1948): p. 121; and Eliot, "The Social Function of Poetry," in *PP*, p. 13.

54. In *Allegories of Reading: Figural Language in Rousseau, Nietzsche, Rilke, and Proust* (New Haven, Conn.: Yale University Press, 1979), Paul de Man argues that the link between metonymy and its referent is contingent and accidental; thus reliance on metonymic fragments of social reality is problematic. Although Hughes is aware that the reader may not understand the historical context of the trope, his poems repeatedly affirm that the meaning of African American experience, in certain instances, may be shared by readers from different social worlds and cultural backgrounds. His insistence on metonymy as a mainstay of his realist poet-

ics is an assertion of his right to creative freedom of expression, even at the risk of incomprehensibility.

55. *Spring and All,* in *The Collected Poems of William Carlos Williams,* ed. A. Walton Litz and Christopher MacGowan, vol. 1 (New York: New Directions, 1986): p. 203.

56. Theodor Adorno, "Fetish Character in Music and Regression of Listening," in *The Essential Frankfurt School Reader,* ed. Andrew Arato and Eike Gebhardt (New York: Continuum, 1982): p. 288.

57. Babette Deutsch wrote that the poems in *Montage of a Dream Deferred* suffered "from a will to shock the reader, who is apt to respond coldly to such obvious devices" ("Waste Land of Harlem," *New York Times Book Review,* 6 May 1951: p. 23).

STEVEN TRACY

# *The Dream Keeper: Langston Hughes's Poetry, Fiction, and Non-Biographical Books for Children and Young Adults*

To say that Langston Hughes never had any children of his own is to state a biological truth and a spiritual falsehood. No, he never fathered any children who carried on his genes from one generation to the next, but he did generate a forever youthful and exuberant art from his own genius, born of a lonely and sensitive childhood and nurtured into print that will speak to his literary and aesthetic progeny, young and old, as long as freedom, perseverance, sensitivity, and integrity continue to resonate in the souls of human beings. Hughes's own approach to the world itself was wide-eyed, exuberant, searching. Witness the titles of his autobiographies: *The Big Sea* (1940), with its important image of casting a wide, single net to harness and embrace the widest possible diversity and volume of experience, and *I Wonder As I Wander* (1956), where this epic hero equates through sound the act of moving through this world with the act of responding deeply and inquisitively to it, as natural and fundamental a part of living as breathing. In a way, we could say that children were alpha and omega to Hughes's career, from his first publication in 1921 in the children's magazine *The Brownies' Book* to the posthumous publication in 1969 of the children's book *Black Misery,* on which Hughes was working during his final hospital stay. Hughes thus framed his artistic life with literary productions for children,

*The Langston Hughes Review,* Volume 17, Centennial Edition, Fall/Spring 2002: pp. 78–94. Copyright © Langston Hughes Society.

165

and those productions should remain a central feature of any portrait of this gentle, caring man and his art.

The African American vernacular music tradition so important to the spirit and style of Langston Hughes's art is replete with references to the isolated, abandoned, orphaned child, very likely a legacy of the kidnapping of the slave trade, the brutal separation of family members on the auction block, and the harsh conditions during and after slavery that made maintaining family ties particularly difficult. Spirituals and blues like "Sometimes I Feel Like a Motherless Child," "Poor Boy Long Way From Home," and numerous individual lyrics lament the loneliness of the individual who feels like an abandoned child, no matter what age he or she may be. Scrapper Blackwell develops the theme at length in "Motherless Boy Blues," with its moving opening stanza:

> Lord, I wished I could see, wished I could see my mama's smilin' face.
> Oh, Lord, I wished I could see my mama's smilin' face.
> Because there's no one a-livin' can ever take her place.

Similarly, Blind Lemon Jefferson sings not just of the motherless child, but of the figure totally bereft of family:

> I am motherless, fatherless, sister- and brotherless, too.

Born out of the conflict between a tradition of African communal unity and wholeness and an imposed slave society bent on dividing and conquering, the lyrics reflect not only an individual tragedy but a concern with cultural conquest that pervades African American vernacular music, even as the stylistic and thematic expression in music itself represents the attempt to restore that communal unity.

Langston Hughes was not an orphan but, as Arnold Rampersad points out in the first volume of his biography of Hughes, "in some respects, he grew up a motherless and fatherless child, who never forgot the hurts of his childhood" (Rampersad, *Life* 1:3). Sisterless and brotherless as well, Hughes was shuttled around among relatives, infrequently with his mother, hating his father, and being raised without much warmth by his grandmother. It was this grandmother, Mary Sampson Patterson Leary Langston, who regaled Hughes with stories of his rebellious, abolitionist ancestors, and though her stories skirted the African American vernacular tradition that later informed so much of Hughes's work, these exciting narratives still provided Hughes with a sense of racial history and responsibility that remained with him, perhaps even influencing him to consider children an important part of his audience as he produced his work later on. Hidden behind his disarmingly boyish, charming smile was this heavy burden of his childhood, as well as the commitment to abolish the indignities of racism and prejudice that was a legacy of his ancestral past. Hughes himself described with wistfulness what he felt he had missed as a child: "My life has been filled with great envy [. . .] for those who have grown up in one place, whose folks stayed put, and who have always had a home to come back to" (Rampersad, *Life* 1:24). That unfulfilled dream of a stable and loving home, a theme so pervasive in African American literature, may well account in part for Hughes's sensitive forays into the genre of children's literature, where he could create a fuller, richer, fairer depiction of African American hopes, dreams, and realities, for those woefully misrepresented or underrepresented in the popular books and magazines of the times.

"Why are they always white children?" Nancy Larrick reported a five-year-old African American girl asking in 1965 about the characters in children's books (63). Embedded in the young girl's query is the reality that the genre of American children's literature frequently committed the sin of omission in representing African Americans in reading matter. It is also a question that could well have been asked about American literature in general throughout American history. Those silences, those blank spaces, represented America's unwillingness or inability to come to terms with the existence of the institution of slavery in a putative democracy and notions of racial supremacy in a country whose founding document declared that all men had been created equal.

But in addition to omission, African Americans had to face the distorted images of themselves when in fact they were portrayed in stories and poems. The other major approach to African American characters in American children's literature from the 19th century on has been to present African Americans from a white supremacist or Eurocentric perspective that mirrors the country's own ambivalence and divisions regarding slavery. As Donnarae MacCann notes: "The simple, transparent images contrived for the young are often an unselfconscious distillation of a national consensus or national debate" (xiii). George M. Frederickson sees this dominant white racist ideology as emerging recognizably around 1830, in some instances occurring as a response to abolitionist attacks, and escalating in the period of emancipation, when racist depictions of African Americans in stories had the effect of helping to undermine whatever advances might have come from the abolition of slavery. The resultant conditions, MacCann asserts, made "the defeated slavocracy [. . .] in many ways a cultural winner" (xiii). Indeed, even the portrayals of African Americans by "sympathetic" abolitionists were stilted, distorted by notions of African American inferiority, idealizations of characters and abolitionist operations, and a paternalism related to the concept of the "white man's burden." Childlike, docile slaves, ridiculous comic figures emerging from the minstrel show tradition, or beasts degraded by the slave system and in need of civilized instruction and uplift by white folks—these were the most common images of African Americans in antebellum literature, and these stereotypes extended and in some cases intensified in the post-bellum period. Dorothy May Broderick's analysis of American children's literature from 1827–1967 shows that African Americans were primarily portrayed as being physically unattractive, musical, devoutly religious and superstitious, dependent upon white folks for advancement, and responsible for the uplift of their people (3). Such a sense of inferiority, limited abilities and options, and social responsibility (the latter imposed by generations of upwardly mobile race leaders and club women as well) placed a heavy burden on generations of African Americans striving to succeed in a post-Reconstruction society whose racist institutions virtually pre-ordained their failures.

As America entered the twentieth century and W. E. B. DuBois identified the problem of the twentieth century as being the problem of the color line, it was clear to some that African American children needed positive portrayals in print to help counteract the preponderance of negative stereotypes in books and magazines aimed at the children's market. The question was, who was going to spearhead those attempts to present more varied and balanced portrayals, and how could they be actualized? Twenty-four answers were supplied in monthly installments beginning in January 1920, and it was there that young Langston Hughes began his professional publishing career in January of 1921. Those responses were the lovingly produced *Brownies' Book,* the October 1919 brainchild of editor W. E. B. DuBois, business manager Augustus Granville Dill, and managing editor and literary editor Jessie Fauset. DuBois was a founding member of the NAACP who was educated at Fisk, Harvard, and the University of Berlin. He already had two scholarly books, a book of essays, a novel, a biography, and poem and essay publications in a variety of journals behind him, in addition to founding and editing *The Crisis* for the NAACP. As one of the "Talented Tenth" race leaders assuming responsibility for leading African Americans in the direction of complete participation in the rights and responsibilities of American democracy, he recognized that "the Children of the Sun," the magazine's poetic designation for African American children (drawn from a poem by Fenton Johnson), also needed to be nourished by knowledge of the positive contributions of people of color world wide. Jessie Fauset's dedication in the first issue of *The Brownies' Book* lays out their intentions in clear, direct, uncluttered language for all to understand:

To Children, who with eager look
Scanned vainly library shelf and nook,
For History or Song or Story
That told of Colored Peoples' glory—
We dedicate *The Brownies' Book.* (Johnson-Feelings 25)

Created as a magazine for adults and children to read together and thus to encourage discussion and connection between generations, the publication provided not only an outlet for professional or aspiring writers and visual artists to submit biographies, short stories, folk tales, poetry, drama, photos, and drawings, but also included a letters section that provided a forum for children and adults to ask questions or raise issues of individual or racial importance. This goal of active participation with the materials published in the magazine was clearly an immediate reflection of the larger goal, which was to raise informed, literate, hardworking, talented, imaginative, compassionate, temperate, and committed race leaders who accepted their responsibilities to their race and country. The well-scrubbed, elegant, earnest children depicted in the photographs in the magazine bespoke the type of image the editors wished to project for their readers to emulate. The intelligent language, meaningful discussions of social issues and political situations, and reverence for the wisdom of elders suggested the type of intellect, community continuity and unity they wished to encourage. Unfortunately, the magazine was unable to generate enough revenue to continue operating past its second year, but during that time it provided a wealth of information for children and, importantly, an opportunity for Langston Hughes to tentatively ease his way into print.

Hughes, of course, would have been excited at the thought of any contact with DuBois. A "race leader" whose public opposition to Booker T. Washington's accommodationist strategies, involvement with the Niagara movement and the NAACP, and distinguished educational and publishing career placed him at the forefront of twentieth century African American leaders, DuBois was well positioned, along with Alain Locke, James Weldon Johnson, and Jessie Fauset, to deliver the New Negro Renaissance into existence. Hughes, in fact, wrote that when he was small, his grandmother read to him from the Bible and *The Crisis,* and that one of the first books he read independently was *The Souls of Black Folk* (1903). An eighteen-year old high school graduate living with his father in Mexico, Hughes sent two poems to the impressive Fauset on September 20, 1920.[1] Fauset, impressed by Hughes's work, asked for pieces on Mexican stories and games (which Hughes supplied for the April and December 1921 issues), along with more poems from which she chose two for publication in the January 1921 *Brownies' Book.* The essays both reveal Hughes's deep feelings for the environment he encountered in Toluca, a love of and respect for an alluring nature, the natives, and native customs, which he describes in vivid detail. Hughes's brief morality play, "The Gold Piece," also published in the July issue of the children's journal, was just the type of literary work the journal sought. The young protagonists are described as a boy and a girl, rendering them easy for young readers to identify with. Their obvious happiness at having money to spend on both necessary and frivolous personal items sets them up for the dilemma they face when an old woman with a blind child happens upon their home needing the exact amount of money they have to help her child see again. Their excitement at being able to "buy and buy and buy" bespeaks a materialism that the journal sought to mitigate by fostering a sense of responsibility to humanity. As a result of their thrift and ultimately their unselfishness, the boy and girl help a fellow human being, a child, enjoy the simple beauties of the world, and find their own true happiness in charity and compassion rather than in material goods. It was, significantly, around the same time that Hughes sent off "The Negro Speaks of Rivers" to Fauset. Whereas Hughes's "very charming" earlier poetry appeared in the children's publication, this new piece was accepted for publication in *The Crisis,* and Hughes moved a notch closer to recognition as a major writer on the American scene. He had reached his chronological and literary majority while affirming his connection with his childhood, writing children's poems and visiting his estranged father in Mexico. He would return to his work in the genre of children's literature in just over a decade, and he would never hesitate to tap the rich feelings of wonder and excitement, often, unfortunately, associated exclusively with childhood, to spark and drive some of his greatest poetry.

Hughes's first volume devoted to children's literature was actually his seventh book. His first, *The Weary Blues,* came on the heels of the title poem winning first prize in the *Opportunity* poetry contest, whereupon Carl Van Vechten arranged for publication in 1926 of a volume of poetry with Knopf. This volume, however, published to generally positive reviews, was followed the following year by *Fine Clothes to the Jew,* which was roundly criticized in the African American press of the time as focusing too much attention on lower class black life to the detriment of the type of image that Old Guard New Negro Renaissance and middle class leaders wished to project. One reviewer in *The Chicago Whip* dubbed Hughes "the poet low-rate of Harlem" (Rampersad, *Life* 1:140), though Hughes had already published in *The Nation* an explanation of his poetic aesthetic in his justly famous essay "The Negro Artist and the Racial Mountain." There Hughes praised the "low down folks" for their unselfconscious *joie de vivre* and refusal to bow to middle class standards of style and propriety (306). They were direct, honest, vital, people whose demeanors Hughes felt many African Americans would do well to emulate. And though there was a bit of romanticization to Hughes's portrait,

Hughes was generally aiming at establishing an approach to life and art that was unfettered by the artificial and externally imposed restraints of a hypocritical and excessively mannered society. While one hesitates to suggest that Hughes's portrait depicts a child-like openness and freedom, some of the elements that Hughes most admires can be related to the carefree innocence often associated with childhood. Those qualities that Hughes admired, then, were not signs of immaturity but independence, an independence unfortunately driven out of many people who succumbed to the social and behavioral demands of an oppressive society.

After graduating from Lincoln University in 1929, Hughes published his novel *Not Without Laughter* (1930). The work is a *bildungsroman* focusing on the path that the young boy Sandy Rogers takes out of the repressive, upwardly mobile middle-class existence of his Aunt Tempy toward an independent life that embraces the arc of itinerant blues singer Jimboy and the life style of Sandy's blues-singing and business-savvy aunt, while not ignoring the benefits of education championed by his grandmother. Clearly Hughes was mining his feelings regarding his own childhood and the unfair criticism of his work by middle class interests, shaping them into art that suggested a way to reconcile the various feelings and interests into a unified and meaningful whole. After two more collections of poetry and a volume that mixed a short play with several poems, Hughes found himself in the third year of America's Great Depression, personally depressed by his separation from the financial support (but artistic restraints) of Charlotte Mason, critiquing capitalism, and siding with the Communist International Labor Defense against the NAACP with regard to the defense strategies for the Scottsboro Boys. In the midst of all of this, Hughes received a request from a white librarian from Cleveland named Effie Lee Power for a selection of his poems that were suitable for children, subsequently published by Knopf in 1932 as *The Dream Keeper*. The "poet low-rate" and budding leftist was recognized as a poet whose work resonated with children of all ages, in part because of his zest and honesty, in part because he eschewed the obscurity and difficulty of many modernists in favor of a willful directness and resounding, affirmative humanity descended from Walt Whitman, Carl Sandburg, and the African American vernacular music tradition.

*The Dream Keeper* was a significant beginning to Hughes's children's literature career in that it collected together not only his poems from *The Brownies' Book* but selections from his other volumes of poetry as well. Hughes was asked to select from his poems those that seemed most appropriate for children, even if not necessarily written just for them. Finding this common audience, or poems that could speak to the children's and adult audience simultaneously, highlights a quality of Hughes's poetry that is sometimes unfairly maligned: the imagining of a multiplicity of voices that can speak for and to his audiences without condescension, but also without the loss of a sense of wonder at the simple beauties, trials, and lessons of life. It was no accident that Hughes entitled his volume, the opening section, and the opening poem "The Dream Keeper," nor that the first and last sections of the book refer regularly to dreams. What better job for the poet than inviting people into his world—"Bring me" he exhorts twice— than the fostering and protecting of dreams, all of them, not just a chosen few, from the man-handling of the prosaic pragmatists. What better way to define people than by their dreams—"you dreamers" he calls them—and the ways in which their dreams help define and sustain their lives as "heart melodies." And what better place to collect and protect them than in "a blue cloud-cloth," with its airy fleeciness a reflection of the color of the vastness of a rich and infinitely beautiful region, though perhaps tinged by the sadness (blues) of an unfulfilled dream that remains forever wrapt and wandering, though visible. Hughes evokes hope and perseverance through the cyclical pairing of sunrise and sunset at the close of the sections "Dressed Up" and "Walkers with the Dawn," the latter ending the book on an optimistic and committed note.[2]

Stylistically and thematically, Hughes does not avoid including poems that employ dialect or utilize blues forms, nor subject matter that appears commonly in blues songs, perhaps a direct rebuke to those "low-raters" who sought to have him eradicate the lives of the low-down folks from his work. Dancing, separation, mistreatment, homesickness, minstrelsy—all are treated in the "Dressed Up" section of *The Dream Keeper* as Hughes acknowledges the blues and the blues life as part of the art and life of African Americans, and a way of persevering, holding onto those dreams. Such poems as "Prostitute," "Beale Street Love," and "Red Silk Stockings" were likely not included by Hughes because they would have been judged inappropriate for young audiences (indeed adult audiences sometimes expressed discomfort with them), but, to his credit, Hughes does not offer just a sugary, artificial world for his readers. Just as significantly, Hughes juxtaposes his "Feet o' Jesus" section with his section of secular/blues poems, recognizing the common source, style, and depth of feeling, even as the appeals seem to be to different sources of relief, and the importance of each related tradition. Indeed, the book depicts the variety of worlds in which we can live—on land and sea, in Africa, America, Mexico, and Paris, in the city or the country, in the sacred or the secular, in youth and old age, of life and of death, in dreams or in mundanities—which are not always so distinguishable, so clearly delineated, so easily separable from each other. Nor should they be. This is the dream, the unity in variety, compassion, and understanding, that Hughes has wrapped between the covers of his book, for all the world, not just children, to see.

In the writing of his 1932 children's book *Popo and Fifina* Hughes capitalized on his longtime friendship with Arna Bontemps and his three month sojourn in Haiti in 1931. Hughes and Bontemps looked enough alike to be brothers, and they established a fraternal friendship from the time of their first meeting in 1923. Bontemps, some nine months Hughes's junior, was a teacher at the Harlem Academy, a school run by Seventh Day Adventists, an aspiring writer impressed by Hughes's art and career, and equally a devotee of literature. Bontemps had already contacted Macmillan publishers about the prospective children's book, and sought to bring Hughes in on the writing project because of Hughes's personal experiences with the "common" folk in Haiti, as well as for their personal and artistic simpatico. Although both writers were experiencing political and social upheavals in their lives at the time of this collaboration, little of their most fervent frustrations and difficulties surfaced in the story. Hughes was moving toward the left under the influence of his various visits to the Caribbean and other artistic and social pressures, and he was experiencing withdrawal symptoms after his break with Mrs. Mason. Bontemps, too, was moving to the left in his response to the effects of the Great Depression on citizens of the United States, and he was also feeling pressure from the Adventists to alter his writing to conform more to their notions of what his literature should try to accomplish—a situation somewhat like that which Hughes had experienced with Mrs. Mason, which ultimately precipitated their break.

Both men had an interest in Pan-Africanism, but they did not find this book to be the proper forum for overtly expressing these pressing concerns. Rather, Hughes and Bontemps crafted a loving portrait of a family poor in wealth but rich in love, strength, traditions, ambition, and pride. In fact, several times the narrative notes the family's strength: the father is a big proud black man with the ambition to own his own boat; the mother is described as a strong woman; Uncle Jacques is tall and dignified; and Popo is depicted as a young boy at first a bit hesitant but ultimately anxious to take his place in the adult world by exercising his creativity in his trade as a cabinet maker. The narrative stresses the necessity of hard work—one of those qualities expressed earlier in *The Brownies' Book*—matched by a firm sense of familial responsibility and solidarity. Although Hughes and Bontemps made no overt political statements in the text, their nuanced portraits of these "common folks," reflected in their portrayals of the richness of the inner and outer lives of these Haitians, emphasized the basic humanity of the characters. This fostered a respect for their lives and culture, and thus made an implicit political statement, in human terms, in the context of Haiti's struggles against insistent European imperialism. In fact, the authors may have embedded a political statement in the kite episode of the story: the kite is a red, star-shaped object, symbol of the Red Army of the Soviet Union, though this meaning is obscured, since it is introduced as red with yellow and green trimmings and compared to a Haitian bird, a natural symbol, before it is described as star-shaped two pages later. Still, when Fifina reflects that she knows that it is not a real star, but just looked like one and made her think of one, it is hard not to see the episode as an expression of the need to bring this red star into existence for the beauty and pride associated with it (Rampersad, *Popo and Fifina* 108). At its heart, *Popo and Fifina* is a sweet, poetically expressed, episodic bildungsroman, almost universally praised upon its release for its local color realism and heartfelt respect for the lives of the central characters, and a fitting expression of the collaborative efforts of two talented writers.

In *The Pasteboard Bandit,* written in 1935 but not published until after Hughes's death, Bontemps and Hughes offer a simple story that reflects a sociopolitical and literary aesthetic as it entertains his young readers with a heartfelt story. It is a multicultural story that explores cultural relativism through the experiences of a young Mexican child, Juanito Perez, whose choice of a small artifact to cherish and share with his American friend Kenny Strange demonstrates the values of sensitivity, friendship, and humanity. The authors' choice of main character and perspective is significant for a variety of reasons. First, the character, Tito, is not human but an inanimate object; however, that fact does not rule out the notion that this object needs consideration and understanding to survive and prosper in the world, nor does it discount the notion that looking at the world from its perspective has a value in forcing us to see the world from the vantage point of the undervalued, underappreciated, or ignored. The intention is to decenter our perspective in order to portray the shades of meaning that arise from an unexpected angle of vision. Second, the character is a small, cheap toy through which Hughes and Bontemps emphasize the importance of recognizing the innate value of all things, humble and simple though they may be. "But he's just a toy," one character exclaims, voicing the thoughts and feelings of many people in this world who used lowly social status as a justification for dismissal, contempt, or oppression. Hughes and Bontemps, however, take the "lowly" seriously and understand how something thought of as a toy, when approached seriously, can become an important tool. Third, the writers caution against judging by preconceptions by making Juanito's toy a bandit, an outlaw, though the status and appearance as a bandit does not make the toy either bad or lawless. In fact, the toy is quite friendly, sensitive, and loyal, not something or someone to fear or marginalize. Certainly the label or appearance of the object ought not to arbitrarily affect the way we respond to it, Hughes and Bontemps caution, especially when, given the thoughts that the authors put in its "head," it is quite as human as the rest of us. In fact, the bandit is not a thief or outlaw in the story, but part of a gesture of friendship that contributes rather than takes away.

Along these lines, the choice of the surname "Strange" for the American boy is significant as well. Though many potential American readers might have expected or found the culture of the Taxco natives to be strange, the authors reverse the perceptions by naming the young American "Strange," thereby generating an alternative perception that reinforces the value of re-orienting one's vantage point as a way of better understanding and appreciating the world. Fourth, though the bandit has a raised fist, it is not a symbol of violence, but, perhaps, through the story, of cultural revolution through the cooperation and harmony demonstrated among the people of different cultures in the story. Ultimately, Hughes and Bontemps emphasize that although this bandit is not the biggest, flashiest, most expensive or meaningful object, it is important to attend to, to cherish, and to share because behind its seeming insignificance lies a meaning and importance that humanity can recognize and appreciate when viewing it fairly and properly. This barely three-dimensional, modest object comes to represent the simple artifact as cultural and aesthetic ambassador, promoting the values of simplicity, humility, and humanity as the proper realms of politics, art, and life.

Not sharing the fortunate publication history of *Popo and Fifina*, *The Sweet and Sour Animal Book* was turned down by eight publishers in 1936, and by others after revisions in 1952 and 1959. Hughes continued to try to get into print this book of abecedarian verse for infants so radically different from the political poetry he was generating for adults in the 1930s. In his description of animals, mostly wild, but two domesticated and one imaginary (the unicorn), Hughes emphasizes several themes important to children and adults alike: the gap between appearance and reality, and the need to realize how one's perspective affects reality; the need to know who we are and be what we are; the importance of finding a place in our world that makes us feel safe, needed, and free; and the need for rules and sympathy in order to help us order our lives. These themes are reflected in the jealousy of the ape poem, the disappointments of the camel, the bravery and cowardice of the dog and elephant, the freedom of the lion, the self-definition of the newt. Hughes stresses the importance of imagination in the unicorn poem, a simple poem that underscores the reality of the imaginative creature by word placement and line breaks, even as the poem denies it. It is, at the end,

Happy unreal
Unicorn! (n.p)

Hughes may in fact have an embedded message on race in this text in his zebra poem, which drops the question "Which is right—/White on black/ Or black on white?" into the pond and then allows the issue of precedence and ascendancy to ripple out in ever-widening concentric circles from the point of impact. This is a gently humorous book, but not a book without its serious messages about the nature of the world.

Surprisingly, given the success of *Popo and Fifina* (though perhaps not surprisingly given the lack of success in placing *The Pasteboard Bandit* and *The Sweet and Sour Animal Book*), it took Hughes twenty years to return to the genre of children's literature. In the interim, though, he remained extremely busy. A flurry of activity found him publishing collections of stories, poetry, and translations; writing plays, operas, movie scripts, radio dramas, part one of his biography, and his famous newspaper column for the *Chicago Defender*, featuring his famous creation Jesse B. Semple; and editing with his old friend Bontemps *The Poetry of the Negro 1746–1949*. He moved further to the left politically for a time, including his founding of the left-leaning Harlem Suitcase Theater in 1938, but ultimately backed away from Communist doctrine. In the post-war civil rights arena, the U.S. Supreme Court banned segregation in interstate bus travel (1946), affirmed the right of African Americans to study law at state institutions at the same time as other citizens (1948), and prevented enforcement of covenants that sought to prevent African Americans from owning or occupying property due to racial discrimination (1948). Meanwhile President Truman established a Committee on Civil Rights (1946), encouraged adoption of a civil rights program (1948), and issued Executive Order No. 9981, which provided for equal treatment and opportunity in the U.S. Armed Forces (1948). Conversely, the NAACP was reporting a rise in the number of lynchings and acts of brutality committed against African Americans, and in 1951 began a serious legal attack on the segregation that was rampant in the nation's elementary and high schools. In this climate, Hughes, committed as he had always been to social justice and advancement of the cause of equality for African Americans, produced a series of children's books that were, like the NAACP's escalating legal actions, an attack on the pernicious effects of segregation and discrimination on African American children. Although the effects of anti-Communist hysteria promoted by Joseph McCarthy threatened at times to derail Hughes from his serious artistic and political work, Hughes persevered in his efforts on behalf of the children, producing a series of books for Franklin Watts and Dodd, Mead that aimed at projecting diverse and positive images and emphasizing the valuable contributions to American and world culture made by people of African descent.

The first of these efforts, *The First Book of Negroes*, was published in 1952 by Franklin Watts. In it, Hughes presents a narrative thread that foregrounds the importance of color, heritage, family, and international contributions of the variety of African peoples. Terry Lane is a young African American boy, "brown as a walnut," living in Harlem, which is touted as a place of distinguished black achievement of which Terry should be justly proud. Terry's middle class father works as a multilingual translator and, with his wife, takes Terry to see a variety of the sights a family can see in New York including a visit to the United Nations where Terry's father works. The grandmother, a graduate of Fisk who only uses improper grammar for the proper delivery of her folk tales, takes Terry places through the stories she tells. She helps educate him about slavery and prepares him for his trip to the Jim Crow South to visit his cousin in Alabama. The stories in the text attempt to highlight the long-standing and worldwide contributions of the diverse Africans, from Pygmy to Watusi, Spaniard to West Indian, American slave to free person of color, griot to writer, explorer to scientist, sports figure to politician, musician to saint. Emphasizing that Terry's ancestors could have come from many places around the world, Hughes places Terry in the global context even as he roots Terry in his American heritage, where the color of Africans "handsome in their blackness" is refracted into a lushly and lovingly described variety of colors: "ebony [. . .]warm cinnamon brown [. . .] tan [. . .] ginger [. . .] golden as peaches [. . .] color of ivory [. . .] coffee and cream" (18). Hughes's focus in a variety of his children's books on rich and loving descriptions of a spectrum of shades of skin hue is likely intended to counter generations of attitudes in American culture that held whiteness as a standard for beauty and stigmatized darker skin as dirty or ugly. Throughout he promotes dignity and pride in the appearance and accomplishments of people of African descent, while speaking frankly about impediments that still exist. Although one mark of the McCarthy-ist times was certainly Hughes's omission of the great contributions of W. E. B. DuBois and Paul Robeson, the volume was still quite groundbreaking and forward looking for its time, with its portraits of strong, intelligent, accomplished women like Terry's grandmother, Harriet Tubman, Harriet Beecher Stowe, Julia Ward Howe, Dr. Ruth Temple, Marian Anderson, Josephine Baker, Charlemae Rollins, Ethel Waters, Althea Gibson, Phillis Wheatley, Gwendolyn Brooks, Mary McLeod Bethune, and Terry's teacher, who makes her classroom a multicultural celebration grounds. Ultimately, the book encourages civic and political interest that will help promote democracy at home and abroad "and help make our country the most wonderful country in the world" (18). The book was published to deservedly excellent reviews, and set a very high bar for children's books on similar subjects that followed, Hughes's own work included.

Hughes's next two children's books, *Famous American Negroes* and *The First Book of Rhythms,* appeared in 1954 for translation into a variety of languages, Hindi, French, and Arabic among them. Growing out of Hughes's experiences teaching at the Laboratory School in Chicago in 1949, *The First Book of Rhythms* is Langston Hughes's resoundingly successful attempt to demonstrate how the rhythmic principle unifies the diversity of elements in the universe. Beginning with a participatory invitation that unites author, audience, and subject matter—"Let's make a rhythm"(1)—and ending once again with a collective designation—"this wonderful earth which is our home" (49)—Hughes defines rhythm in its broadest possible sense as any type of patterned movement, encompassing all of the senses, precluding the exclusion of any sensory experience and thus preparing the way for a remarkable series of associations and connections that make discovering rhythms a constantly momentary and momentous adventure. From Isaac Newton to the Rockettes, Ravel to nursery rhymes, the human heart to the Grand Canyon, thoughts and emotions to pyramids and skyscrapers, Hughes connects the macro to the micro, the unity of the world to the distinct, special, individual identity, sometimes through startlingly novel statements that make us see the world in new ways. He describes the Grand Canyon as "an immense rhythmical cleft across the land." He rhapsodizes with a wisdom true to anyone who has played baseball that "You, your baseball, and the universe are brothers through rhythm." Most importantly, Hughes does not conceive of this book as being directed exclusively toward African American children. Avoiding the trap of racist stereotyping of all African Americans as possessing a special sense of rhythm that others do not have, Hughes addresses the multiplicity of rhythms and their worldwide sources—France, Africa, Spain, Egypt, America. His narration for the 1955 recording for the Folkways LP "Rhythms of the World," companion album to the book, reinforces his universal approach. If there is any text that manifests the principle of *e pluribus unum* in its sensibility, references, and artistry, it is *The First Book of Rhythms*.

Of course, a great many of those rhythms that enlivened Hughes's poetry were born of African American vernacular music, so it was only natural that Hughes would eventually translate his love for music onto the written page for children. In 1955, the year that Marian Anderson debuted as the first African American singer in the history of the Metropolitan Opera House, the year Charlie Parker took his final bow among the living, and the year the folk music boom, which grew in part out of the Leftist interest in singers like Big Bill Broonzy, Josh White, and Leadbelly, was not far away from the American mainstream, Hughes published *The First Book of Jazz* and *Famous Negro Music Makers*. Jazz had attracted a popular audience since its inception, and, more and more with the emergence of the swing and big band era. After the war, the creativity of a new generation of musicians confronting the post-war climate of expectation and disillusionment helped produce an electrifying new sound, built on earlier blues, boogie woogie, and jazz styles, but with shifting rhythms and a searching, nervous energy and impatience that caught the mood of the younger generation eager to carve out a place for themselves separate from the middle class complacency and status quo politics of the pre-war era. This diversity produced types of jazz for many different audiences, from the "mouldy figs" yearning for a Dixieland revival to lovers of Basie-Ellington-Goodman big band swing to the boppers with their revolutionary ideas, virtuoso technique, exclusive language, and stance outside of the stultifying bounds of middle class America. With this increased visibility (and audibility) of jazz, clearly what was needed was a jazz primer for youngsters. Hughes, who had appreciated, championed, and employed jazz and blues from the beginning and had several children's books to his credit, was certainly one to capture the tenors of the times—even if, in fact, he felt he needed a number of jazz critics, folklorists, and aficionados (he lists twenty-seven, plus Louis Armstrong, in his acknowledgements) to verify his details for him, his knowledge of jazz being less systematic and encyclopedic, more temperamental and visceral.

*The First Book of Jazz* emphasizes the universal appeal and relevance of American jazz in the context of a variety of world musical genres, including references to West African roots; Russian, French, and other European composers; discussions of New England hymns; Appalachian ballads; and American Indian tribal music. Again, Hughes seems to be attempting to draw together the community of world music and place the importance of African American music among them, with the very important residual benefit of encouraging young people to explore these other musical traditions as well. He traces the history of jazz from West Africa to New Orleans, through work songs, jubilees, spirituals, minstrel songs, ragtime, blues, and boogie woogie. In a significant passage he discusses how Louis Armstrong, whose story offers a narrative thread along which Hughes develops his ideas, combines elements of these various influences into the music we know as jazz. Hughes comments on the soundtrack for the Folkways LP *The Story of Jazz* that jazz is "American music," and this African American music that is American music finds a beautiful synthesizer in Armstrong. Louis the synthesizer represented a source for Langston the synthesizer to call on America, with its ideals firmly rooted in synthesis, to strive to rise to the level of its ideals. The book's particular appeal to children results from its clarity and obvious warmth, as well as the repeated notion that jazz is supposed to be fun. The opening section of the book is entitled "Just For Fun," a middle section labeled "Jazz is Fun," and the volume ends with the sentence "The world is jazz-happy."

Hughes makes it clear that, although jazz emerges from a culture of people who were kidnapped and enslaved (though he mentions this only obliquely in the text), and although jazz has its serious and intellectual elements, jazz is a music intended for entertainment, not only of the audience, but for the musicians who play it. Performance invites participation, as Hughes delineates in depicting the young Armstrong joining in with the second liners as they march down a New Orleans street. Eschewing the macho swagger of Muddy Waters' 1955 hit "Manish Boy," which proclaimed

No B
O, child,
Y
That mean manish boy
I'm a MAN,

the book confidently asserts the strength, pride, and worthiness of the African American artist. With its interesting and useful text that names important figures and explains ideas like syncopation clearly, and an excellent glossary and index, the volume is a fine first book of jazz for children, one that, like Hughes's other children's books, casts a wide net to encompass and welcome all readers and hearers into its world.

Two of Hughes's next trio of books reflected the Pan-African interest he had manifested since his New Negro Renaissance days in the Harlem of Marcus Garvey and W. E. B. DuBois. *The First Book of the West Indies* (1956) and *The First Book of Africa* (1960), both published by Franklin Watts, are sociopolitical histories that aim at fostering an honest and proper understanding of people of color in these geographical locations.

In contrast to the Africa of Hollywood's Tarzan movies and the voodoo zombies of Hollywood and pulp fiction, Hughes tells the stories of a long and proud history of colored peoples whose demeanors and contributions extend far beyond the maligning portraits that characterize the describers far more than the described. The West Indies are explored in their various locations and cultures, again with references to the shades of complexion "from deep, dark chocolate or cinnamon brown to coffee-and-cream or peach or white" (*West Indies* 35), and to the various religions, musics, and natural beauty of the tropical locations. Hughes examines the religions of the various locations, including but not limiting his references to zombies, casually describing the paintings at Port-au-Prince that depict dark-skinned angels and disciples without comment, though the political, religious, and spiritual implications are obvious. The children are depicted as hard-working, fun-loving members of a cooperative family that strives together toward the common goal of survival, learning how to become skillful craftspeople and, importantly, passing along the stories and songs of their ancestors in place of the radios and televisions of mass culture that threaten to extinguish this important element of folk culture in the world.

The book on Africa addresses the encroachment of the contemporary Western world on the culture and economy of Africa as it tries to dispel the myths put forth about this continent by the Western world. After a look at Africa's ancient history and distinguished past, Hughes makes frank but not strident condemnatory references to materialistic Europeans bent on empire building at the expense of native Africans. He even signifies cleverly on

Cecil Rhodes, putting the characterization of him as an "unscrupulous land grabber" in other peoples' mouths. Hughes emphasizes that many parts of Africa are primitive but not savage, and that Africans' ancient civilizations have been plundered and undermined by outsiders. Primitiveness, however, is not a pejorative term in the sense of the humanism of Africans: Hughes describes a cooperative community with clean homes and art that is useful as well as beautiful, with musical traditions other than the employment of drums and story traditions that are functional as well. Contemporary Africa is seen as a continent of change, moving with the direction of intelligent leaders, like Nkrumah, into the 20th century in a gradual but concrete fashion, struggling to reconcile ancient traditions with modern technology and to rid the continent of exploiters, in general and the apartheid of South Africa in particular, while looking to the U.N. to help solve these difficulties and accepting the assistance of well-meaning countries of the world. Hughes sums up his intentions well as the book draws to a close.

Hughes was working on *Black Misery* on his deathbed in 1967. In the midst of his circumstances and the sometimes strident, acidic sarcasm of revolutionary writers of the Black Arts Movement, he crafted a quiet, introspective, melancholy, and profoundly moving book about the deliberate and incidental tragic ramifications of discrimination. Like *The First Book of Rhythms,* the text revisits or discovers for readers those momentary and momentous reflections of the larger whole of prejudice in American life. Organized in a fashion that reminds in some ways of the definition poems of Emily Dickinson, the book offers twenty-seven instances that help characterize misery for the African American child. Significantly, the definitions begin "Misery is when," not "Misery is if," suggesting the tragic inevitability of the circumstances described. The misery described occurs in a variety of arenas, a number of them in schools, stores, and other public places, treating not only actions but also the hurtfulness of language. Hughes reveals the network of linguistic, intellectual, emotional, moral, social, and ethical attitudes and actions that African Americans had and have to endure. He ends appropriately with a school setting: "Misery is when you see that it takes the whole National Guard to get you into the new integrated school." The miserable, fragile psyche that he delineates does not seem to wish to load weaponry to force kindness and friendship. It is not the child's way, Hughes says, to make the world right. These quiet words represent a plea for humanity, expressed in words that children can, and that adults ought to understand.

Finally, then, this is the source of the great beauty of Hughes's work. Sometimes criticized as overly simple or superficial by people who confuse obscurity with depth, Hughes's work aims at speaking to people in words that bring them together, that reach out to and embrace rather than lashing out and fragmenting. He attempts a comprehensive and universal vision frequently filtered through his specific and personal experiences as an African American. Intelligent, sympathetic, proud, committed, articulate—these are qualities we would like to nurture in our children, and would like to believe that we possess as well. To use these qualities to foster understanding and justice, crafting direct, uncluttered, memorable language that resonates deeply and broadly over generations: what could be more important?

It is not as simple as it sounds.

## NOTES

1. Fauset was Phi Beta Kappa at Cornell, received an MA from the University of Pennsylvania, and studied at the Sorbonne.

2. The book was inscribed "To My Brother," actually stepbrother Gwyn "Kit" Clark, who was the son by a previous marriage of Homer Clark, who Hughes's mother had married and with whom Hughes went to live in 1915 in Lincoln, Illinois. This very personal gesture is perhaps a hallmark of Hughes's work: one can bear the voices speaking one on one, one to one, even as they deliver larger, more generalized messages to the masses who read his poetry, and this singling out of the individual through the voice of the poem accounts in some degree for the particular success of Hughes's work with children.

## WORKS CITED

Blackwell, Scrapper. "Motherless Boy Blues." Champion 50000, 1935. Reissued on *Scrapper Blackwell: Complete Recorded Works 1928–1958 in Chronological Order*, Volume 2 (1934–1958). Document BDCD 6030.

Broderick, Dorothy May. "The Image of the Black in Popular and Recommended American Juvenile Fiction, 1827–1967." Diss. Columbia University, 1971.

Hughes, Langston. *The First Book of Negroes*. New York: Franklin Watts, 1952. N. pag.

———. *The First Book of Rhythms*. 1954. New York: Oxford University Press, 1995. N. pag.

———. "The Negro Artist and the Racial Mountain." 1926. *Voices From the Harlem Renaissance*. Ed. Nathan I. Huggins. New York: Oxford University Press, 1976.

Jefferson, Blind Lemon. "Broke and Hungry." Paramount 12443, 1926. Reissued on *Blind Lemon Jefferson: Complete Recorded Works in Chronological Order*, Volume 1 (1925–1926). Document DOCD 5017.

Johnson-Feelings, Dianne, ed. *The Best of the Brownies' Book*. New York: Oxford University Press, 1996.

Larrick, Nancy. "The All White World of Children's Books." *Saturday Review* (11 September 1965): p. 63.

MacCann, Donnarae. *White Supremacy in Children's Literature*. New York: Garland, 1998.

Waters, Muddy, "Manish Boy." Chess 1602, 1955. *The Complete Muddy Waters, 1947–1967*. Charly CD RED BOX 3, 1992.

Rampersad, Arnold. *The Life of Langston Hughes*. 2 vols. New York: Oxford University Press, 1986.

———. ed. *Popo and Fifina*. By Langston Hughes and Arna Bontemps. New York: Oxford University Press, 1993.

WILLIAM HOGAN

# Roots, Routes, and Langston Hughes's Hybrid Sense of Place

Reading the major works of Langston Hughes's early career, one is struck by his gravitation toward figures of landscape, and particularly by the way that the language of landscape and place help him articulate a vision for a strong, modern African American culture. In his 1926 essay "The Negro Artist and the Racial Mountain," for example, the figure of the mountain makes the case that black artists must embrace and celebrate their racial identity, rather than denying it. Similarly, in "The Negro Speaks of Rivers," his first published poem and still one of his best known works, the river comes to stand for the common history and common experiences connecting people of color over distances of time and geography:

> I've known rivers:
> I've known rivers ancient as the world and older than the
> flow of human blood in human veins.
>
> My soul has grown deep like the rivers.
>
> (Hughes, *Collected Works* 1:36)

And finally, in calling his first autobiography *The Big Sea*, Hughes emphasizes the many routes he followed as a young man, from America to Europe

*The Langston Hughes Review*, Volume 18; Spring 2004: pp. 3–23. Copyright © 2004 Langston Hughes Society.

and Africa, in an effort to discover who he was and where he had come from. *The Big Sea* is a book of wide experiences, and of wonder at the diversity of life; Hughes makes this point with Whitmanesque gusto in the book's epigraph:

> Life is a big sea
> full of many fish.
> > I let down my nets
> > and pull.

My argument in this essay is that one of Hughes's cultural projects, particularly in his early years, was to try to build new and stronger types of African American community by reimagining the connections between African American culture and place. The landscapes Hughes imagines, whether they are nourishing rivers that connect and strengthen communities of color or mountaintops that black artists must ascend in order to be heard, work to unite the African American community. They try to envision a new kind of rootedness in a historical moment that through the Great Migration and Jim Crow social structure in the post-emancipation South seemed intent upon uprooting African American communities.

By creating poetic landscapes that emphasize fluid connections and dynamic continuities among peoples of color, Hughes grounds his ideas about black communities in the physical world, lending them substance and legitimacy. The solid, tangible presence of mountain and river lend authority to his argument for the proud history of African American culture. Yet in wedding that culture to certain landscapes—for example, the river as a symbol of both rooted connectedness and fluid mobility—he also posits, as it were, a distinctly African American sense of place. By defining new connections between culture and environment, Hughes works toward establishing the basis for a common African American identity, an idea around which the community might cohere.

Recent work in African American history and cultural studies has focused attention on the connections between place and African American culture, imagining new ways of resolving place-oriented dichotomies like home/homelessness, rootedness/rootlessness, and community/isolation.[1] Paul Gilroy, for example, has proposed that traditional geographical models of the community/place relationship do not apply to the particular situation of African Americans. He argues for a political/sociological/geographical model of race called the Black Atlantic, in which communities of color on both sides of the Atlantic cohere not according to rooted connection to one particular place, but according to a kind of flowing connection between and among communities. The idea of a geographically grounded African American community, in other words, is less significant for Gilroy than the notion of a hybrid, interconnective racial identity that crosses national boundaries. In many respects, Gilroy's theory resonates with Hughes's geographical model in "The Negro Speaks of Rivers," in which the soul of the narrator grows deep with the waters of all the rivers of the Black Atlantic.

While Hughes's work must be contextualized according to currents in African American history and culture, I also want to suggest that his reimagining of place can be understood as more than a sociological phenomenon particular to African Americans. A range of modern and modernist writers, from W. B. Yeats and Wallace Stevens to Jean Toomer and Marianne Moore, confronted the problem of reimagining the relationship between place and culture; thus, it is important to understand Hughes's work in this regard not only sociologically, but historically as part of a broad response to the changing meanings of the physical environment in the early twentieth century. In working towards a definition of place that posits cultural communities among people separated by diaspora and migration, Hughes participates in this broad historical response to the changing relation of cultures and their environment. If Yeats's understanding of Irish landscapes, for example, was conditioned by the broader rise in European nationalist movements, and if Moore's sense of place responds to the changing status of wilderness in an industrializing America, then Hughes's mapping of the routes of African American culture imagines a new meaning of "rootedness" that proposes to strengthen communities even across physical separation.

"The Negro Artist and the Racial Mountain," which is still regarded as one of the strongest essays of Hughes's career, makes a useful first example of the way culture and landscape interact in his early work. The mountain functions as a shifting metaphor, representing at first the obstacles to African American literary expression, and then symbolizing the solid, if nascent, strength of an ethnic community united. He imagines himself at the beginning of a new era of cultural possibility, foreseeing a hopeful future in which black people would stand atop "the racial mountain," free to express themselves individually and genuinely, rather than in an attempt to please white America. In strident language, he foresees the blossoming of African American cultural production:

> Now I await the rise of the Negro theater. Our folk music, having achieved world-wide fame, offers itself to the genius of the great individual American Negro composer who is to come. And within the next decade I expect to see the work of a growing school of colored artists who paint and model the beauty of dark faces and create with new technique the expressions of their own soul-world. (692–694)

Building momentum, as if he were writing a sermon, Hughes comes to argue not only for the legitimacy of African American art, but also for its relentless movement toward full fruition, the inevitability with which black writers and artists will overcome difficulty to create new and innovative forms.

In the opening paragraphs of the essay, the mountain is not an enabling device for black culture; on the contrary, it symbolizes the many obstacles to free and truthful self-expression faced by black American artists:

> [T]his is the mountain standing in the way of any true Negro art in America—this urge within the race toward whiteness, the desire to pour racial individuality into the mold of American standardization, and to be as little Negro and as much American as possible. (692)

In this formulation, the mountain is a huge and immovable monolith blocking the path to authentic expression. By the end of the essay, though, the mountain has shifted in meaning, becoming less an intimidating obstacle to free expression, and symbolizing instead the dizzying heights African American culture seems poised to achieve, the cultural and spiritual mountaintop from which to sing freely:

> We are beautiful. And ugly too. The tom-tom cries and the tom-tom laughs. If colored people are pleased we are glad. If they are not, their displeasure doesn't matter either. We build our temples for tomorrow, strong as we know how, and we stand on top of the mountain, free within ourselves. (694)

In this respect, the mountain serves Hughes as a rhetorical device allowing him to turn a potential obstacle into an avenue to freedom. The essay turns on this rhetorical pivot, becoming an inspirational call to action, a shout of encouragement not to shrink from the mountain but to ascend and conquer it.

Hughes uses the mountain for more than its rhetorical effectiveness, however; it is also a way to ground his argument, which is largely cultural in nature, to the tangible world of landscape, to locate it spatially. His argumentative objective is quite daunting: he sets out not only to celebrate African American artistic production, but also to define it, to imagine what a distinctly African American mode of expression might look like. In some sense, he wants to make African American art forms possible. In the face of this rhetorical task, he gravitates toward a metaphor of solid earth: the mountain becomes a way to ground his proposal, and to create a physical place (the mountaintop) for African American art to occur. In the remainder of this essay, I will look more closely at Hughes's recalibration of the culture/place relationship. I examine the general parameters of Hughes's sense of place and look at his construction of Harlem as a particular cultural site.

In "The Negro Speaks of Rivers," Hughes develops a theory of racial community whose strength derives not from geographical isolation, but from movement, from cultural flow between communities of color across both space and time:

> I've known rivers:
> I've known rivers ancient as the world and older than the
>     flow of human blood in human veins.
>
> My soul has grown deep like the rivers.
>
> I bathed in the Euphrates when dawns were young.
> I built my hut near the Congo and it lulled me to sleep.
> I looked upon the Nile and raised the pyramids above it.
> I heard the singing of the Mississippi when Abe Lincoln
>     went down to New Orleans, and I've seen its muddy
>     bosom turn all golden in the sunset.
> I've known rivers:
> Ancient, dusky rivers.
>
> My soul has grown deep like the rivers.
>
> (*Collected Works* 1:36)

The river, both deep and "ancient as the world," is on one hand a symbol of rootedness; it is part of the earth, a feature that connects culture to place. Yet the river also flows, connecting the ancient cultures of Egypt and Africa with post-emancipation African America. And while the river's flowing movement might seem the opposite of rootedness, Hughes brings the two characteristics together. Indeed, in the logic of the poem, the flow of the river reinforces the strength of black culture in the United States, nourishing it with history and continuity. With the image of the river, with its connotations of movement, rejuvenation, rootedness, Hughes creates a picture of black culture that is both steeped in tradition and vibrantly able to reinvent itself when necessary.

In "The Negro Speaks of Rivers," therefore, Hughes manages a kind of recalibration of the relationship between culture and place: rather than relying on a conventional definition of rootedness inappropriate to the historical situation of African Americans, he creates a new rootedness that draws its strength precisely from diaspora and migration. Instead of denying or ignoring the historical pattern of forced uprooting and separation that characterized African American experience, he uses that pattern to his advantage, emphasizing the solidarity and strength of communities of color across space and time. Throughout his early work, Hughes works toward merging the meanings of "roots" and "routes" in the relation between culture and place. In his model, the many "routes" historically taken by black culture only strengthen the "roots" of the community, by emphasizing the global connections and cultural continuities between people.[2]

When Hughes wrote the first draft of "The Negro Speaks of Rivers" in 1920, there was certainly no shortage of "routes" in African American culture. In 1917, America's entrance into the first World War had created a wartime labor shortage in the northern industrial metropolises, which increased the northward migration of African Americans from the rural south to the urban centers of New York, Chicago, Cleveland, and Detroit. Between 1916 and 1919, about 500,000 African Americans moved north, and during the 1920s, almost a million more followed (Grossman 3–4). This exodus, both in search of work in the North and in retreat from entrenched racial prejudice in the South, frequently separated husbands from wives and nearly always disrupted southern black communities in favor of new, unfamiliar, and radically different surroundings in the cities. This huge demographic shift has become known as the Great Migration, and in recent years it has attracted a great deal of both scholarly and popular attention as one of the major cultural phenomena in the shaping of the modern United States.[3] Hughes wrote "The Negro Speaks of Rivers" within the historical and sociological context of the Great Migration. As African Americans, were uprooted in great numbers again, pressed to move in search of work, Hughes's poem recognizes the need for a new kind of rootedness, one that embraced a history of migration and resettlement.

"The Negro Speaks of Rivers" is one of Hughes's most reprinted poems. It appeared first in 1921 in *The Crisis*, the magazine of the NAACP edited by W. E. B. DuBois. It later appeared in Alain Locke's *New Negro* anthology; in *The Dream Keeper*, Hughes's 1932 book for children; and in numerous magazines, anthologies, and collections of Hughes's work. It was one of the centerpieces of *The Weary Blues* (1926), his first volume of poetry. If "The Negro Speaks of Rivers" helps articulate Hughes's ideas about rootedness and the need for a new kind of connection between African American culture and place, the rest of *The Weary Blues* provides a more complete elaboration of those ideas.

In the rare instances in which critics have read *The Weary Blues* as a complete volume, it has been interpreted as a potpourri of Hughes's early styles. The book contains blues poems, more traditional lyrics, and it features Hughes working in both longer and shorter forms. It has also been read as a catalog of his many travels. Many early reviewers of *The Weary Blues* call attention to the "nomadic" quality of the volume, attributing the geographical diversity of the book to the fact that Hughes traveled extensively in his early years, living (among other places) in Cleveland; Mexico; Kansas; New York; Washington, DC; Chicago; Paris; and on board the SS *Malone,* a commercial ship that traveled to Europe and Africa. I would suggest, however, that the volume is more than a grab bag of stylistic experiments or a testament to Hughes's nomadism; rather, reading the volume as he published it, with the arrangement of poems intact, it is possible to read *The Weary Blues* as a coherent whole. Seen as a deliberately arranged volume rather than as a convenient grouping of early poems, *The Weary Blues* comes into sharper focus as a book about place, and particularly about describing a new kind of relation between black culture and its many geographical roots.[4]

The volume Opens with "Proem," whose title implies not only its position at the beginning of the book, but also its role as a prologue to the collection, establishing the terrain the whole volume will explore. The title also suggests a mythological aspect. This is a poem (and a volume) about origins, about making a new beginning, and telling the story of a culture. The poem supports this reading:

> I am a Negro:
>> Black as the night is black,
>> Black like the depths of my Africa.
>
> I've been a slave:
>> Caesar told me to keep his door-steps dean.
>> I brushed the boots of Washington.
>
> I've been a worker:
>> Under my hands the pyramids arose.
>> I made mortar for the Woolworth Building.
>
> I've been a singer:
>> All the way from Africa to Georgia
>> I carried my sorrow songs.
>> I made ragtime.
>
> I've been a victim:
>> The Belgians cut off my hands in the Congo.
>> They lynch me now in Texas.
>
> I am a Negro:
>> Black as the night is black,
>> Black like the depths of my Africa.
>
> *(Collected Works* 1:22)

We can see that this is a volume that begins with the internal subjectivity of the black narrator ("I am a Negro"), but quickly expands outward in both space and time. We travel from ancient Rome and Egypt to the African Congo; we follow the continuity of "sorrow songs" from Africa to Georgia to the urban context of ragtime. Yet despite the geographical and temporal reach of the poem, we come back to where we began, in the individual consciousness: "I am a Negro." As in "The Negro Speaks of Rivers," the many places of the poem do not, finally, scatter or uproot the narrator's consciousness; rather, in the incantatory cadences of the poem, the multiple sites of black culture strengthen the narrator's pride and confirm his identity. "Proem" opens *The Weary Blues* with a new kind of geography of race, based around movement and flow between places and cultures, centered in strengthening the roots of community by proliferating the routes of culture.

After opening *The Weary Blues* in this way, with an argument for a multiple rootedness, Hughes proceeds to explore some of these many roots more fully. He takes pains to focus his attention on places both international and domestic, rural and urban, and even real and imaginary. In short, the book becomes an attempt to build a new sense of place out of a diversity of geographical reference, expanding outward, as in "Proem," from the individual subject toward the global community. Moreover, the routes outward from the self ultimately lead back inward, and the self is strengthened by the hybrid combination of places.

After "Proem," the book is divided into titled sections, each containing a series of poems depicting a different site of black culture. The first section, "The Weary Blues" is set largely in Harlem, and particularly in the jazz and blues clubs of Lenox Avenue. Then, like the pattern in "Proem," the sections of the book radiate outward from this home base: a section called "The Negro Speaks of Rivers" examines more rural, and frequently southern, American scenes; "Water Front Streets" is a gathering of seafaring and maritime poems, representing a departure from a particularly American context toward wider roots; "Shadows in the Sun," offers poems about Mexico, the Caribbean, and South America; and the final section of the book, "Our Land," focuses on Africa and the cultural connections between Africans and African Americans. The whole of *The Weary Blues,* then, describes an ever-widening arc of cultural continuity. As the sections unfold themselves, Hughes gradually embraces a wider and wider diversity of places as part of his cultural background.

Hughes ends the volume with "Epilogue" ("I, too, sing America!"), another of his most famous poems, which resolves the book's many cultural routes into a single, complex identity:

I, too, sing America.

I am the darker brother.
They send me to eat in the kitchen
When company comes,
But I laugh,
And eat well,
And grow strong.

Tomorrow,
I'll sit at the table
When company comes.
Nobody'll dare
Say to me,
"Eat in the kitchen,"
Then.

Besides,
They'll see how beautiful I am
And be ashamed,–

I, too, am America.

(Collected Works 1:62)

*The Weary Blues* pursues African American identity in many different directions, but ultimately, Hughes's goal is to build community, to create a common idea around which people can unite, despite their geographical distance from each other.

I have been suggesting that one of the effects of *The Weary Blues* is to imagine and articulate a new relation between place and African American culture, a relation based on intra- and international vectors of cultural continuity that connect places and peoples. One of the ways Hughes establishes these vectors is to explore widely different geographical locations in the poems themselves and show how each of them contributes to the hybrid construction of African American culture; yet the content of the poems is only one of the ways that *The Weary Blues* argues for an African American culture strengthened by routes as much as by roots. The book itself, in its blend of tonal and stylistic approaches, as well as in its physical attributes such as cover design and publishing imprint, functions as a material enactment of Hughes's hybrid cultural geography.

It has been frequently noted that Hughes, particularly in his early work, was a deft manipulator of poetic styles. In *The Weary Blues*, for example, he includes a visceral paean to nightlife, "Negro Dancers" ("Me and ma baby's / Got two mo' ways, / Two mo' ways to do de buck!"), right alongside "Young Prostitute" ("Her dark brown face / Is like a withered flower / On a broken stem.") which reads as if it might have been included in an anthology of imagist poetry. Scholarship on the Harlem Renaissance has, in the last fifteen years, questioned the distinctions frequently drawn between the work of Hughes and other Harlem Renaissance writers on one hand, and that of "High" modernists like Eliot and Pound on the other.[5] James Smethurst, for example, in a recent study of African American writing in the period, points to the surprising "range of addresses and addressees" in Hughes's early poetry and to stylistic "polyphony" as a marker of Hughes's modernism (93–116). To this reading of Hughes's tonal diversity, I would add that in *The Weary Blues,* writing in multiple voices is another way for Hughes to build a theory of culture based not around locally hermetic communities, but around dynamic vectors of cultural exchange. In *The Weary Blues,* his tonal and stylistic polyphony reinforce the book's tendency to spread outward in its cultural references.

Nowhere is the volume more a site of ethnic hybridity than in its physical appearance, with a cover illustration by the Mexican caricaturist Miguel Covarrubias, an introduction by the white writer Carl Van Vechten, and with an imprint from the Jewish publisher Alfred A. Knopf. As was the case with many modernist book productions, the making of *The Weary Blues* must most accurately be called a collaborative project. Van Vechten knew Covarrubias, a young artist who had moved to New York from Mexico City in 1923, and essentially chose him to contribute the cover design. This was a decision of which Hughes heartily approved. He was familiar with Covarrubias's artwork from the drawings he had contributed to Alain Locke's *New Negro* anthology in 1925.[6] In his cover design Covarrubias depicts the Lenox Avenue blues pianist from the title poem, making music "by the dull pallor of an old gas light" (*Collected Works* 1:23). The illustration is somewhat typical of Covarrubias's work. With its cabaret setting and exaggerated ethnic characteristics, his drawings have become some of the most recognizable visual icons of the Harlem Renaissance.

*The Weary Blues*'s publication by Alfred A. Knopf was also a marker of the volume's national and international hybridity. As recent criticism on the print culture of the Harlem Renaissance has shown, Knopf was a relatively new press at the time, particularly unusual for the national and ethnic diversity of its published authors. In addition to publishing several important black writers of the time, including James Weldon Johnson and Nella Larsen, Knopf also published Wallace Stevens, Vachel Lindsay, and Thomas Mann (Hutchinson 342–386). In short, when *The Weary Blues* appeared from Knopf, with a cover by Covarrubias and an introduction by Van Vechten, it enacted in its material appearance the same kind of inter- and intranational cultural blending that Hughes pursues within. *The Weary Blues*, taken as a thematic and bibliographic whole, exemplifies the kind of cultural geography established in Hughes's early work. By focusing on the development of community roots based in cultural continuities across distances, rather than in traditional, fixed geographical communities, he builds a connection between culture and place strengthened, not weakened, by geographical dispersion.

No discussion of Hughes's constructions of place would be complete without an examination of Harlem, undoubtedly the cultural site with which he is most frequently associated. In 1921, at the age of nineteen, he arrived in New York City for the first time, ostensibly to attend Columbia. But Harlem made a stronger impression on the young Hughes than did the university at the neighborhood's edge. In his autobiography *The Big Sea*, he describes the sense of wonder he felt upon emerging for the first time from the 135th street subway station:

> I came out onto the platform with two heavy bags and looked around. It was still early morning and people were going to work. Hundreds of colored people! I wanted to shake hands with them, speak to them. I hadn't seen any colored people for so long—that is, any Negro colored people. (*Big Sea* 81)

In this early experience, Hughes seems awed by Harlem, taken in by the idea of a genuinely African American "city within a city," as James Weldon Johnson had described it in *The New Negro* ( Johnson 301). Yet by the end of the twenties, the young, awed visitor had transformed into an established, if still young, writer. Hughes and Harlem became strongly linked during the twenties as the place and the writer helped shape each other. It is this process of mutual construction I want to examine focusing particularly on Hughes's role in the emergence of Harlem not merely as a cultural center for African Americans, but also as a cultural crossroads through which passed many currents of American life and art in the 1920s.

That Hughes has become icon of the Harlem Renaissance is somewhat ironic since he lived in Harlem only for short periods of time during the Renaissance's height. Indeed, many of the writers we associate most closely with the Renaissance, including Zora Neale Hurston, Jean Toomer, and Claude McKay, resided only sporadically, or indeed, not at all, in the neighborhood. The Harlem Renaissance, seen in this way, is something of a misnomer, not only because many of its writers and artists did not live in Harlem, but also because the name implies a "movementhood," a thematic unity and a geographical rootedness that the period's African American literature decidedly lacked. Literary historians have argued convincingly over the last decade that the Harlem Renaissance was anything but a hermetic cultural movement confined to the blocks north of 125th street (see Hutchinson, Douglas). These studies have instead revealed the collaborations, across both ethnic and geographical lines, that helped create the Harlem Renaissance.

If the Harlem Renaissance might be a slightly misleading way of describing the period literature of a place, it is also somewhat misleading to describe Harlem itself as a well established thriving center of black culture when Hughes arrived in 1921. In fact, Harlem was a new African American neighborhood. As its name suggests, it had originally been a Dutch settlement, and through its history until the early twentieth century, the blocks north of Central Park in Manhattan had been populated primarily with Irish, then Jewish, and finally German immigrants. The first African American residents did not move in until 1905, only sixteen years before Hughes arrived, wide-eye at the possibilities for a vital, progressive black community in New York (Watson 11).[7] The neighborhood was changing extremely rapidly through the early decades of the twentieth century. When black people began to arrive, they came from all over the country, and indeed, from all over the world, with new arrivals from the southern United States as well as from Cuba, Haiti, Jamaica, and Puerto Rico.

Given Harlem's constant demographic reconfiguring, it makes more sense to think of the neighborhood as a cultural crossroads, a place in the process of becoming, rather than as an established neighborhood with a fixed identity. By the mid-1920s, with its vibrant intellectual life, innovative musical culture, and hugely successful nightclubs, Harlem was indeed a center of African American culture in the United States. But it is important to illuminate the cultural processes that helped it acquire that identity. Without a long history as an African American neighborhood, Harlem's identity was, in some sense, invented: it was brought into existence by the people moving into the neighborhood and changing it day by day, and also by writers and artists such as Hughes who represented Harlem in their work and helped define what it might become.

In the 1920s, Hughes, along with other black writers and intellectuals, hoped fervently that Harlem might become something great. His work during this decade attempts to construct it as a place for cultural change, a community that could expand outward and incorporate the diversity of its constantly-arriving new residents. Earlier I suggested that his general vision for African American cultural geography was based around vectors of cultural connection. The Harlem of his early work is a point of convergence for those vectors, a collage of different people and different modes of expression. In Hughes's first two poetry collections, *The Weary Blues* and *Fine Clothes to the Jew,* Harlem emerges as a blend of folk culture mixed with urban living, of lyrical beauty, gritty realism, of sensual joy combined with anger and despair. In his vision of cultural blending, he is ultimately optimistic about the possibilities for Harlem. Though he does not shy away from the poverty and racism faced by African Americans in the neighborhood, he works to invent a city strengthened by its diversity.

From early in his career, Hughes's work was intimately connected to Harlem. As a young African American writer in the 1920s, he inevitably became associated with the increasing notoriety of Harlem, and his work, despite his own frequent traveling, came to be seen as representative of the neighborhood. In 1925, when Hughes was a relatively unknown younger poet, he was a featured contributor in a special issue of *Survey Graphic* magazine, entitled "Harlem: Mecca of the New Negro." The issue can be read as an early draft of Alain Locke's *New Negro* anthology; its goal was to publicize and examine the emergence of Harlem as a center of African American culture. In his introduction to the issue, Locke argued that Harlem was more than a predominantly black neighborhood; rather, it was a "race capital," a crucible for the forging of a "new soul" among African Americans. Locke was palpably optimistic for Harlem's future prospects:

> [W]e shall look at Harlem . . . as the way mark of a momentous folk movement; then as the center of a gripping struggle for an industrial and urban foothold. But more significant than either of these, we shall also view it as the stage of the pageant of contemporary Negro life. In the drama of its new and progressive aspects, we may be witnessing the resurgence of a race; with our eyes focused on the Harlem scene we may dramatically glimpse the New Negro. (Locke 630)

Locke's heraldic tone is sustained throughout much of the *Survey Graphic* "Harlem" issue, and it is characteristic of a prevalent attitude toward Harlem in the 1920s, an attitude that acknowledged the possibilities for Harlem, but which also recognized that for Harlem to realize its potential would require a concerted effort on the part of its residents, and on the African American community more generally. His introduction announces that the *Survey Graphic* issue is part of that struggle, that the issue itself aims to be part of Harlem's process of becoming.

In this context, we can see Hughes's seven-poem contribution to the magazine as the poet's first public intervention in the shaping of Harlem's identity. In a section entitled "Youth Speaks," his series of shorter poems appear in a single-page layout. None of the poems makes direct reference to Harlem, or to the city more generally, but in the textual context of the *Survey Graphic,* they become optimistic and inspiring visions of Harlem's possibility. In "Poem," for example, Hughes's general entreaty to move forward toward the future becomes a dream for Harlem:

We have to-morrow
Bright before us
Like a flame

Yesterday, a night-gone thing
A sun-down name

And dawn to-day
Broad arch above the road we came,
We march. ("Poem" 633)

In another piece, also entitled "Poem," Hughes writes stridently, "We are not afraid of night / Nor days of gloom, / Nor darkness, / Being walkers with the sun and morning" (633). The general, inspirational tone of these poems become in the *Survey Graphic* forward-looking visions for Harlem. The city has yet to be defined, and will be shaped by the community that works toward shaping it.

Other poems in the *Survey Graphic* dream of a "safe haven" for African Americans, a paradise free of racism and oppression. In "Dream Variation," for example, Hughes writes:

To fling my arms wide
In some place of the sun,
To whirl and to dance
Till the bright day is done.
Then rest at cool evening
Beneath a call tree
While night comes gently
Dark like me. (633)

The night, so often associated with danger and fear, becomes in this poem a symbol of gentleness, of comfort. The "darkness" of the night reassures the dark-skinned narrator. By inverting prevailing myths about darkness, Hughes dreams of a place that welcomes and nurtures people of color. In the context of the *Survey Graphic,* this place inevitably resonates with Harlem. Hughes thus constructs the neighborhood as a promised land for African Americans. In vision, Harlem awaits new arrivals from wherever they might originate. It is not exclusive or set in its ways; rather, it is poised to become stronger and more robust for the diverse community that seeks it out.

Later in 1925, the *Survey Graphic* issue was expanded and published by Alfred and Charles Boni as *The New Negro* anthology. As Arnold Rampersad notes in his introduction to a recent edition, the anthology was widely regarded, almost immediately upon publication, as the definitive collection of the Harlem Renaissance (*New Negro* ix). As such, it was widely influential in defining Harlem as a cultural center during the twenties. In *The New Negro*, Hughes's poems have a similar effect as they do in the *Survey Graphic;* they construct Harlem as a diverse and open-ended community, waiting to be defined and capable of absorbing the dreams of its many inhabitants. But as recent scholarship has shown, *The New Negro*, particularly in early editions, was a deeply collaborative project, including contributions from both white and black artists and commentators.[8] In this, the anthology was characteristic of the many cultural and ethnic hybridities that combined to shape and define Harlem in its early years. Thus, in *The New Negro*, the cultural openness of Hughes's poems becomes even more prominent. In this textual site, the poems work to imagine a Harlem whose identity contains and embraces multitudes.

In *The Weary Blues* and *Fine Clothes to the Jew*, Hughes's own books during the twenties, he continues to construct Harlem as a site of cultural convergence, a place defined and strengthened by cultural blendings. One of the most prominent blendings he pursues is the commingling of folk and urban culture. Hughes uses the blues to resolve folk and urban elements in African American culture and to exemplify cultural formations that move between and connect communities over geographical distance. The blues are important to *The Weary Blues*, but they are even more central to his second volume, *Fine Clothes to the Jew* which appeared in 1927 hard on the heels of both *The New Negro* and *The Weary Blues*. In *Fine Clothes to the Jew* whose unfortunate title comes from the poem "Hard Luck," which tells of a poor man forced to "Gather up" his "fine clothes / An' sell 'em to de Jew," Hughes focuses his attention on the speech and lives of ordinary African Americans. Some early reviewers of the volume, particularly in African American intellectual circles, detested the book, complaining that in depicting the lives of poor blacks, Hughes was pandering to the worst stereotypes of white America. More recent critics have begun to find favor with *Fine Clothes to the Jew*, however. Arnold Rampersad, for example, considers it "Hughes's most radical achievement in language," and compares it to Whitman for its use of common experience and vernacular as the material for art (*Life of Langston Hughes* 1:141).

I am interested in *Fine Clothes*'s implications for Hughes's vision of Harlem. In his focus on the blues, I want to suggest that he blurs the boundary between rural and urban cultures in the African American community. In this way, he contributes to his vision of Harlem as a point of convergence for the disparate currents of African American culture. By creating a blues set in the city but steeped in rural musical traditions, Hughes envisions a Harlem that is modem, urban, and forward-looking, yet also grounded in local black

communities around the country. An early reviewer of *Fine Clothes* noticed
Hughes's attempt to give voice to a new urban aesthetic:

> For his present volume young Hughes has gone for material to the
> more primitive types of American Negro, the bellboys, the cabaret
> girls, the migratory workers, the singers of blues and spirituals
> and the makers of folk songs. The plantation Negro of yesterday is
> no more, and in his place has come the city worker, the struggler
> in the industrial maelstrom of modern life and inhabitant of the
> Harlems of American cities.
>
> ("Negro Poet Sings of Life" 5F)

Yet even as *Fine Clothes* does indeed focus attention on the modern city, it
is also important to notice the cultural connections Hughes establishes with
communities outside the urban environment.

In *Fine Clothes*, the urban and the rural are held in tension with one
another. While many of the poems in the volume depict stark portraits of
African American life in the city, memories of the south, both positive and
negative, run throughout the volume. "Po' Boy Blues," for example, tells the
story of a narrator recently arrived in the northern city thinking longingly of
the south he has left behind:

> When I was home de
> Sunshine seemed like gold.
> When I was home de
> Sunshine seemed like gold.
> Since I come up North de
> Whole damn world's turned cold.
>
> (*Collected Works* 1:79)

This narrator is suspended between two worlds, the rural world left behind,
and the harsh new city life he has begun. The blues structure of the poem
reinforces that sense of between-ness. By participating in a musical tradition that is both rural *and* urban, and that is itself constantly changing,
constantly in a state of becoming, Hughes retains both north and south as a
vital presence in the poem.

This sense of between-ness, of a city life built on the uneasy resolution
of north and south, is characteristic of *Fine Clothes to the Jew.* The volume
has urban snapshots such as "Railroad Avenue": "Dusk dark / On Railroad
Avenue. / Lights in the fish joints, / Lights in the pool rooms" (*Collected
Works* 1:81), and depictions of blue collar city work, such as "Elevator Boy"
and "Porter." These poems coexist, however with a section towards the end

of the book entitled "From the Georgia Roads," which reads as if it is a memory of a previous life that will not fade. In "Sun Song," for example, Hughes writes:

> Sun and softness,
> Sun and the beaten hardness of the earth,
> Sun and the song of all the sun-stars
> Gathered together,—
> Dark ones of Africa,
> I bring you my songs
> To sing on the Georgia roads.

*(Collected Works* 1:103)

The result is a volume that is unmistakably urban in quality. The narrators are primarily recent migrants and urban workers. But with the southern scenes and the echo of the blues throughout, Hughes creates a picture of Harlem that resists geographical fixity and rather gains vitality precisely from the diffusion of its cultural references. The city in *Fine Clothes to the Jew* is not necessarily friendly or welcoming; but if it is to grow, and to house a strong community for African Americans, it must carry in it the memory of the past, a memory that is both cultural and geographical. In his construction of Harlem Hughes works to retain that memory.

Much later in his life, in 1948, Hughes finally bought the house he would occupy for the rest of his life, three blocks from Lenox Avenue in the center of Harlem. In 1951, he published his famous poetic sequence *Montage of a Dream Deferred*, which he saw as his career's definitive statement about Harlem. Since I am concerned primarily in this essay with his earlier work and with the way he connected race and place in Harlem's earlier, more optimistic days, I will not treat *Montage* at length here; yet, it should be noted that in a letter to Arna Bontemps upon the completion of *Montage*, Hughes wrote that it was a "tour de force." It represented Harlem using what he saw as the definitive aesthetic mode of the twentieth century, the collage (Rampersad, *Life of Langston Hughes* 2:151). It captured the essence of the place not by mere description or by a definitive statement, but rather by blending together the diversity of the neighborhood and presenting it directly. And in this, *Montage* perhaps crystallizes and summarizes the cultural geography Hughes develops in his earlier work. In response to the Great Migration, in response to the uncertain yet heady optimism surrounding Harlem in its early years, in response to the forced uprooting faced by African American communities both during and after emancipation, Hughes worked to create community roots and cultural continuities not by definitive statement, but by blending together cultural formations from across geographical distances. In establishing a theory of place based around routes as much as roots, and in imagining a Harlem not provincial or hermetically sealed but open to new arrivals and strengthened by diversity, Hughes recalibrated the relationship between culture and place. In this quality of his work it is possible not only to see his progressiveness, but also his modernism.

## NOTES

1. Paul Gilroy's work in *The Black Atlantic* has been very influential in this regard. See also Hazel Carby, *Cultures in Babylon.* Patricia Yeager, ed., *The Geography of Identity,* collects a number of provocative essays theorizing a "postnational geography."

2. This distinction between "routes" and "roots" is helpfully articulated by David C. Nicholls in *Conjuring the Folk.* Nicholls uses the distinction to describe the relationship between migration and folk culture in his analysis of African American literature.

3. Nicholas Lemann refocused attention on the Great Migration with his widely popular *The Promised Land* which became a television miniseries. Joe William Trotter, ed., *The Great Migration in Historical Perspective* is also helpful in understanding this movement. For a literary critical perspective on the Great Migration, see Nicholls, *Conjuring the Folk* and Lawrence R. Rodgers, *Canaan Bound.*

4. With Arnold Rampersad's new edition of Hughes's poems in the University of Missouri Press's *Collected Works of Langston Hughes* series, reading *The Weary Blues* as a volume has become much easier to do. The new edition gathers Hughes's poems in their original volume arrangements, including epigraphs, forewords, and titled sections of poems within volumes. Previously, the standard edition of Hughes's poems had been Rampersad's and Roessel's *The Collected Poems of Langston Hughes* (New York: Alfred A. Knopf, 1994); in this earlier edition, poems were arranged chronologically, with only Hughes's 1951 volume *Montage of a Dream Deferred* appearing intact. The new edition enables critical readings of larger, volume-wide patterns in Hughes's work, readings that had been difficult since his individual volumes have been largely out of print for decades.

5. Houston Baker in his influential *Modernism and the Harlem Renaissance* argues that the Harlem Renaissance was a crucial moment in the development of twentieth century literature, and questions definitions of modernism that arbitrarily exclude African American writing. In another essay, Arnold Rampersad argues that African American writers "responded to the age" in ways equally diverse and innovative as their white counterparts see Rampersad, "Langston Hughes and Approaches to Modernism." For information on the social construction of modernist texts, see Jerome McGann, *Black Riders.*

6. In a letter to Van Vechten, in response to the news that Covarrubias would be working on *The Weary Blues,* Hughes wrote enthusiastically: "I am so glad Covarrubias is going to do the cover. I like his work and it should go well with the book" (Bernard 15).

7. For other accounts of rapid demographic shifts in Harlem between 1880–1920, see Lewis, and Huggins.

8. George Bornstein in his study *Material Modernism* recuperates bibliographic elements from the early editions—color illustrations by the white artist Winold Reiss, for example—which highlighted the collaborative quality of the anthology.

## WORKS CITED

Baker, Houston A. Jr., *Modernism and the Harlem Renaissance*. Chicago: University of Chicago Press, 1987.

Bernard, Emily, ed. *Remember Me To Harlem: The Letters of Langston Hughes and Carl Van Vechten, 1925–1964*. New York: Knopf, 2001.

Bornstein, George. *Material Modernism: The Politics of the Page*. Cambridge: Cambridge University Press, 2001.

Carby, Hazel. *Cultures in Babylon: Black Britain and African America*. London: Verso, 1999.

Douglas, Ann. *Terrible Honesty: Mongrel Manhattan in the 1920s*. New York: Noonday, 1995.

Gilroy, Paul. The *Black Atlantic: Modernity and Double Consciousness*. Cambridge: Harvard University Press, 1993.

Grossman, James R. *Land of Hope: Chicago, Black Southerners, and the Great Migration*. Chicago: University of Chicago Press, 1989.

Huggins, Nathan. *The Harlem Renaissance*. Oxford: Oxford University Press, 1971.

Hughes, Langston. *The Big Sea*. New York: Knopf, 1940.

———. *Collected Works of Langston Hughes: The Poems*. Ed. Arnold Rampersad. 3 vols. Columbia: University of Missouri Press, 2001.

———. "Dream Variation." *Survey Graphic* (March 1925): p. 633.

———. "The Negro Artist and the Racial Mountain." *The Nation* (23 June 1926): pp. 692–694.

———. "Poem." *Survey Graphic* (March 1925): p. 633.

Hutchinson, George. *The Harlem Renaissance in Black and White*. Cambridge: Belknap Harvard, 1995.

Johnson, James Weldon. "Harlem: The Culture Capital." *The New Negro: Voices of the Harlem Renaissance*. 1925. Ed. Alain Locke. New York: Touchstone, 1997.

Lemann, Nicholas. *The Promised Land: The Great Black Migration and How it Changed America*. New York: Vintage, 1991.

Locke, Alain. "Harlem." *Survey Graphic* (March 1925): p. 630.

McGann, Jerome. *Black Riders: The Visible Language of Modernism*. Princeton: Princeton University Press, 1993.

"Negro Poet Sings of Life in Big Cities." *Washington Post,* 6 February 1927, 5F.

Nicholls, David C. *Conjuring the Folk: Forms of Modernity in African America*. Ann Arbor: University of Michigan Press, 2000.

Rampersad, Arnold. Introduction. *The New Negro: Voices of the Harlem Renaissance*. 1925. Ed. Alain Locke. New York: Touchstone, 1997.

———. "Langston Hughes and Approaches to Modernism." *Harlem Renaissance: Revaluations*. Ed. Amritjit Singh, et. al. New York: Garland, 1989: pp. 49–71.

———. *The Life of Langston Hughes*. 2 vols. Oxford: Oxford University Press, 1986.

Rodgers, Lawrence R. *Canaan Bound: The African American Great Migration Novel*. Urbana: University of Illinois Press, 1997.

Smethurst, James. *The New Red Negro: The Literary Left and African American Poetry, 1930–1946*. Oxford: Oxford University Press, 1999.

Trotter, Joe William, ed. *The Great Migration in Historical Perspective*. Bloomington: University of Indiana Press, 1991.

Yeager, Patricia, ed. *The Geography of Identity*. Ann Arbor: University of Michigan Press, 1996.

JONATHAN SCOTT

# Advanced, Repressed, and Popular: Langston Hughes During the Cold War [1]

You don't make things popular just because you want them to be simple, but because you want people to understand them. But when people understand things, then they demand more. And so I think the question is, how do you combine the advanced with the popular?

—Amiri Baraka

In 1948, the Langston Hughes canon included twenty volumes of fiction and poetry, a broad range of magazine and journal articles, a host of short stories, a Broadway play, a Broadway musical, a Hollywood screenplay, eight radio scripts, and more than a dozen song lyrics. By 1952, Hughes told friends that his books were getting "simpler and simpler and younger and younger" (Berry 1983, 320), for it was during the 1950s that he returned to writing for young people, and his popular Jesse B. Simple character, producing four "Simple" books as well as seven history texts for young people. But the announcement also revealed the particular social and political circumstances that he faced as a professional African American writer during the high period of the cold war. Despite an outpouring of writing in every genre and literary form within his reach, more than a hundred appearances on the lecture circuit in the United States and Canada, and (belated) canonization by the American Academy of Arts and Letters, Hughes remained unable to support himself as a writer. Ironically, it was not proceeds from his published

*College Literature*, vol. 33, no. 2 (2006), pp. 30–51. Copyright © 2006 *College Literature*.

works but a $1,000 cash grant from the Academy—the largest single sum he had ever received during his career—that provided the down payment on his first permanent residence, a Harlem townhouse that he moved into in July 1948.

By comparison, William Faulkner was making $1,250 a week as a professional writer during the 1930s and 40s, and he was bringing in thousands of dollars a piece for screenplays and the movie rights to his short stories and novels, in one case $50,000 for *Intruder in the Dust* (Minter 1980, 220). While Faulkner was securing a lucrative writer-in-residence position at the University of Virginia, Hughes was being denied a poet-in-residence job at Texas Southern, a position offered and then withdrawn after threats and intimidation from anticommunist and white supremacist groups at the University. In fact, Hughes was an early victim of the kind of political firing that would eventually force hundreds of left-wing American college and university professors from the academy (Wittner 1974, 124).

Hughes described his situation as "literary sharecropping," a term he would use for the rest of his career (Nichols 1980, 292). The term drew attention more to the persistence of racial oppression in the United States than to the punishing effects of the anticommunist movement on political writers and artists like himself, since African American artists had been victims of "blacklisting" long before the creation of the House Un-American Activities Committee. "Negro writers, being black, have always been blacklisted in radio and TV," Hughes told the Authors League of America in 1951 (1957, 46). Unwilling to accept that his participation in the communist movement of the 20s and 30s had made all subsequent attempts to enter the U.S. mainstream doubly hard, Hughes pushed forward, taking on projects that he was less than passionate about, or that he could never finish. His literary agent in the 1950s, Ivan von Auw, characterized Hughes's response to the cold war conjuncture thusly: "He didn't concentrate enough on just one project. Instead, he seemed easily distracted, always running all over the place. He honestly believed that the way to get ahead was to take on everything offered. I think he was wrong; but perhaps he had no choice, really" (Rampersad 1988, 196).

Yet, as I will argue, to say that Hughes "had no choice really" is an undialectical way of seeing things, for the circumscribed choices he did make during the cold war were based on a rather systematic approach to writing, teaching, and producing literature. The treatment of Hughes's method in this essay aims to accomplish three things. First, to challenge the prevailing "common sense" view of Hughes in the U.S. academy that sees him, almost exclusively, as a folk poet, which has come at the expense of his other advanced contributions to aesthetics; second, to dispel the myth that Hughes abandoned socialist politics after being targeted directly and relentlessly by the anticommunist movement; and third, to show, pedagogically, the felicitous uses today of his theory of English composition, which is laid out in his 1954 text *The Book of Rhythms,* the basis of which was a writing workshop he directed in Chicago in 1949.

### More Than a Folk Poet: Hughes's Theory of Aesthetics

Three decades after announcing famously in "The Negro Artist and the Racial Mountain" his purpose as a writer—to help win self-determination for African American artists—Hughes found himself at an impasse. Writing geared for the mass market brought harsh criticism from the literary establishment, while erstwhile publishers replied to writing from the left with one rejection slip after another. To make matters worse, his opportunities on the lecture circuit dwindled, largely due to the success of a decade-long propaganda campaign against him by the white supremacist, anticommunist group, America First (Berry 1983, 316). The anticommunist right's aim was to force Hughes, one of the world's most recognizable left cultural workers, to renounce socialism, and to undermine the new links he had begun to make between African American writers and a new African American reading public. The crusade against Hughes culminated in 1953 when he was summoned to appear before Senator Joseph McCarthy's Permanent Sub-Committee on Investigations. In the assessment of Hughes scholar George Cunningham, "He hoped that his readings would help to build a Negro reading public for the works of Negro authors, and at the same time, to stimulate and inspire the younger Negroes in the South toward creative literature, and the use of their own folklore, songs, and racial background as the basis for expression" (1994, 35). His situation as a writer deeply circumscribed and overdetermined by a repressive nexus of anti-black and anticommunist political forces, Hughes returned to work on two unfinished projects: his *Simple Saga* and a series of popular histories for children. That the *Simple* stories saved his career is certain; less clear are the relations between popular culture and literature in his writing during the height of the cold war, and how Hughes approached the problem as an intellectual.

As a literary response to the cold war, both projects are interesting objects of study. Hughes's shrewd point in his *Simple* columns about the dual function of the color line—to keep not only black folks down and out but reds too—could be easily applied to popular culture and social democracy, for it was during the early stages of the cold war that American anticommunist intellectuals launched the first organized attack on popular culture. On trial were specific art forms, styles, genres, mediums, and aesthetics, since the sole criterion for determining guilt or innocence was the subject's mainstream or popular *accessibility,* including children's literature, photographic essays, the "New Hollywood," writing workshops, Broadway musicals, and other forms favored by Hughes.

As the 1954 U.S. Army pamphlet *How to Spot a Communist* revealed, the attack on popular culture from the anticommunist establishment was a logical corollary of the U.S. right wing's intention to destroy all forms of popular democracy in the society. The pamphlet, for example, asserted that a communist could be identified by his or her "predisposition to discuss civil rights, social and religious discrimination, the immigration laws, [and] antisubversive legislation"; communists could also be spotted by their use of the terms "chauvinism," "book-burning," "colonialism," "demagogy," "witch-hunt," "reactionary," "progressive," and "exploitation" (Caute 1978, 296). For creative artists like Hughes, the anticommunist movement's narrowing of themes and subjects, as well as genres and forms by which they could be expressed, to only those which affirmed God, family, and country helped to create the conditions for a systematic, negative critique of U.S. society. In response, Hughes utilized the idea of negative critique, or "negative resonance," to borrow Adorno and Horkheimer's formulation, in his writing for young people. The attack on "affirmative culture" by the right—the foreclosure of anything that affirmed socioeconomic equality and the enforcement of civil rights in U.S. society—left wide open, dialectically, whole fields of popular culture through which the ideals of high art, such as rupture and dissonance, could be carried out by American artists.

What Hughes's output during the high period of the cold war illuminates is twofold: first, the sea-change in American popular culture from "affirmative culture" to the arts of "negative resonance"; and second, the fresh line of intervention by which socialist intellectuals and artists could imagine a political unity of the U.S. working classes. In addition to bringing to light the emergent popular-democratic movements for social change, such as the struggle for desegregation, another goal of the international alliance of scientists and cultural workers was the dismantling of atomic weaponry in the United States and Europe. For Hughes, the task was to attract American workers to civil rights struggle and social democracy with an advanced literary aesthetic and a steady diet of aesthetic forms and structures that raised their standards, that met their own desires, and that mirrored their own way of seeing and feeling the world.

In 1942, Hughes described succinctly his intellectual formation. If read next to the anticommunists' condemnation of popular culture, his list of influences and favorite public figures amounted to a total self-indictment:

> My chief literary influences have been Paul Laurence Dunbar, Carl Sandburg, and Walt Whitman. My favorite public figures include Jimmy Durante, Marlene Dietrich, Mary McLeod Bethune, Mrs.

Franklin D. Roosevelt, Marian Anderson, and Henry Armstrong. I live in Harlem, New York City. I am unmarried. I like Tristan, goat's milk, short novels, lyric poems, heat, simple folk, boats, and bullfights; I dislike Aida, parsnips, long novels, narrative poems, cold, pretentious folk, busses, and bridge. . . . My writing has been largely concerned with the depicting of Negro life in America. I have made a number of translations of the poems of Negro writers in Cuba and Haiti. In 1931–32 I lectured throughout the South in the Negro schools and colleges there, and one of my main interests is the encouragement of literary ability among colored writers. The winter of 1934 I spent in Mexico, where I translated a number of Mexican and Cuban stories. I was the only American Negro newspaper correspondent in Spain, in 1937—for the Baltimore Afro-American. I am executive director of the Harlem Suitcase Theater, the only Negro Worker's Theater in New York. I received the Palms Intercollegiate Poetry Award in 1927, the Harmon Award of Literature in 1931, in 1934 was selected by Dr. Charles A. Beard as one of America's twenty-five "most interesting" personages with a "socially conscious" attitude, and in 1935 was granted a Guggenheim Fellowship for creative work.

(Kunitz and Haycraft 1942, 684)

In the context of Hughes's relationship to children's literature, which would figure prominently in his career during the 1950s, Dwight MacDonald's denunciation of the genre in his 1953 essay "A Theory of Mass Culture" can be read as openly jingoistic. MacDonald's problem with the children's literature of the 30s and 40s was that it had "adultized children," replacing the popular symbol of Uncle Sam with that of Peter Pan (Rosenberg 1957, 66). Under the aegis of anticommunism, MacDonald's attack on juvenile literature was both a realignment of the ideologies of patriarchy and American empire and a thinly-veiled argument for reversing the democratic gains made in American literature and culture during the Popular Front period, the popularization of children's literature being one such significant gain. For as Christopher Lasch has argued in his perceptive essay "The Cultural Cold War," the principal stratagem of American anticommunism during the 50s was to conflate the aims and ideals of bourgeois liberalism with those of revolutionary socialism. For fellow travelers such as MacDonald, Lasch writes, anticommunism

represented a new stage in their running polemic against bourgeois sentimentality and weakness, bourgeois "utopianism" and bourgeois materialism. That explains their eagerness to connect Bolshevism with liberalism—to show that the two ideologies sprang from a common root and that it was the softness and sentimentality of bourgeois liberals that had paradoxically allowed communism . . . to pervade Western society in the thirties and early forties.

(Lasch 1969, 68)

Thus, the claim that Hughes's response to the rise of American anti-communism was to choose a less "political" kind of writing (children's literature and the *Simple* stories, among other popular, sentimental literary forms) is belied by the fact that the anticommunist movement considered genres and forms such as these to be no less "red" than radical political organizations. To be sure, Hughes took no chances with the anticommunist right, severing ties with leftist organizations, including the American Labor Party and the National Council of American-Soviet Friendship, which had come under investigation by the FBI and the Special Committee on Un-American Activities (Rampersad 1988, 198). But his turn toward popular literature and culture cannot be read in the same light, a fact that Hughes was reminded of constantly.

For example, when the first book-length collection of his *Simple* stories, *Simple Speaks His Mind,* went to press in the spring of 1950, Hughes's editor at Simon and Schuster made a concerted effort to disguise the politics of the book, describing it as a "charming portrayal" of Negro life in Harlem. The editor dismissed Hughes's objections to the advertisements, insisting that Simon and Schuster could not afford to "frighten prospective readers away by indicating that it is, in any sense, a tract" (Rampersad 1988, 178). In terms of his own position on American popular culture, since the mid-30s Hughes had been an outspoken critic of white racism in Hollywood and on the air. In 1945, for instance, he responded to Columbia University Professor of Communications Erik Barnouw's query about race and radio thus:

Radio furnishes some very good Negro entertainment, but comparatively little more, seldom touching on the drama or the problems of Negro life in America . . . And it continues to keep alive the stereotype of the dialect-speaking, amiably moronic Negro servant as the chief representative of our racial group on the air.

(Barnouw 1945, 284)

As Barnouw noted at the time, not only had Hughes himself expressed a strong interest in writing a daytime serial about an African American family, but also his name was the first mentioned whenever the subject was raised in radioland (1945, 285). In fact, Hughes's first impulse was to make the would-be popular *Simple* stories into a radio program, not into short fiction or a novel; the networks, however, remained either indifferent or openly hostile to such a proposal (Rampersad 1988, 155). Reading his unaired 1945 radio drama "Booker T. Washington in Atlanta"—an experimental piece based on the forms and concepts of arena theater—it is clear that American radio listeners, as well as the medium itself, missed out when Hughes was banished *de facto* from the airwaves (Barnouw 1945, 283–294).

Exiled from Hollywood, radio, and television, Hughes still managed a twenty-year march through the fledgling sites of American popular culture. His two main interventions in popular aesthetics were the *Simple* stories and his popular histories for young people. But there were other interventions as well, interventions that laid the groundwork for his work on Simple and in children's literature. In the 50s and 60s, Hughes worked on several collaborations that established the creative method by which he would carry out these later interventions. They are worth noting also for what they show about the specific obstacles he faced as a socialist African American writer in cold-war America.

The first collaboration of the 50s was a photo-essay with African American photographer Roy DeCarava, *The Sweet Flypaper of Life* (1955), and the second was a pictorial history of African Americans co-authored by the Jewish American scholar Milton Meltzer, *A Pictorial History of the Negro in America* (1956). Finding a publisher for *A Pictorial History* proved extremely frustrating for Hughes and Meltzer, as more than ten firms turned down the project. According to Meltzer, "Two or three even said that blacks don't read, so why bother with them? And a few suggested going to a foundation, since no normal publisher would take on such a pointless task" (Rampersad 1988, 248). In the case of *The Sweet Flypaper of Life,* a publisher was not hard to find; the problem was that Simon and Schuster had cut costs on the book, unbeknownst to Hughes and DeCarava, by printing pocket-size paperback editions rather than the big and glossy coffee table books that were standard for works of popular photography. In the mid-60s, Hughes worked again with Meltzer on a pictorial history, *Black Magic: A Pictorial History of the Negro in American Entertainment* (1967), arguably the most comprehensive history of African American popular culture ever published.

*Black Magic* is an exhaustive account of the origins of virtually every African American popular art form, from major elements such as hand-clapping, stick dancing, and the drum-beating rhythms of the eighteenth and nineteenth centuries, as well as the spirituals and folk culture, to constitutive elements such as the making of homemade banjos and drums, and a list of the first African American radio commentators and newscasters. The text is filled with an amazing array of esoterica, the *stuff* of any lasting book on popular culture. For example, in their ninth chapter, "Just About

Everything," Hughes and Meltzer provide a fascinating history of the first African American "exhibits" in P. T. Barnum's traveling circus. Barnum's first set of Siamese Twins—the fourteen-year-old Carolina twins, Millie and Christina—are discussed, along with Barnum's first "Fat Ladies," who were actually blues singers looking for steady work—Big Maybelle and Beulah Bryant. There's also a story about Barnum's first "Giants," one of whom was an African American Civil War veteran named Admiral Dot. Admiral Dot stood 7 feet 11 inches tall and weighed 600 pounds; the text is accompanied by a rare daguerreotype of the Admiral. There are also brief histories of forgotten pioneers such as "the world's most beloved nightclub hostess," Ada "Bricktop" Smith Du Conge. Made into a celebrity in Paris during the early 20s with the help of Louis Aragon, Bricktop ran the most popular nightclub in Paris for nearly twenty years. In addition to the brief histories of individual pathfinders, there are short histories of institutions such as the Lincoln Theater in Harlem, the Lafayette Players, and the American Negro Theater, which began in the basement of the New York Public Library. But perhaps the most delightful and useful aspect of the book is, not surprisingly, the graphics. Mixed throughout the text are playbills, posters, signed photographs, advertisements, rare photographs of artists at work, newspaper clippings, drawings, and diagrams.

These three texts belong to the coffee table book genre, and as such constitute one of three main lines of intervention into popular literature chosen by Hughes in the cold war period. Contemporary critics have placed the other two—short story fiction and juvenile literature—into the category of "high" literature, yet the relations between the final form of these works and the "wreckin' shop floor" from whence they came have not been recognized or explored. The following notes are meant to elucidate these relations and to advance a concept— the "collage aesthetic"—that could account for the logic and direction of Hughes's astonishingly diverse and prolific literary output during the cold war. The dialectic of Hughes's literary production during the 50s and early 60s is precisely the diversifying of popular aesthetic forms, preferences, and practices from within an increasingly narrow, monolithic, segregationist, and antipopular system of mass culture.

### Art for the Sake of Conscious Youth: Making Politics Popular

When Hughes's writings for young people are mentioned by literary scholars and critics, his juvenile poetry and short fiction are ranked above the popular histories he wrote, if the latter are acknowledged at all. Like his radio scripts in the 40s and 50s, it can be argued that Hughes's histories for young people are neglected today *in spite of* their certain success in the market place and the classroom. In this way, the aim of the present essay is to situate these writings in the context of the cold war in order to better understand the unrecognized vitality of Hughes's relations with socialist politics and popular aesthetics, and to appreciate his overriding purpose in these works through an analysis of one in particular, *The Book of Rhythms*.

In terms of African American youth culture and political education, the veteran rapper Chuck D issued in 1996 a blueprint on the topic, which he titled "Ten Resentments of the Industry." The ideas expressed in Chuck D's blueprint reflect important elements of Hughes's relationship to mainstream American culture; it is helpful, then, to quote generously from his piece. Four of Chuck D's resentments are:

> I resent the fact that between ownership and creativity in the entertainment and music industry, blacks are not presented the options on how they can participate in it, besides singing, rapping, dancing, telling jokes or acting. . . . I resent the pedestal that we human beings place on others based on minimal manufactured achievements. The illusion of so-called stars has created, through culture, the imaginary perception of falling off. You never fall off if you know where you are. Star spelled backwards is rats. And the attitude of a rat is what many have adopted and portrayed to its public: slam-dunking, rhyming, singing when it meant nothing a hundred and fifty years ago in the United States. So what's the big deal now? . . . I resent the cowardly lack of voice leadership by industry blacks under the spotlight projected by the media, on real issues, on their refusal to name and acknowledge real leaders without that spotlight, to make real changes in life regularly. . . . I resent the fact that we do not keep and store facts about us, leaving others to create facts about us. Television and radio has a serious imbalance of entertainment and information, imbalances of show and business, therefore steering youth culture to focus goals on only that of being an athlete or entertainer.
>
> (Chuck D 1996)

Chuck D's resentments illuminate a series of questions relevant for considering Hughes's likewise conflicted relationship with American popular culture. Given the persistence of racial oppression in United States society, which has given us a white racist national-popular culture, how do African American popular artists develop their own popular audiences and independently carry out their own artistic plans and projects? To phrase the problem differently, how do African American artists create popular art independent of white privileged mass culture so long as popular democratic culture itself remains dependent on it? Moreover, how could independent

African American voices be raised up (Chuck D's concept of "voice leadership") in a system designed at every level to reduce them to one undifferentiated social status? For Chuck D, every constraint on African American popular expression, and every form of exploitation and co-optation obtaining in the American entertainment industry, is a result of "white Americanism," in the sense given it by W.E.B. DuBois in *The Souls of Black Folk:* the glorification of "dollars and smartness" at the expense of "light-hearted but determined Negro humility" (1969, 52).

My suggestion is that Chuck D's ten point critique of U.S. media culture is Hughesian in aim and conception. To put it differently, Chuck D's critique, presented perspicaciously on his CD *The Autobiography of Mistachuck* (1996), was enabled by Hughes's work during the 50s. Although each of Chuck D's ten points could easily generate separate empirical research projects in American popular culture, these four in particular serve as fruitful departure points, or concepts, for an analysis of Hughes's popular histories for youth, including specifically his writing workshops, the basis of the *Book of Rhythms*. First, the need to independently store facts about African Americans in order to counter the media's invention of "facts" about African Americans is the premise of both Hughes's books about African American heroes and *First Book of Rhythms*, among his other works for children. Second, because the whole star system of U.S. media culture helps reproduce some of the most pernicious anti-Black tropes and images in the American national-popular—from the use and abuse of sports stars like O.J. Simpson and Dennis Rodman to politician-stars like former Detroit mayor Coleman Young (a target of the white national media throughout the 1980s) and Marion Barry (the target of the 1990s)—this system must be counter-attacked. Third, because "the imbalance," as he puts it, "between ownership and creativity in the entertainment and music industry" has forever delimited "the options on how they [aspiring African American creative artists] can participate in it, besides singing, rapping, dancing, telling jokes or acting," a new relationship between popular aesthetics and independent intellectual and political work is the order of the day. In my view, Hughes accomplished this task through his role as a producer of popular culture and a teacher of writing.

The need to independently store facts about African Americans was always linked for Hughes to the nurturing and development of politically active and independent African American popular audiences. What is at stake is the writer's *method*. In terms of method, Hughes approached writing during the 30s and 40s from two angles simultaneously. Politically, he served as a Black national advocate for international socialism, mainly through his journalism and poetry, while as an artist he asserted the international scale of the American national struggle to abolish racial oppression, precisely by making his interventions at the level of national popular culture and through the formation of *national* popular aesthetic tastes and preferences. In contrast to Black communists like Claude McKay and Richard Wright, for instance, Hughes approached literature as a dynamic site from which these two battles could be fought at the same time, "not singly but together, not successively but together, each growing and aiding each," in the words of DuBois (1969, 52). Especially in his popular histories for youth, Hughes set out to answer DuBois's call, and through literary forms newly accessible to the masses of American society.

As Cedric Robinson has observed astutely in his history of the black radical tradition *Black Marxism* (1983), what distinguished McKay and Wright from their black radical co-workers was the fact that they came to communism directly through black nationalism: McKay through Garvey-ism and Wright through the black working class of the American South. According to Robinson, this is why they ended-up rejecting the communist solution to racial oppression (1983, 417–418). Yet had he studied Langston Hughes—in fact, not a single mention is made of Hughes in *Black Marx-ism*—a different conclusion might have come from his book: that commu-nism and black radicalism are not irreconcilable ways of seeing the world, and not therefore doomed to mutual distrust and indifference, but rather are actually one of the more successful crossovers of our times, a far more successful crossover than that between, say, European-American trade unionism and communism, or environmentalism and communism. More-over, that these supposedly antithetical worldviews could find common ground in popular literature—in the literary collage form and in children's literature—calls into question Robinson's thesis. Hughes's remarkable suc-cess as a black socialist writer goes a long way in explaining his omission from Robinson's study.

Although the conclusions drawn in *Black Marxism* cannot be ade-quately addressed here, they do provide a starting point for understanding Hughes's writings for youth. First, Hughes's emphasis on the worldliness or internationalism of African American culture circumvented the polar opposition between black nationalism and international communism by presenting and promoting a way of thinking that depended on both for its "historical uniqueness," to use one of Robinson's central terms. Second, his writings for children in particular revealed as a strategic site of political struggle, at the height of the cold war, the task of winning over to social-ism America's youth. Despite the fact that many of these works left out DuBois, for instance—a point repeated needlessly in the scholarship on Hughes, since the works in question were not about intellectuals—or that several were grossly censored by anticommunist editors, there are excellent reasons to study them. That they have not been studied at all tells us two things: that Chuck D's resentments of white American media culture speak directly to a failure of method and not so much to questions of media access and representation, nor to the commodification of African American culture, which have been the main *foci* of antiracist media critique; and that, more obviously, a great deal of critical work remains to be done on the writing of Hughes.

As Chuck D stresses, the opportunity to participate in the mass production of popular art has worked insidiously against its historic creators by "steering youth culture to focus goals on only that of being an athlete or entertainer." By saturating the U.S. media with affirmations of one-sided conceptions of blackness, the task of regulating all the imaginary social relations needed to continue racial oppression in U.S. society has been made doubly easy. According to the terms laid out by Chuck D, the pillars of the American national-popular are four white racist tropes, reinvented as the current conjuncture requires: 1) African American contentedness (singing); 2) fear of, and lust for, blackness (rapping); 3) loyal and patriotic ex-slaves (dancing); and 4) African American incompetence and buffoonery (telling jokes and acting). If DuBois' concept of Black America's "three gifts"—the gifts of story and song, of sweat and brawn, and of cheer (1969, 275)—is kept in mind, the missing literary trope here is transparent: "sweat and brawn," or labor power. The creative path through which African American labor could be made into a new archetype, while at the same time undermining the reigning four, would open up new creative methods for *all* American writers. As Ishmael Reed nicely put it in his Introduction to *19 Necromancers from Now,*

> the inability of some students to "understand" works written by Afro-American authors is traceable to an inability to understand the American experience as rooted in slang, dialect, vernacular, argot, and all of the other put-down terms the [English department] faculty uses for those who have the gall to deviate from the true and proper way of English.
>
> (Reed 1970, x)

Among those forms that Reed believes "deviate" from what is taught in the American academy are detective novels and dime-store westerns, a point that helps illuminate boldly the specific direction of Hughes's interventions in the 50s. In a phrase, *the liberation of American literature,* to borrow the title of V.F. Calverton's work of literary history and criticism from the 1930s, must come through the popular in order for artistic autonomy to become possible in U.S. society. For Hughes, the path of the "popular" went directly through young people.

### Hughes' Rhythm Writing Workshops: Dynamic Conformism

"There is no rhythm in the world without movement" is how Hughes opens *The First Book of Rhythms,* the second of six children's books he wrote for Franklin Watts during the 50s and 60s. The first, *The First Book of Negroes,* had been criticized by Negro intellectuals for leaving out any mention of DuBois or Paul Robeson. In 1965, however, he explained the circumstances that he had faced at the time:

> It was at the height of the McCarthy Red baiting era, and publishers had to go out of their way to keep books, particularly children's books, from being attacked, as well as schools and libraries that might purchase books. . . . It was impossible at that time to get anything into children's books about either Dr. DuBois or Paul Robeson.
>
> (Rampersad 1988, 230–231)

As Arnold Rampersad has noted, "it was taken for granted by . . . [Hughes's] various publishers that even brief references to DuBois and other radicals were out of the question in a text aimed at children. Such books were virtually indefensible when attacked by the right wing" (1988, 230). To give just one example, Rampersad points out that the first edition of *First Book of Negroes* had featured a picture of Josephine Baker, but after a New York columnist threatened to attack the book unless all references to her were removed—on the grounds that Baker was a communist—she disappeared from the text in the next printing (1988, 230). Not only were Hughes's children's books vulnerable to anticommunist attack, but his critically acclaimed poetry suffered too:

> Just about everyone at the firm of Henry Holt who had been involved in publishing Hughes's *Montage of a Dream Deferred* in 1951 and *Laughing to Keep from Crying* in 1952 had been summarily fired and various contracts canceled. Stock of the books, including *Montage,* was sold off cheaply—all because of pressure, Langston was told, from reactionary groups backed by oil-rich conservatives. "That Texas oil money suddenly found them their list!" Hughes joked desperately about the fired editors. "All due to a few little poetries."
>
> ·  (Rampersad 1988, 85)

Next to his series of "First" books, his photo-essay with Roy DeCarava (*The Sweet Flypaper of Life*), as well as his history of the NAACP entitled *Fight for Freedom, Montage of a Dream Deferred* and *Laughing to Keep from*

*Crying* were indeed "little poetries." The children's books brought him a much wider audience, as did *The Sweet Flypaper of Life*. More importantly, the whole mode of writing was different. *First Book of Rhythms*, for example, came directly out of Hughes's teaching experiences at the Laboratory School in Chicago, where in 1949 he led interdisciplinary writing workshops for eighth graders. In contradiction to Ivan von Auw's opinion that Hughes's method during this period was scatterbrained, the project in fact demanded rigorous planning and execution. Synthesizing his research on the subject, Hughes scholar Robert O'Meally writes:

> According to his carefully wrought lesson plans, Hughes led a series of discussions of rhythm in plants, animals, and the universe, as well as rhythm in human body movements, speech, music, visual arts, and, of course, poetry. His notes indicate that for homework students were to prepare reports comparing rhythms they had observed. One was scheduled to make a presentation on music and baseball, another on swimming and modern dance
>
> (O'Meally 1995, 50)

Like his 1929 cultural studies project at Lincoln University, Hughes's cross-disciplinary intervention twenty years later (e.g., to see in baseball the same logic of development and change that one finds in popular music) witnessed a kind of formal meeting between two distinct partners. This approach gives a sense of Hughes's purpose as an intellectual and how he understood his own role as writer in the world. In terms of the Chicago workshops, his role was to assist in the intellectual-moral development of youth through wide ranging forays in popular culture.

In this regard, *Book of Rhythms'* table of contents is instructive: it indicates some of the truths that Hughes wanted the students of his experimental laboratory to discover on their own. Organized according to seventeen chapters, each proposes a different research possibility, line of inquiry, and independent writing exercise. The first chapter, "Let's Make a Rhythm," presents the method of discovery, which constitutes the first half of the book's object of study. The second half begins with the ninth chapter, "Athletics," which relies on Hughes's concept of "organic data," such as the operation of industrial equipment and other mass-organized activities, as well as their result: the *artifacts* of mass production. From a formalist, grammar-centered pedagogical standpoint, seeing in a book on writing a chapter entitled "Furniture" is beguiling. Here, though, Hughes is interested not so much in deconstructing and "rephrasing" the bland schematisms of Anglo-American English studies as in laying the groundwork for a kind of "dynamic conformism" where young people could be socialized into what

Hughes termed in his Simple columns the art of "listening fluently." In this new situation, however, the verb "to listen" is replaced by the verb "to move," for as he plainly states in the opening page of *Book of Rhythms*, "rhythm comes from movement" (1954, 1).

To move fluently requires coordination skills, first and foremost. Since the workshops were writing workshops, Hughes's students started with pad and pencil. "Make a point of a triangle, then a smaller one, then a smaller one than that, then still a smaller one, so that they keep on across a sheet of paper, all joined together," he instructed. "Again, you have made a rhythm. Your hand, your eye, and your pencil all moving together have made on the paper a rhythm that you can see with your eyes" (1954, 1). Then shifting quickly to other sensory skills, the aural and the aerobic, he prepares them for the second part of this start-up exercise. "You can make a rhythm of sound by clapping your hands or tapping your foot," Hughes told them. "You can make a body rhythm by swaying your body from side to side or by making circles in the air with your arms" (1–2). At this point, the students go from making triangles to making circles: "Now make a large circle on a paper. Inside your circle make another circle. Inside that one make another one. See how these circles almost seem to move, for you have left something of your own movement there, and your own feeling of place and roundness. Your circles are not quite like the circles of anyone else in the world, because you are not like anyone else. Your handwriting has a rhythm that is entirely your own. No one writes like anyone else" (2).

This first writing exercise is also the first lesson of dynamic conformism: the exercise is common, as are the tools and the procedures, yet the outcome is highly personalized, even idiosyncratic. In other words, to arrive at the axiom "No one writes like anyone else," the student writers must first engage in a collective writing activity and then follow, in their own unique way, the teacher's general directive to all. But before this can happen, students must learn how to write. "How do you write?" begins the next section of the first chapter. Verb-subject agreement is not the focus, nor is the rule for avoiding run-on sentences, the use of a period and a capital letter, etc. Instead, Hughes has them create their own illustrated rhythm patterns. "Make a rhythm of peaks, starting from the bottom of one peak," he instructs. "Make another rhythm like it, but start from the top. Then do the same thing again, but put one rhythm over the other, and you have a pattern. Fill in with your crayon and you have a pattern of diamond shapes. Rhythm makes patterns" (1954, 2–3).

As far as learning the skills of coordination, it would be appropriate here to make a link between Hughes and Bontemps' collage method in *Poetry of the Negro* and *Book of Rhythms*, not only because the rhythm writing workshops took place the same year they completed their landmark anthology, but because the workshop exercises themselves often produced, spontaneously, a collage aesthetic. The basis of the literary collage is repetitions and the use of "multistrip" patterns. As Robert Farris Thompson has it in his brilliant study of West African aesthetics, *Flash of the Spirit,* one of the signal features of multistrip composition is a strategy "for recovering in a special West African way spontaneity in design, without which there can be neither vividness or strength in aesthetic structure" (1984, 211). In fact, the different patterns illustrated throughout *Book of Rhythms* follow closely the logic of West African textile making—the "rhythmized textiles" documented by Thompson (207). Moreover, a look at the illustrations gives a good indication of how Hughes proceeded in the writing workshops.

Created by the graphic artist Matt Wawiorka, the illustrations doubtless try to match the kinds of writing produced by Hughes and his students in the experimental laboratory. There are two good examples of rhythmized writing and drawing in the book that follow directly from Hughes's initial guidelines: the first a multistrip illustration consisting of a row of bowls and a row of plates, which curls up the right side of chapter fourteen, "Rhythms in Daily Life"; and the second a multistrip pattern that tries to capture the rhythms that moisture makes when it forms snowflakes, hail, rain, and icicles. The second illustration is in the fourth chapter, "Sources of Rhythm." Here, Hughes prefaced his remarks on the sources of rhythm by saying, in Hughesian fashion, that when it comes to rhythmical design, no race—to paraphrase Aimé Césaire—has a monopoly on beauty, strength, and intelligence, that there is room for *everybody's* rhythm at the rendezvous of victory. The opening page of chapter four reads as follows:

> Artists have used animals, trees, men, waves, flowers, and many other objects in nature for rhythms. In France 25,000 years ago the cave men made animal drawings on the walls of their caves.
>
> Later the flag lily, fleur-de-lis, became a rhythmical design that is the national symbol of France.
>
> African artists a thousand years ago made beautiful masks with rhythmical lines.
>
> In the sixteenth century a Spanish artist named El Greco sometimes made a man look like this.
>
> (Hughes 1954, 11)

A sketch of a tall and thin man accompanies the text, as does a drawing of the *fleur-de-lis.* Two pages later is the drawing of rain, snow, hail, and icicles. Thompson has suggested that one of the main variables in the making of West African rhythmized textiles "is a vibrant propensity for off-beat phrasing in the unfolding of overall design" (1984, 209). That is, major accents of one strip are staggered in relation to those of an adjoining strip, which does not become clear or purposeful until the whole of the composition is taken into account.

In the *Book of Rhythms* drawing, this same technique is in motion. First, there are three rhythmized lines or strips: rain, snow, and icicles. Second, the strips are juxtaposed according to their edges, by their roughest or boldest side; third, the snowflake rhythm designs—there are four—serve as the drawing's major accent. And four, the balls of hail are there to remind us that this design was made through constructive and purposeful human rhythm, and is not an accidental manifestation of desire nor a symptom of lack of desire. In terms of Hughes's fourth rhythm strategy—the *preempting of any assumption of accident,* to use Thompson's precise formulation—the balls of hail come in many different shapes and sizes yet always at the same interval of time, or section of space, on the page. The balls of hail function as satellites of the snowflakes, usually in groups of four or five. Likewise, the bursts of rain come in many different lengths and widths yet their frequency is a strict form of syncopation, with the accent on the long line (or the off-beat line) occurring every three rain-bursts, forming a 3/2 rhythm structure. Another strategy of rhythmized writing in the drawing is that, while the icicles provide the top of the drawing's border, as if hanging from a gutter, the bottom has none, and the left and right borderlines are given shape only by a group of two bursts of rain and a ball of hail.

Thompson says that this kind of strategy confirms "a love of aesthetic intensity" (1984, 209). What we can say in Hughes's case is that it also establishes a dynamic beginning for the instructor of writing. Hughes's method is an ingenious way of getting students thinking in terms of the rhythm patterns of prose and poetry writing, of lyrical flow, of word sequences, transitions, cadences, and caesuras. Already there is the room to start and stop as suits the writer, but in a disciplined, rhythmized way. In other words, many of the frustrations of the college writing instructor—run-on sentences, comma splices, improper use of punctuation, etc.—are answered in this exercise: how to give life to the rhythms of the natural world (in this case, moisture) on paper. Great novelists have a hard enough time putting these rhythms to words, so the task is simply to draw them. And here the elegance of the design belies the claim that the task is too "elementary." Indeed, knowledge of rhythms is a prerequisite for great architectural design, as Hughes convincingly explains in the closing lines of "The Sources of Rhythm":

> Perhaps the curve of a waterfall or the arching stripes of the
> rainbow suggested the rhythms for the arches of the houses and

temples and tombs and bridges of men long ago—the arch of
Tamerlane's tomb at Samarkland, the arch of a bridge in ancient
China, or the Moorish arches at Granada.

When the Egyptians built their tombs and temples over a thousand
years before Christ, they knew how to combine the rhythms of
nature with the possibilities of stone and sun-dried brick in the
structure of their buildings. And the more harmoniously they did
this, the more beautiful were their buildings. In splendid palaces
the pharaohs lived.

The Greeks, hundreds of years before Christ, knew the rhythmical
beauty of the soaring line in a column. The rising lines of its many
columns made the Parthenon one of the most beautiful buildings
ever created.

The columns of Greek temples go upward.

The pyramids of the Egyptians point upward.

The skyscrapers of American cities rise into the skies.

Like the blades of grass and the stems of flowers and the trunks
of trees, the houses and temples and other buildings of man rise
toward the sky where the sun is. Almost nobody builds a house,
church, or any kind of building underground.

(Hughes 1954, 14–15)

Hughes places emphasis on the constructive power of rhythm, for his
one line paragraphs in this passage serve as a figurative homology of the
physical columns they describe. He also allows us to see the practical importance of rhythms in terms of building an equalitarian national-popular
school curriculum. If to make far-flung connections between disparate histories, ancient and modern alike, as well as between world civilizations, also
ancient and modern, is the occupation of the philologist, then the process
by which young people internalize both the method and the values of such
generalism is the work of the composition teacher of writing rhythms.

Hughes's sweeping account of the role of rhythms in the construction of more than a thousand years worth of architectural landmarks, from
bridges in ancient China to skyscrapers in New York, is motivated by his
*non-specialized* method, which must strike today's reader in the United
States as alien, even sentimental. As Timothy Brennan has put it cogently

with respect to the generalism of Edward Said, "In the United States today, such a gesture is a calculated rebuke to technological panaceas and professionalist poses in the academy and in official public culture" (1993, 82). Yet for Hughes a generalist method for teaching young people about world history and geography, of great civilizations and their historic contributions to human social progress, was not a calculated rebuke but a beginning point, a place from which youth could be fully socialized into the rhythms of equalitarian everyday life: for Hughes, the consummate worldly sphere of existence and for that reason precisely the place to carry on the struggle for a democratic American society.

In a discussion of the pedagogical implications of Hughes's *Book of Rhythms,* the question arises: But what difference does Hughes's method make? What different kinds of student writing does Hughes's pedagogical approach enable? In the future, this question will be answered more systematically, for as of now his "rhythm writing" approach to teaching English composition is unknown in the discipline of composition studies.

## Pedagogical Implications: A Case Study

For the past several years, I have received grants to explore the pedagogical implications of Hughes's method for freshman composition, and with those grants I have been able to begin such a study. As co-coordinator of the composition program at the large, urban community college where I work, I have been able to experiment practically and creatively with Hughes's originary method. What I can share in this respect is, therefore, provisional and very partial but at the same time promising and concrete. Embarking on the Hughesian path of writing instruction along with me have come hundreds of students who have participated directly in the experiment and produced many hundreds of "rhythm writing" composition pieces in my writing courses. Naturally, however, it is very difficult to select one or two in particular that embody all the elements and objectives of a Hughesian approach. Nevertheless, I have included several below that help substantiate the claim that Hughes's theory of composition, developed in the 1950s, is more relevant today than ever.

One of the tenets of the Hughesian method is to establish the student writer's own unique standpoint, but not in the abstract sense of "perspective," "opinion," or "feeling." Hughes had his writing students look closely at themselves, not as others see them but as they feel and think about themselves in relation to the world. Yet, the idea is not to write a personal memoir but instead to focus on a concrete aspect of themselves that could tell a whole story of their social relations—where they come from, where they are, how they got there, and where they are going. Following Hughes, the first writing assignment I give is to have students examine their own unique hands and to allow what they observe directly to shape a story about their lives. One student wrote:

> I have long fingers with brittle nails on each of them. They're very light with color and a have a few battle scars. My two pinkies are crooked but one is not fully. It looks like they were broken when I was a baby and no one knew so it healed on its own. My palms used to be so soft and moist but now because of hard labor at work, they are cracked and rough. My palms' skin is red and tight. I love to look at my prints because they are so obvious to see. I have a mole on two fingers and one inside my right palm. Also one on my left wrist. My hands have completed many jobs. Braiding hair, washing dishes, cleaning everything, mopping, or even always being washed away from dirt. My fingers have been cut, jammed, smashed, and more. But they are mine. I think I have beautiful hands no matter what they look like and no matter what kind of labor they have done.

This story is told from a subjective position, but the Hughesian method encourages students to see this *felt* subjectivity in relation to the real social world. Consequently, it is not enough to instruct writing students, for example, to "describe someone you know"—they need to describe that person in relation to others, including themselves. The second writing assignment I give is to have students portray the rhythms of a person they know, not in the mode of portraiture—that is, in a stationary or static position—but rather in a condition of movement. One student produced this piece:

> When I think about Samora, I think about things like: sunsets, a summer breeze and tranquility. Everything about her is sensual, even her name, Samora. When she enters a room she quietly takes it over. She has such a smooth way of handling herself and can make herself comfortable in almost any situation. When she walks, she seems to glide. Talking with her is a tranquil experience; her voice has this calming, relaxing quality, and the way she moistens her lips with her tongue she can hold your attention for hours. I once had the chance to see her under the setting sun. The sun brought this wonderful glow to her caramel complexion. Samora has thick black hair which she wears in a short tapered style, along with these dark piercing eyes that just dance with mystery. She has this provocative way of raising her left eyebrow to let you know that what you are saying is questionable. It's surprising to know that she

has so many female friends. She just has a way about her that is attractive to both male and female; you just want to be around her. The most incredible thing about all this is that she's not aware of any of it. She is free of any pretentious ways, it's almost innocent. When I first met her it was at a party that I was invited to. She was having a great time mingling and getting others to relax and enjoy themselves. I was surprised to find out that she was not the host. Samora is a gem, it's just the way she is.

By writing like this, have students become more "politically aware"? That depends on how one defines politics. Hughes was not interested in having his writing students discuss "social issues" or comment critically on current events. Nor was he concerned that they read the New York *Times* every day. For Hughes, "political awareness" in the writing classroom, as in life generally, is mastering the dialectical unity of the individual and the collective, which is the base of socialism, i.e., the social relations of production. Hence, what is political about Hughes's pedagogy is the new social relation it establishes between teacher and student, and between students and the actual world in which they live, through the production of popular, critical writing. No longer a hierarchical relation (master and pupil), the teacher-student social relation becomes under Hughes's method one of friendly guide and open mind. And in the case of the social relation between students and others, in everyday life, students develop the confidence to approach the world not as passive observers or spectators but instead as individual subjects willing to assert their own desires, preferences, and demands in the face of immensely complex, confusing, and often oppressive environments. In Hughesian terms, by discovering their own writerly conscious, students are now in a position to shape their own destiny in relation to the fate of the society in which they live every day.

In American studies, Hughes is known, in the main, as a "folk poet." It is not difficult to support such a general categorization, yet it misses two important elements. The first is that Hughes applied his lyrical genius to concrete tasks and objectives, such as writing popular histories, as well as directing writing workshops, for American youth. Some of the fine points of this first element have been highlighted, in the light of the rapper Chuck D's blueprint for transforming African American youth culture. The second is that the folk poet description cannot begin to appreciate the strategies, themes, motifs, and images that unify Hughes's work over five decades. The overall aim of this essay is to suggest several central themes in his work that could enable a unified analysis of Hughes's literary legacy. One theme is the education of youth for their active participation in American civil society, and the other is the aesthetic preference for collage. While the two themes are present in virtually every project he undertook in the 50s and 60s, they are put into practice systematically in *Book of Rhythms,* a text that was, according to the dominant anticommunism of its time, decidedly radical and socialist. Here the limits of the "folk poet" characterization of Hughes are felt most acutely, since the evidence of his life and work during the high period of the cold war paints a different picture: rather than simply a folk poet, Hughes was, especially during the anticommunist purges, a mastermind of method, constantly figuring out new ways to make old equalitarian ideals dynamic and freshly popular.

## NOTE

1. The main argument in the present essay is developed further in the author's book-length study of Hughes entitled *Socialist Joy: Reflections on the Writing of Langston Hughes* (2006).

## WORKS CITED

Barnouw, Erik, ed. 1945. *Radio Drama in Action.* New York: Rinehart & Co.

Berry, Faith. 1983. *Langston Hughes: Before and Beyond Harlem.* Westport, Connecticut: Lawrence Hill.

Bigsby, C. W. E. 1994. "The Theater and the Coming Revolution." *In Conversations with Amiri Baraka,* ed. Charlie Reilly. Jackson: University Press of Mississippi.

Brennan, Timothy. 1992. "Places of Mind, Occupied Lands: Edward Said and Philology." In *Edward Said: A Critical Reader,* ed. Michael Sprinker. Oxford: Blackwell.

———. 1993. "The National Longing for Form." In *Nation and Narration,* ed. Homi K. Bhaba. New York: Routledge.

Caute, David. 1978. *The Great Fear: The Anticommunist Purge Under Truman and Eisenhower.* New York: Touchstone, 1979.

Chuck D. 1996. *The Autobiography of Mistachuck: Report from the Commissioner.* Mercury Records.

Cunningham, George. 1994. Afterword to *The Sweet and Sour Animal Book,* by Langston Hughes. New York: Oxford University Press.

DuBois, W.E.B. 1969. *The Souls of Black Folk.* New York: Penguin.

Hughes, Langston. 1926. "The Negro Artist and the Racial Mountain." *The Nation* (23 June): pp. 692–694.

———. 1954. *First Book of Rhythms.* New York: Franklin Watts.

———. 1957. "Negro Writers Have Been On A Blacklist All Our Lives." *Mainstream* (July): p. 46–48.

Hughes, Langston, and Arna Bontemps, eds. 1949. *The Poetry of the Negro, 1746–1949.* Garden City, NY: Doubleday.

Hughes, Langston, and Roy DeCarava. 1955. *The Sweet Flypaper of Life.* New York: Simon & Schuster.

Hughes, Langston, and Milton Meltzer. 1967. *Black Magic: A Pictorial History of the Negro in American Entertainment.* Englewood Cliffs, NJ: Prentice-Hall.

Kunitz, Stanley J., and Howard Haycraft, eds. 1942. *Twentieth Century Authors.* New York: H. W. Wilson.

Lasch, Christopher. 1969. *The Agony of the American Left*. New York: Alfred A. Knopf.

Minter, David. 1980. *William Faulkner: His Life and Work*. Baltimore: Johns Hopkins University Press.

Nichols, Charles H., ed. 1980. *Arna Bontemps–Langston Hughes Letters, 1925–1967*. New York: Dodd, Mead.

O'Meally, Robert G. 1995. Afterword to *Book of Rhythms,* by Langston Hughes. New York: Oxford University Press.

Rampersad, Arnold. 1988. *The Life of Langston Hughes*. Vol. 2. New York: Oxford.

Reed, Ishmael. 1970. *19 Necromancers from Now*. Garden City: Doubleday.

Robinson, Cedric J. 1983. *Black Marxism: The Making of the Black Radical Tradition*. London: Zed.

Rosenberg, Bernard, and David Manning White, eds. 1957. *Mass Culture: The Popular Arts in America*. New York: The Free Press.

Thompson, Robert Farris. 1984. *Flash of the Spirit: African and Afro-American Art and Philosophy*. New York: Vintage.

Wittner, Lawrence S. 1974. *Cold War America: From Hiroshima to Watergate*. New York: Praeger.

# Chronology

1902      James Mercer Langston Hughes is born on February 1 in Joplin, Missouri.

1915      Moves to Lincoln, Illinois, to live with his mother and stepfather.

1916      Elected class poet for grammar school graduation.

1920      Graduates high school; spends summer in Mexico.

1921      Publishes first poem in *The Crisis* magazine; enters Columbia University, New York.

1923      Works on ship travelling to Africa.

1925      Wins first prize for poetry in *Opportunity* contest.

1926      Publishes first book of poetry, *The Weary Blues;* enters Lincoln University.

1929      Graduates from Lincoln University.

1930      *Not Without Laughter* is published.

1932      Travels to U.S.S.R.

1934      *The Way of White Falls* is published; father dies.

1935      First play, *Mulatto,* opens on Broadway.

1937      Travels to Spain as war correspondent.

1938      Mother dies.

1940    *The Big Sea* is published.

1942    *Shakespeare in Harlem* is published.

1943    Begins *Chicago Defender* column.

1947    Teaches at Atlanta University.

1949    Teaches the Labratory School, University of Chicago.

1950    *Simple Speaks His Mind* is published.

1951    *Montage of a Dream Deferred* is published.

1956    *I Wonder as I Wander* is published.

1959    *Selected Poems of Langston Hughes* is published.

1966    Journeys to Dakar, Senegal, to attend the first World Festival of Negro Arts.

1967    Dies after surgery of infection on May 22.

# Contributors

HAROLD BLOOM is Sterling Professor of the Humanities at Yale University. He is the author of 30 books, including *Shelley's Mythmaking* (1959), *The Visionary Company* (1961), *Blake's Apocalypse* (1963), *Yeats* (1970), *A Map of Misreading* (1975), *Kabbalah and Criticism* (1975), *Agon: Toward a Theory of Revisionism* (1982), *The American Religion* (1992), *The Western Canon* (1994), and *Omens of Millennium: The Gnosis of Angels, Dreams, and Resurrection* (1996). *The Anxiety of Influence* (1973) sets forth Professor Bloom's provocative theory of the literary relationships between the great writers and their predecessors. His most recent books include *Shakespeare: The Invention of the Human* (1998), a 1998 National Book Award finalist, *How to Read and Why* (2000), *Genius: A Mosaic of One Hundred Exemplary Creative Minds* (2002), *Hamlet: Poem Unlimited* (2003), *Where Shall Wisdom Be Found?* (2004), and *Jesus and Yahweh: The Names Divine* (2005). In 1999, Professor Bloom received the prestigious American Academy of Arts and Letters Gold Medal for Criticism. He has also received the International Prize of Catalonia, the Alfonso Reyes Prize of Mexico, and the Hans Christian Andersen Bicentennial Prize of Denmark.

ARNOLD RAMPERSAD is Wilson Professor of Humanities at Princeton University. His two-volume biography *The Life of Langston Hughes, Volume 1: 1902–1941: I, Too, Sing America* (1986) and *The Life of Langston Hughes, Volume 2: 1941–1967: I Dream a World* (1988) won the American Book Award.

GERMAIN J. BIENVENU is library associate at the Hill Memorial Library, Louisiana State University.

KAREN JACKSON FORD is associate professor of English at the University of Oregon. Her *Split-Gut Song: Jean Toomer and the Poetics of Modernity* was published in 2005.

DAVID CHINITZ is associate professor of English at Amherst College. His *T. S. Eliot and the Cultural Divide* was published in 2003.

JOSEPH MCLAREN is professor of English at Hofstra University. He has written extensively on black literature and culture; his books include *Langston Hughes: Folk Dramatist in the Protest Tradition, 1921–1943* (1997) and *Langston Hughes's African Connection* (1992).

H. NIGEL THOMAS is professor of American literature at Université Laval in Quebec City, Quebec. He has written poetry, short stories, a novel, and *From Folklore to Fiction: A Study of Folk Heroes and Rituals in the Black American Novel* (1988).

ROBERT O'BRIEN HOKANSON is associate professor of English at Alverno College.

ANITA PATTERSON is associate professor of English at Boston University. She is author of *From Emerson to King: Democracy, Race, and the Politics of Protest* (1997).

STEVEN C. TRACY is professor of Afro-American Studies at the University of Massachusetts, Amherst. He is author of *Langston Hughes and the Blues,* (1988) and editor of *A Historical Guide to Langston Hughes* (2003).

WILLIAM HOGAN teaches British and American modernism at Providence College.

JONATHAN SCOTT is Assistant Professor of English at Al-Quds University in Jerusalem. His *Socialist Joy in the Writing of Langston Hughes* was published in 2007.

# Bibliography

Bernard, Emily. *Remember Me to Harlem: The Letters of Langston Hughes and Carl Van Vechten, 1925–1964.* New York: Knopf, 2001.

Dace, Tish, ed., *Langston Hughes: The Contemporary Reviews.* Cambridge & New York: Cambridge University Press, 1997.

Duffy, Susan. *The Political Plays of Langston Hughes.* Carbondale: Southern Illinois University Press, 2000.

Emanuel, James A., *Langston Hughes.* New York: Twayne, 1967.

Fraden, Rena. *Blueprints for a Black Federal Theatre, 1935–1939.* Cambridge: Cambridge University Press, 1994.

Gates, Henry Louis Jr. and K. A. Appiah, eds., *Langston Hughes: Critical Perspectives Past and Present.* New York: Amistad Press, 1993.

McLaren, Joseph. *Langston Hughes: Folk Dramatist in the Protest Tradition, 1921–1943.* Westport, Conn.: Greenwood Press, 1997.

Metzer, Milton. *Langston Hughes: A Biography.* New York: Crowell, 1968.

Mikolyzk, Thomas A., *Langston Hughes: A Bio-Bibliography.* New York: Greenwood Press, 1990.

Miller, R. Baxter. *Langston Hughes and Gwendolyn Brooks: A Reference Guide.* Boston: G. K. Hall, 1978.

Miller, R. Baxter. *The Art and Imagination of Langston Hughes.* Lexington: University Press of Kentucky, 2006.

O'Daniel, Therman B., ed. *Langston Hughes: Black Genius: A Critical Evaluation.* New York: Morrow, 1971.

Rampersad, Arnold. *The Life of Langston Hughes*, 2 volumes. New York: Oxford University Press, 1986, 1988.

Tracy, Steven C., *Langston Hughes & the Blues*. Urbana: University of Illinois Press, 1988.

Tracy, Steven C., editor. *A Historical Guide to Langston Hughes*. Oxford, England: Oxford University Press, 2004.

# Acknowledgments

"Langston Hughes's *Fine Clothes to the Jew*" by: Rampersad, Arnold; *Callaloo: A Journal of African American and African Arts and Letters,* 1986 Winter; 9 (1 (26)): pp. 144–158. © The Johns Hopkins University Press. Reprinted with permission of the Johns Hopkins University Press.

"Intracaste Prejudice in Langston Hughes's *Mulatto*" by: Bienvenu, Germain J.; *African American Review,* 1992 Summer; 26 (2): pp. 341–353. Copyright © 1992 Germain J. Bienvenu. Reprinted by permission of the author.

"Do Right to Write Right: Langston Hughes's Aesthetics of Simplicity" by: Ford, Karen Jackson; *Twentieth Century Literature: A Scholarly and Critical Journal,* 1992 Winter; 38 (4): 436-56. Copyright © 1992 *Twentieth Century Literature,* Hofstra University. Reprinted by permission of the publisher.

"Rejuvenation through Joy: Langston Hughes, Primitivism, and Jazz" by: Chinitz, David; *American Literary History,* 1997 Spring; 9 (1): pp. 60–78. Copyright © 1997 Oxford University Press. Used by permission of Oxford University Press.

"From Protest to Soul Fest: Langston Hughes' Gospel Plays" by: McLaren, Joseph; *Langston Hughes Review,* 1997 Spring; 15 (1): 49-61. Copyright © Langston Hughes Society.

233

"Patronage and the Writing of Langston Hughes's *Not Without Laughter: A Paradoxical Case*" by: Thomas, H. Nigel; *CLA Journal,* 1998 Sept; 42 (1): pp. 48–70. Copyright © 1998 The College Language Association. Reprinted by permission of The College Language Association.

"Jazzing It Up: The Be-Bop Modernism of Langston Hughes" by: Hokanson, Robert O'Brien; *Mosaic: A Journal for the Interdisciplinary Study of Literature,* 1998 Dec; 31 (4): pp. 61-82. Copyright © *Mosaic: A Journal for the Interdisciplinary Study of Literature.* Reprinted by permission of the publisher.

"Jazz, Realism, and the Modernist Lyric: The Poetry of Langston Hughes" by: Patterson, Anita; *Modern Language Quarterly: A Journal of Literary History,* 2000 Dec; 61 (4): pp. 651–682. Copyright © 2000, University of Washington. All rights reserved. Used by permission of the publisher.

"The Dream Keeper: Langston Hughes's Poetry, Fiction, and Non-Biographical Books for Children and Young Adults" by: Tracy, Steven; *Langston Hughes Review,* 2002 Fall-Spring; 17: pp. 78–94. Copyright © Langston Hughes Society.

"Roots, Routes, and Langston Hughes's Hybrid Sense of Place" by: Hogan, William; *Langston Hughes Review,* 2004 Spring; 18: pp. 3–23. Copyright © Langston Hughes Society.

"Advanced, Repressed, and Popular: Langston Hughes During the Cold War" by: Scott, Jonathan; *College Literature,* 2006 Spring; 33 (2): pp. 30–51. Copyright © 2006 *College Literature.* Reprinted by permission of the publisher.

# Index